/ SNOWBOARD GIRL /

SNOWBOARD GIRL

SHANNON
DUNN-DOWNING

THE PEARL

PEARLMAG.CO

Scripture quotations are taken from the Holy Bible, New Living Translation, copyright ©1996, 2004, 2015 by Tyndale House Foundation. Used by permission of Tyndale House Publishers, Carol Stream, Illinois 60188. All rights reserved.

Developmental editing: Vella Karman.

Copy editing: R.J. Catlin.

Interior book design: Noah J. Matthews.

Cover design by Gigi Gabarino. Cover editing by Levi Matthews.

Cover Photo: Aaron Blatt/Burton.

Library of Congress Control Number:

Print ISBN: 978-1-960230-21-8
E-book ISBN: 978-1-960230-23-2

Printed in the United States of America

To my family:
my parents, my brother Sean, my husband Dave, and my sons Logan and
Dillon—you are my roots, my wings, and my courage.

/ Forgotten Medal /

SNOWBOARDING HAD ALWAYS BEEN about moving forward—standing on the edge of a cliff, heart pounding, and pushing myself past the limits of what felt possible.

But there I was, sitting in the driver's seat of a silver Toyota mini-van—of all things—realizing that life has a way of catching up with you.

It was a typical Southern California afternoon, warm enough to make you forget it was late October. The salt from my morning surf session had dried on my skin, leaving familiar, taut streaks across my arms. My hair was tangled. The oversized sunglasses I had grabbed on my way out barely hid the exhaustion etched across my face. I had traded podiums and adrenaline for the school pick-up line—but today, something felt different.

I pulled into the circular drive of the elementary school, the cars crawling forward in the stop-and-go rhythm of after-school chaos. Kids darted between cars, backpacks swinging, their voices a mix of laughter and pent-up energy. A group of boys sprinted toward my van—Logan, my eldest, leading the charge with his untucked uniform and wild excitement scrawled across his face. His best friend Max was right behind him, arms flailing like he'd just won the lottery. A few more kids trailed behind, sneakers slapping the pavement in a chaotic chorus. As the van's side door slid open with a mechanical whoosh, they skidded to a stop, eyes wide, practically vibrating with whatever news they couldn't wait to unload.

"Mom! Are you famous?" Logan practically shouted, throwing himself against the passenger door.

I blinked, caught off guard. *Famous? Where was this coming from?*

Dillon, my youngest, breathless from keeping up, grinned wide. His gap-toothed smile stretched from ear to ear. "Max found you in a book at the library! It says you were in the Olympics!"

There it was—a piece of my past, long buried under school lunches, soccer practice, and grocery lists, suddenly unearthed by elementary school gossip. I let out a small laugh, glancing at Max, who looked downright triumphant, like he'd solved a great mystery.

"Yeah, I guess I did," I said, as if it were no big deal.

But Logan wouldn't let it slide. "Why didn't you ever tell us? Can we see your medal? Are you, like, a champion or something?"

The rest of the kids leaned in, their curiosity electric. They weren't just asking for my boys—they wanted to know too. I shook my head, smiling.

"Okay, okay," I said, holding up my hands in surrender. "When we get home, I'll show you the medal."

Truthfully, I hadn't thought about that medal in years. It was packed away somewhere in the back of my closet, tucked beside old snowboards, bindings, and boots that once defined the first half of my life.

As we drove home, Logan and Dillon whispered in the backseat, already building their own version of my story. I caught glimpses of their animated faces in the rearview mirror. Logan leaned in toward his little brother, hands flying as he described my supposed competition days. Dillon's wide eyes soaked it in, his backpack clutched tight like he was holding onto something precious.

And me? I gripped the steering wheel a little tighter, feeling the weight of something I hadn't acknowledged in years. For so long, my life had been about chasing the next trick, the next contest, the next mountain to conquer. I had stood atop podiums, traveled the world, and been part of something bigger than myself.

But that had been another lifetime.

Now I was a mom. A wife. Somewhere in the blur of raising kids and running a household, I had tucked that version of myself away, just like that medal. As I pulled into the driveway, I sat for a second before shifting into park. The house was the same as always—bikes strewn across the lawn, a half-finished chalk masterpiece on the driveway, a soccer ball wedged in the bushes. But something had shifted.

I don't know why it hit me so hard, but something told me—this wasn't just about the medal. It was about everything I had left buried with it.

CHAPTER 1
/ The Move /

I DIDN'T BELONG HERE.

Not in Steamboat.

Not at school.

Not anywhere.

At least, that's how it felt when we left the Chicago suburbs and moved to the small mountain town of Steamboat Springs, Colorado. We weren't chasing adventure—we were starting over.

My dad had built a handful of businesses: hockey shops, golf course concessions, even an ice-skating accessory company that stamped NHL hockey pucks. That last one was supposed to be our successful family business. Instead, the guy who sold it to him lied—the equipment didn't exist.

The business collapsed. And so did everything else.

Bankruptcy changed everything. Dad gave up chasing big risks and became a State Farm Insurance agent. Mom left behind a career she enjoyed, as a secretary to the president of a paper company. But it wasn't just her job she left—it was our tight-knit family: her parents, three brothers, a twin sister, and all their kids—my grandparents, uncles, aunt, and cousins. In Illinois, we never had to go far to be surrounded by people who loved us.

Dad's dream was always to move to Colorado someday—the place we'd gone on ski vacations, the place he sang about on his acoustic guitar with full-on John Denver vibes. So, when an insurance agency location opened up in Steamboat, he took it. And then, suddenly, we left everything I'd ever known.

At first, I was excited. A new town, a fresh start—it sounded like an adventure. We packed up everything we owned and hit the open road for Colorado. My brother Sean was twelve. I was nine.

As we drove over the Rocky Mountain passes, fresh streams tumbled down cliffs beside us, flashing in the sunlight. At one point, a mountain goat wandered right up near the road, completely unfazed by our car. It was wild and beautiful, so different from the busy, flat neighborhoods we'd left behind. We were in awe.

But by the time fifth grade rolled around that fall, reality had set in. The loneliness crept in slowly, like a fog I didn't notice until I was standing in the middle of it. I had never known what it was like to feel avoided. I wasn't the type to sit alone at lunch, but there I was—picking at my sandwich in silence, watching friendships form around me like I was invisible.

Back in Illinois, I had belonged to my neighborhood, to my school, to a life I hadn't realized I would miss so much. But in Steamboat? I was just there—the new kid, the shy kid. It wasn't in my nature to aggressively seek friendships or force myself into circles that didn't have space for me. So I waited. Patiently. Hoping things would just...work out.

And then I met Betsy.

In sixth grade, we were paired together in class, and from the start, we couldn't stop talking, couldn't stop laughing. The teacher tried separating us—twice—but it didn't matter. We were insta-besties, like we'd been waiting to meet each other our whole lives.

For years, we did everything together: sleepovers, road trips, pranks that sometimes got us into trouble (though mostly we avoided it).

We had our own universe, but we weren't closed off. We floated between different friend groups. At the core of it all, though, it was always us.

Pretty much inseparable.

Before Steamboat, my heart was set on the Olympics—gymnastics especially, but I also loved figure skating. That was the dream. I had committed to a more elite gymnastics training regimen, and figure skating was a mix of ice shows and lessons. I poured everything I had into those sports. They weren't just something I did—I loved them.

But Steamboat was an Olympic town built for skiers. Sure, it had a rink, but it was just a patch of ice on the rodeo grounds. No real figure skating programs. No elite gymnastics training either. I tried to find something new, but nothing clicked.

One day, I saw a sign: **SKI JUMPING TEAM SIGN-UPS.**

Ski jumping looked terrifying—but also kind of amazing. I figured if my older brother Sean could send it off the seventy-meter jump on his skis, maybe I could learn how to fly too.

Mom was thrilled. Finally, something I showed interest in. She walked me into the building for sign-ups, smiling, ready to help me find my thing. The coach glanced at me, then shook his head. "No girls."

Mom's face froze. "Excuse me?"

He repeated it like it was nothing. "No girls. It's too dangerous."

I was ready to back down. The jumps were massive—the thought of launching myself into the air felt insane. Beginners started on smaller jumps, slowly working their way up. But eventually, the goal was the ninety-meter Olympic-sized monster looming overhead.

Mom wasn't backing down, though. She casually walked me outside, her voice calm but clipped.

"Wait here," she muttered, then turned on her heel and stormed back inside. I stood there, staring up at the jump, my stomach flipping. From this angle, it looked even bigger—impossibly big. My heart pounded just imagining what it would feel like to launch off that thing.

A few minutes later, she walked out, all calm and her voice smooth. "Okay, you're in."

I blinked. "What?"

"You can be part of the team," she said, a small smirk tugging at her mouth. Whatever had happened in there, it was handled.

I hesitated.

The coach hadn't wanted me there. I didn't want to be the girl he expected to fail. I didn't want to be terrified out of my mind, training under someone who didn't believe in me.

So I backed down.

And after that? I stopped looking for my thing. I loved sports and participated, but nothing felt worth putting everything I had into it.

Until Sean handed me a snowboard.

The winter season of 1987–1988 was Steamboat's first year allowing snowboarding. I was sixteen. Betsy had already learned—one more reason for me to try.

"You're gonna love it," Sean told me. "Skiing's fun, but this—this is different."

Sean had picked up snowboarding first, and like everything he did, he went all in. With his thick brown hair and intense blue eyes, he had that stocky, athletic build that made him a natural at everything he tried.

He spent an entire day teaching me how to ride, pushing me, encouraging me every step of the way.

I wasn't on the bunny slope for long, though. Sean was a patient coach, but I was determined to progress faster than my body could handle.

I've got this, I thought, cruising down the run, proud of myself for figuring out my turns.

And then *wham*. Face-first. Eating snow. *How is it possible to crash this hard?!* I wondered.

But even with the bruises, I was in love. I ended up buying the same board I had rented that day because I knew—there was no turning back.

And I wasn't the only one. More and more riders were showing up on the mountain, each of us drawn to something about snowboarding that just felt...different. Snowboarding was raw, unfiltered, and completely our own. There were no coaches, no rules—just us, figuring it out as we went.

Skiers hated us. They didn't need to say a word—though, trust me, we heard plenty of colorful language. The way they stiffened and edged away as we passed said it all. To them, we were nothing but knuckle-draggers wrecking their pristine slopes with every slash and carve.

You were either a skier, or a skateboarder who had taken to snowboarding. The only ones still skiing were those too stubborn or hesitant to break from tradition.

Snowboarders carried a wild energy that didn't belong on their mountain. Like punk rock cowboys blazing into town, we created our own paths—launching off side hits, inventing new ways to ride, leaving fresh lines in the snow that skiers wished would disappear.

We didn't care. We weren't trying to be like skiers anyway. That wasn't the goal. We wanted to be like skateboarders—fluid, creative, free.

Betsy and I weren't great riders yet, but that didn't matter. We were carving out our own space—a place where we didn't have to try to fit in. For the first time since the move, I had found something I wasn't willing to walk away from. It didn't feel like just a new hobby—it felt like home. And somewhere deep down, I knew this was only the beginning.

CHAPTER 2
/ Punk Rock Princesses /

THIS WAS JUST A TYPICAL, RANDOM, hilarious day in the life of Betsy and me.

There wasn't enough snow to ride, and the restless itch was setting in. We needed something to fill the gap between storms—something ridiculous enough to keep us entertained. Thanksgiving break in 1989 had left the town half-empty—most people were traveling or holed up with family—which made everything feel even quieter, even slower.

That's how we ended up in my basement, rummaging through my mom's storage box—the one where she kept her old prom dresses. My parents had recently hosted a prom-themed party, and the dresses hadn't been put away yet.

Betsy's voice rang out from across the room. "Check these beauties!" She held up two of my mom's old dresses like trophies.

I raised an eyebrow. "Oh yes."

She pressed a pale blue satin dress to her chest, twirling in place. "Think she'll care?" Her sparkly blue eyes lit up with mischief as she tossed me the other one. I held it up.

Strapless. White. Red velvet polka dots.

Oh, I love this.

"These things are ancient. How much worse can we really make them?" I laughed, stepping into it.

Betsy—with her 5'7" model frame, straight brunette hair, and effortless charm—could make anything look good. I, on the other hand, was short and athletic, 5'2" and lean, a build passed down from my dad's side. While she looked ready for a magazine cover, I was still rocking braces and wondering if puberty had just skipped me entirely. But when it was just us? None of that mattered.

Minutes later, we were outside, bouncing on the trampoline in full prom dress glory, our skirts billowing as we launched into the air. The fabric flapped in the cold, making it feel like we were at some wild, upside-down ball.

Then I spotted it—my snowboard, leaning against the house.

I stopped bouncing. "I'm grabbing the snowboard," I said, hopping off the trampoline. I strapped my Sorel boots into the bindings and started bouncing again. The familiar weight of the board grounded me.

Sean and I had spent countless hours dialing in grabs, studying every tweak and hold from the snowboard magazines. Grabs came from skateboarding—skaters weren't strapped in, so they had to hold their boards midair to stay in control. Snowboarders didn't have to grab—we were strapped in—but we copied the style anyway. Freestyle was all about expression. A clean grab could make or break a trick—tightening your form, giving you control, and most importantly, making everything look better.

This time, though, Betsy and I were seriously upping the style factor—unmatched, literally. Who else was throwing melancholy grabs in prom dresses and Sorels?

Betsy clutched her stomach, already giggling. "Prom-o-rama, send it!"

I grinned, bouncing higher and higher.

The key to real airtime?

Timing.

If your friend jumped and hit the mat just as you were lifting off, the rebound could launch you sky-high—like a slingshot.

"Double bounce me!" I yelled. Betsy crouched low and timed it perfectly. The trampoline snapped back, and I shot into the air—twice the height, all hang time.

Now I had enough time to bend down, reach for my board, and put my front hand on my heel-side edge for a melancholy grab—a trick borrowed straight from skateboarding. The name had some weird origin story, like everything in skate culture, but all that mattered was that it looked sick. And then—

A telltale *riiip* cut through the cold.

We collapsed onto the trampoline, gasping between fits of laughter. Betsy barely got the words out. "That was hilarious! You almost nailed it, Queen Shreds-a-lot!"

I glanced down. My mom's dress was toast—torn fabric hanging in jagged strips. It must've caught on my binding somehow. And after Betsy's inspection, I realized I'd also managed to blow out the zipper. Worth it.

These were the moments we lived for.

But it was freezing, and our short-lived trampoline session was officially over. Of course, we had to stay in our outfits—continuing the adventure in prom dresses was half the fun. A few safety pins fixed my blown-out zipper, and just like that, we were good to go. We threw on jackets over our dresses and laced up our matching red-and-white Air Jordans, scuffed from countless skate sessions but still the coolest shoes we owned.

Our next stop was Totally Board—our favorite snowboard shop, just a few miles from my house in the mountain village area. Just as we were about to climb into my car, Betsy nudged me. "Don't forget the package."

I smirked. "Oh yeah—almost forgot." I ran back outside to the front steps and grabbed the plastic bag we'd stashed earlier—frozen dog poop, solid as a rock.

Betsy grinned. "Mission Merde."

She was fluent in French thanks to her mom, who was from France.

"Merde" was one of the first French words she taught me. I tossed the bag onto the floor of the backseat and cranked the stereo—Oingo Boingo blasting as the adrenaline still buzzed through us. We had a secret plan to execute—but we weren't exactly sure where to make it happen. But today was the day.

The second we pulled into the Totally Board parking lot, our focus shifted. What's the latest cool stuff? Who's hanging out? Any plans for the night? Totally Board wasn't just a shop—it was our spot.

As we walked in, Conrad spotted us from behind the counter, smirking as a Social Distortion track blared over the speakers. "Ladies, what's with the formal wear? Did I miss an invitation?"

"Testing new gear," I shrugged, like it made perfect sense.

Sean was in the back, waxing his board, laser-focused as usual. He looked up, saw our prom dresses, and shook his head, a mix of amusement and disbelief crossing his face. "What the— What are you guys up to now?"

Betsy and I exchanged a look.

"Nothing to see here," I said, quoting *The Naked Gun*, which sent us into another fit of laughter. I settled in beside Sean, my eye catching the latest issue of *Transworld Snowboarding magazine*, still wrapped in plastic. I grabbed it and tore the packaging open—I knew I was going to buy it anyway.

Then I saw the cover.

And froze.

Amy Howat, midair, hand hovering near the nose of her snowboard as she launched out of the halfpipe. Bright neon green and yellow jacket. Contest bib tied at the sides.

Betsy leaned over. "Are you kidding me? Finally, a girl on the cover!"

I nodded, staring at the image. It wasn't just about a girl making it— it felt like snowboarding itself was saying, "*You belong here.*"

Sean glanced up. "You could pull that grab better than her, Shan," he said casually. I laughed it off.

But his words stuck. I studied the image. She wasn't fully grabbing her board. It wasn't a perfect shot.

And that made it real. Attainable.

Something sparked inside me—a fire I hadn't expected. Could I actually go pro? The thought flickered—both exciting and terrifying. I folded the magazine under my arm, tucking Sean's words into the back of my mind. For later.

Betsy nudged me—sharp and sudden.

"Grocery store," she whispered. I didn't need more than that. We were practically telepathic after all these years. I paid for the magazine, tossed out quick see-ya-laters, and we headed for the door. We had walked in with no agenda, just killing time. Now we had a mission.

Minutes later, we were inside the grocery store, scanning for a target. Betsy spotted her first.

"There—perfect," she whispered, nodding toward a woman in the bulk foods section, scooping chocolate-covered raisins into a bag.

I clutched the frozen prize, heart pounding. *Okay, here goes.*

As we walked past, I slipped the bag into her cart and kept moving, forcing myself not to laugh. Betsy and I ducked behind a display of canned soup, barely holding it together. Betsy elbowed me. "What if she thinks they're some kind of fancy chocolate turtles and actually buys them?"

I covered my mouth, shoulders shaking. We peeked around the display just in time. The cashier grabbed the bag, holding it between two fingers. "Ma'am...what is this?"

The woman frowned. "I—I don't know. Did I get that from bulk?"

Betsy gripped my arm, snorting into her jacket sleeve. The cashier squinted. "Wait... Is this...dog poop?"

I spun around, pretending to study the tabloid rack. Right at eye level: "Oprah Abducted By Aliens!"

I lost it. Not just because the headline was ridiculous—but because once the first laugh escaped, it was over. Betsy caught sight of my face and doubled over, gripping the candy rack for support. Still in our prom dresses, we bolted—full sprint—out the door, skirts flying. We barely made it to the parking lot before collapsing against my car, gasping between deep belly laughs.

"Oh my gosh, you actually dropped the doodie balls in that lady's cart without her even noticing!" Betsy howled, tears streaming down her face.

I could barely breathe. "Her face when she saw it!"

Still riding the high, we jumped into my Geo Tracker—tiny, boxy, Jeep-ish, with a soft-top perfect for summer—and cranked the heat, music blasting. We weren't ready for the night to end. When we pulled into the empty parking garage near the mountain, I rolled down the windows, letting the mixtape echo through the cold, stale air. The headlights carved sharp lines across the concrete—crushed beer cans, broken pallets—ghosts of past skateboarding sessions scattered around us.

This was our space. Our time.

As "Sour Grapes" by the Descendents blasted from the cassette deck, we skated—still in our filthy, shredded prom dresses—trick after trick under the halo of my car's headlights. The scrape of our wheels, the sting of the cold air, the steady beat of the music—it felt perfect.

Sean's words from the shop kept sneaking into my mind. *Maybe I could ride like the pros.*

But for now, we weren't chasing anything but the rush of the moment—punk rock princesses in a forgotten parking garage, skating until the night blurred into music and laughter. I didn't know it yet, but that night was the start of everything changing.

CHAPTER 3

/ Goin' Pro /

DAD PULLED OUR CHEVY BLAZER into the nearly empty parking lot at Arapahoe Basin ski area, just a couple hours from home in Colorado. Sean sat up front while I stretched out in the back, trying to wake up.

It was April 29, 1990—the day of the Professional Snowboarding Tour of America Body Glove Snowbout 1—and we were here to throw ourselves into the unknown. The contest was open to pros and amateurs alike, but the $25,000 prize purse—basically a million bucks in snowboarder terms—had drawn the sport's heaviest hitters. Legends. The ones we'd seen in glossy two-page spreads, launching above halfpipe walls and frozen mid-trick.

Today, they wouldn't just be in the magazines—they'd be standing next to us at the top of the halfpipe. And we'd have to prove we belonged.

Sean had spotted the contest flyer in a snowboard magazine a month earlier, and the second he showed it to me, the buzz hit. His excitement was contagious, the kind that plants a seed and doesn't let go. We had no idea if we'd even make it past the qualifying round, let alone place in the top ten. But it didn't matter. Just being here—lining up at the same drop-in as our heroes—felt like a win already.

The parking lot slowly filled as riders trickled in, car doors slamming, boards sliding out of backseats, laughter echoing into the thin, mountain air. Patchy snow clung stubbornly to the rocky terrain, refusing to melt. A-Basin, perched above ten thousand feet, was an endless-winter kind of place: cold, rugged, unapologetic.

Dad snagged a front-row parking spot, naturally. "Front-row-er!" he said with a grin, like he always did when he beat the odds. His optimism was relentless—and, somehow, always caught on. He jumped out in his Columbia jacket and Sorel boots, eyes twinkling with energy. Big blue eyes—my eyes. Dad lived for days like this. Sports ran in his veins. He played semi-pro hockey, coached youth leagues, and believed competition revealed character. He didn't just cheer us on—he believed in us like it was a fact.

Getting out of the car, I thought of Mom. She rarely came to our contests—she got too anxious, convinced her nervous energy would jinx us. She preferred pacing at home. I understood...but still, this felt like something worth witnessing.

Dad was the opposite. All in. Calm but intense. Unshakable—and absolutely guaranteed to strike up a conversation with every human within a five-mile radius.

We walked toward registration, the old A-frame lodge standing firm in the fog, its faded green siding barely visible behind bright yellow Body Glove banners snapping in the breeze. We were early enough to beat the chaos, just a handful of riders stretching and shaking off sleep.

That's when Dad threw it out there: "You should enter the pro division."

I blinked. "What?"

"Why not?" he shrugged. "You've ridden against most of these kids in the Rocky Mountain Series. Might even win some money."

I laughed—but then looked up. Just across the lot, a familiar car pulled in, packed with riders we'd seen all season. I recognized faces from the Rocky Mountain Series, where I'd placed second overall. That part didn't scare me.

But this contest wasn't just about outriding a few locals. It meant seeing our names on the same start list as the pros we'd studied, idolized, and practically memorized. The ones we'd watched from the crowd at the Breckenridge World Cup—trailing camera crews, backed by big sponsors, their names always in bold.

I don't think Dad grasped the full weight of his suggestion—but to me, the possibility of going pro carried real magnitude. It wasn't just an idea. It felt like a turning point.

The pro division entry cost one hundred dollars. Amateur entry was just ten dollars.

My pen hovered. Pulse pounding. *Was I kidding myself? Was I about to get obliterated?*

Sean had already marked his form without blinking. He caught my eye, and grinned. "Come on, Shan. What's the worst that could happen?"

Everything in me twisted. But everything in me also knew—I had to go for it. If I wanted to make it in snowboarding, I had to go up against the best—the ones proving themselves in contests. Halfpipe was becoming the main stage.

For years, racing had been snowboarding's dominant path. But I never liked it. It was stiff. Predictable. Just a straight shot down the hill, chasing a stopwatch on someone else's line. Freestyle was different. It was creativity. Style. Freedom. You chose your line, left your mark, rode the mountain your way.

Even Jake Burton Carpenter—the founder of Burton Snowboards— once thought racing would define the sport. But Craig Kelly flipped that script. When he pivoted to freestyle, Burton followed. Halfpipe rose with him.

Snowboarding, to me, was an expression. Risk. Art. It wasn't just a sport—it was a lifestyle.

Craig was right. Everything was changing. Halfpipe wasn't a sideshow anymore—it was the spotlight. And if I wanted in, I had to commit. Not safe. Not comfortable. Not "ready."

Now.

I pressed the pen down. Marked the box: Pro Division.

Just like that, my fate was sealed.

"Well," I said, laughing nervously as I handed in the form, "I guess we're officially pros now."

Dad was already working the scene, chatting up officials, asking about the format. Turns out, it was based on surf contests: heats, eliminations, prize money at every round. Survive and advance.

Simple in theory.

Sean and I loaded up our backpacks—water, snacks, sunscreen, windbreakers—and started hiking toward the halfpipe.

The halfpipe cut clean through the slope like a white U-shaped ditch. Its five-foot walls were hand-shaped, sharp, and precise—built for speed. Workers drilled fencing into place along the sides, marking the boundaries between competitors and the expected crowd of spectators. At the bottom, a towering scaffolding structure loomed above the pipe, giving judges a bird's-eye view of every run.

Sound techs ran mic checks over booming speakers: "Check one, check—" followed by bursts of static and feedback. A narrow five-foot-wide deck flanked each side of the pipe, giving riders a way to hike back up between laps. Bright banners and sponsor flags flapped. Photographers with huge lenses were ready to capture every stomped trick—and every brutal fall.

We chucked our backpacks into the roped-off competitor area at the base, then began the climb. No lift access. Just your legs and lungs. And at 10,500 feet, your lungs notice fast.

Practice would start soon. Over one hundred men were registered, and maybe thirty girls. The energy was thick with anticipation. We were in it now.

At the top of the halfpipe, riders exchanged heys and high-fives—casual, upbeat. Sean and I hugged and fist-bumped familiar faces from the amateur circuit. Everyone agreed—it was surreal to be here, lining up with the pros.

Then the loudspeaker crackled to life: "Practice starts in five minutes."

And just like that, everything shifted. The chatter dropped. Focus locked in. Riders bent over their boards, strapping in—tightening each ratchet until their boots were locked down solid. Loose bindings meant disaster in the pipe. You needed full control when you were launching above icy walls.

You could drop from either side—left or right—but there were no start gates, no structure. Just 150 riders, all trying to get in at once. It was about to get wild.

Like grains of sand squeezing through the neck of an hourglass, everyone fought for position.

Sean nudged me. "Get aggressive," he said under his breath. "If you hesitate—even a little—they'll snake you."

Before I could nod, the practice window opened—and the whole scene exploded. Riders jammed toward the pipe's entrance, yelling "Droppin'!" over each other, in a nonstop blur of neon jackets and flying boards.

It was chaos. Timing was everything.

Be bold. Drop in. Own it.

Sean charged in. I followed right on his heels. The second I pointed my board down the hill, nerves evaporated.

The pipe was pure—fast, smooth, rhythmic. I carved up the wall, launched into the air, and landed clean in the transition, driving every move to build speed for the next hit. No thinking. Just riding.

At the bottom, I turned to Sean, breathless, grinning.

"This is gonna be so fun," I said, feeling free.

As if on cue, the fog lifted, and the sun broke through, warming the scene. I pulled off my hat, gathered my hair into a high half-up ponytail with my scrunchie, letting the rest flow down, and swapped goggles for my sunglasses.

Sean nudged me as we hiked up the side of the halfpipe, so I followed his gaze. My heart skipped a beat.

Craig Kelly was hiking ahead of us. Yellow Burton pants, a gray jacket with pink sleeves, and yellow Oakley goggles—he was unmistakable. His brown hair was buzzed short, with a thin goatee framing his chin. That slightly protruding nose gave his profile a look I'd seen a hundred times in magazines.

This was Craig Kelly—the legend himself.

And here I was, riding the same snow as him.

Then we saw Shaun Palmer finish his run, unstrap, and linger at the bottom of the pipe—chatting, totally at ease. He oozed swagger and wild energy, his bleached tips only adding to the reckless vibe. If Craig Kelly was smooth precision, Palmer was the wild card—untamed, fearless, always pushing the edge. He moved like he had a chip on his shoulder. Maybe he did. Beneath the bravado, there was a sharp, relentless focus—he just didn't care if anyone noticed.

Craig and Palmer were rivals in every sense. Craig rode with calm control, every movement clean and dialed. Palmer was all chaos—faster, bigger, riskier. His style was raw and unfiltered, but somehow still cool. Craig was the polished pro. College-educated, thoughtful, methodical. Palmer? The rock star rebel—wrecking rental cars and trashing hotel rooms like it was part of his training plan. Everyone I knew loved both—for totally different reasons.

It felt like two worlds colliding: Craig, low crouch and laser focus. Palmer, a force of nature—unpredictable, electric, impossible to ignore.

It was intimidating to be surrounded by riders like them—and just as inspiring.

My brother gravitated toward Palmer's bold, all-out style—rebellious, fearless, always charging. Me? I saw myself in Craig—the thinker, the strategist. Or at least, that's what I liked to believe.

We fell into a rhythm during practice, hiking so fast we were nearly running up the pipe to the beat of the blaring music. Then we'd drop in, dialing in our runs. I stuck with Sean, matching his pace and feeding off the momentum. I was locking in my favorite tricks, fine-tuning my line until everything clicked. A couple of times, I had to cut my run short when someone dropped in unexpectedly and cut me off—so frustrating. But I stayed focused, tightening each run to make sure it all flowed. The sidelines were starting to fill with spectators, adding even more energy to the scene.

I kept an eye on my competition, and with each run, my confidence grew. I felt like I was in the mix—riding just as strong as the top girls. Dad cheered us on from the sidelines, grinning. "You're looking great. Just as good as the best out here."

With the crowd and the rising temps, the pipe was getting slushier by the minute. We all had to adapt on the fly—the walls were breaking down fast, ruts forming in the transitions. Every run felt different, and keeping speed was getting trickier.

The loudspeaker announced the end of practice, but riders kept squeezing in last-minute drops from halfway up the pipe. I stopped to take a break, my legs burning, my mind racing. A flicker of panic crept in—*Was I really ready for this?* But then I reminded myself—*I had a few solid runs. Good enough.*

That's when I heard a voice from just uphill. "High altitude, huh?"

I looked up. Tina Basich stood there, her neon Kemper board jammed into the snow beside her. My stomach flipped. *Is she talking to me?* I glanced back—no one was behind me. *Yep. She's really talking to me.*

"Hi—I'm Tina," she said, smiling.

"Hi, I'm Shannon," I replied, suddenly feeling like a fish out of water. "Yeah, it's pretty intense up here." Scrambling, I blurted, "I love your scrunchie! It totally matches your pants!"

Her pants were impossible to miss—a bold salmon shade that popped even in a sea of neon, perfectly matched by her scrunchie. Tina laughed. "Thanks! I made it myself."

I grinned, relaxing a little. "I make them too, but mine usually fall apart."

We laughed, and suddenly, everything felt lighter. As we hiked up the pipe, we kept chatting, and Tina introduced me to more riders. Everyone smiled, gave nods, and even broke into a chorus of "Happy

Birthday" for Michelle Taggart's twentieth. There was no cutthroat competition among the women—just support and excitement to be part of something cool. They weren't as wild as the guys, but they were just as fierce, strong, confident, and welcoming. The camaraderie was a relief.

The contest kicked off, and everything shifted. The music cranked louder. The crowds swelled—there were now more spectators than competitors. According to the announcer, it was the biggest crowd in snowboard contest history. Fans lined the sidelines and packed the base area, turning the mountain into a full-on amphitheater of stoke. At the top of the pipe, riders gathered—nerves sharpening into adrenaline.

Sean's heat dropped first. He rode like a madman—pure "balls to the wall" riding, skate-style energy, fast and loose—and the crowd ate it up. So far, he was landing clean and holding his own with the top guys.

Between heats, Dad found the start list and brought it over. I was grateful. Knowing where I slotted in and how many riders were ahead helped me focus. I liked being prepared. Understanding the structure, thinking through a strategy—it calmed me. I scanned the list again, counting down until my heat. Just my habit—making sure I was set to go.

And then, it was my turn. Nerves hit hard—until Sean found me right before my run.

"Relax, Shan," he said. "You've got twenty minutes to put down two good runs—no problem. Just go for a clean, smooth first one, then try your tricks." He took the edge off my nerves. "No girls are doing anything you can't do," he added. "You just have to be smooth and controlled. Nothing special—just make it through this round."

His words sank in. The pressure loosened its grip. And once I dropped into the pipe, the nerves melted. I was just riding. No fight for space like in practice. The crowd was cheering. The sun was shining. The music pulled me into another world.

Heat after heat, Sean and I kept advancing. The field narrowed. The pressure built. Then suddenly—it was finals time.

The final men's heat wrapped up as Craig Kelly dropped in last. That signature low crouch—every movement precise, clean, surgical. It was mesmerizing to watch.

Off to the side, Shaun Palmer stood mid-interview with a journalist, grinning. When asked about the possibility of a win, I heard him say, "I'm not sure, but I think I've got this." No hesitation. Just Palmer being Palmer—half trash talk, half truth.

This was it. No more playing safe. It was time to throw down.

My trick list wasn't huge, but it was solid. I opened with an alley-oop—a stylish uphill spin that played against gravity, floating midair before dropping smoothly into the transition. For my closer, I threw a clean frontside 360, landing switch. It was foundational, but when executed well, it was enough to earn extra points from the judges.

The final heat was twenty minutes. As many runs as we could squeeze in. Best two counted.

My first few runs were fine, but not finals-worthy. A bobble here, a slowdown there. I was holding back, and I knew it. Now, it all came down to this. One run left. If I wanted a shot at the podium, this had to be it.

I dropped in—legs burning, brain on autopilot. Trick by trick, I linked the cleanest run I'd put together all day. The carves were smooth; the grabs, locked in. Momentum carried me, even through the slush. Then the final hit—time to go.

I wound up, popped, and tucked into the spin. Mid-rotation, the world blurred—then sharpened. Landing in sight. I spotted it, stomped it, and rode away clean.

That was it. The run I came for.

At the bottom, my chest heaved, heart pounding. Sean caught my eye and gave a nod—he felt it too. His finals had been rough. He fought to keep speed in the melting pipe, but he rode with heart. The spring sun was breaking down the walls, turning the pipe to slush. We all had to adapt.

The announcer climbed onto the stage, mic in hand. The late afternoon light cast long shadows across the snow. Riders gathered, boards scattered at their feet, faces sunburned and raw. The whole mountain seemed to lean in, listening.

Sean ended up seventh—which was pretty legit—and walked away with $275. A local Coloradan pulled off a surprise win, bumping Craig Kelly to second and Shaun Palmer to third.

Now it was time for the women's results.

I braced.

"In fifth place," the announcer called, "we have a tie...Tina Basich and Shannon—"

My stomach flipped. Tina Basich. *I tied with Tina Basich?*

But then—

"Shannon...Smith!"

Wait. What? Not me. Maybe I didn't make the top five. Whatever. I'd shown up. That was enough.

I turned to Dad. He frowned, confused. "I'm pretty sure...you're on the podium."

Before I could react—

"In third place... Let's hear it for the Colorado local—Shannon Dunn!"

I froze. I'd actually done it.

Sean and Dad tackled me in a hug, lifting me off the snow. The crowd exploded.

Still dazed, I stepped up beside first-place finisher Michelle Taggart and runner-up Carla Dalpiaz, check in hand, heart thundering. I'd made the podium at my first pro contest—and walked away with $400 in cash.

Just five months ago, I had stood in a snowboard shop, staring at a photo of a girl soaring out of a halfpipe, wondering if I could ever be her. Now, standing on that podium—clutching my winnings, adrenaline still surging—my focus had changed. I didn't just want a podium.

I wanted to win. I wanted to chase this with everything I had.

CHAPTER 4

/ Small Talk to Big Reality /

I SHOVELED A BITE OF FLUORESCENT ORANGE mac and cheese into my mouth, the color clashing with our mustard-yellow countertops in a way that summed up my life—unexpected, messy, and a little bit ridiculous. It was a weird breakfast, but options were slim: this or a frozen dinner. Mom was supposed to go shopping later, but for now, I was making do with what was left in the cabinets. Some mornings just started sideways. I figured the weirdest part of my day would be eating mac and cheese for breakfast.

I was wrong.

Just as I sat down with my bowl, the front door flew open, slamming against the wall. Sean barreled in, snowboard magazine in hand, his face lit with excitement. Scarlet, our scruffy, long-eared cocker spaniel, trailed at his heels, tail wagging wildly, paws caked in mud. It was mud season—mid-May in Steamboat. The snow was melting, turning everything into a swampy mess of brown and slush.

Mom, still on the phone, covered the receiver just long enough to shoot us a look. "Scarlet's tracking mud everywhere! Clean her paws!" she hissed, then snapped back into her conversation like nothing had happened.

Scarlet had been my sixteenth birthday gift—a pound puppy from the local humane society, a distraction after Sean had graduated high school and started community college. Even though he was still in town, things felt different without him home full-time. He'd been my buddy since the day I was born, and I'd been chasing him ever since.

Classes were over, and summer break felt amazing. I'd graduated high school early—after just one semester of senior year. That winter, I took community college courses, including a business class with Sean.

School was only part of the picture.

My real focus was snowboarding. I'd been training harder than ever, competing in the Rocky Mountain Amateur Snowboard Series—and that podium at the A-Basin pro event had lit a fire in me. I was obsessed with progressing.

Snowboarding wasn't just something I loved—it was my escape. The second my board touched snow, everything else—stress, expectations, uncertainty—faded away.

But reality loomed. I'd been accepted to the University of Colorado Boulder in the fall—Betsy had too. Going to college meant putting snowboarding on hold. It gnawed at me. Still, I kept moving forward. Things usually worked out.

"Shan, check this out!" Sean's voice boomed through the kitchen as he waved the magazine like it held the secret to life.

Mom, still mid-call, shot him a death stare. The curly phone cord stretched taut as she turned away, pressing a finger to her lips. "Yes...that sounds great," she murmured into the receiver, pacing like she always did when business was on the line.

Dad strolled in, morning routine in full swing—straight to the coffee pot, splash of cream, stir, slurp.

"Dad, c'mon. No slurping," I groaned.

Mom had trained us that it was impolite, but Dad never cared about those kinds of details. Oblivious, Sean shoved the magazine in my face.

"Look at this," he said, flipping to a spread in *Snowboarder Magazine* that read, "Summertime Bruise: Getting Schooled at Craig Kelly's World Snowboard Camp."

He spun toward Dad, already scheming. "What do you think about us heading to Whistler, Canada this summer?"

Dad raised an eyebrow mid-sip. "Whistler?"

Sean jabbed at the page. "Craig Kelly's summer camp. If we're serious about going pro, we need to ride with guys like him. They've got a half-pipe on a glacier. In the summer!"

Sean explained, and I nodded along, agreeing with every word—the setup, the pros, the snow, the edge it could give us for next season. I was already hooked, even though I barely knew what I was getting into. Just then, Mom hung up the phone with an exaggerated sigh and rubbed her forehead.

"How many times have I told you to be quiet while I'm on a call? Sheesh, you guys." She shook her head, looking between us. "What has you so riled up?"

Sean didn't miss a beat. "Craig Kelly's summer camp—check this out, Mom." He held up the magazine and read aloud, "'Summer camp is just an excuse to get you out of your mother's hair.'"

I flipped the magazine around so she could see the spread. "It's a training camp with the best riders. We'd get to practice in a real halfpipe all summer." I added, "And you'd finally get a break from us."

Mom's irritation shifted to full-on skepticism. "You're going to drive all the way to Canada? Just the two of you?"

"We'll be fine," Sean said. "It's not that far."

"It's fifteen hundred miles!" she shot back. "And what car are you driving? Yours won't make it. What if something happens?"

Sean shrugged. "We'll plan our stops, use a map, call every night. We're not clueless."

"I've got prize money from the last contest," I said. "And I'll pick up extra shifts at Top Cookie."

It was the little tourist shop where I worked selling T-shirts, slabs of fudge, and homemade cookies that smelled like pure sugar.

Sean grinned. "And I'm sure Betsy will keep prank-calling just to hear you answer the phone. 'Hi, Top Cookie!'" he said in a sing-song voice.

I rolled my eyes. "She never gets tired of that."

Mom sighed and glanced at Dad. "I just don't know," she muttered. Then, almost like an afterthought: "That was Janice, the realtor, on the phone. She mentioned a house out in the country, near the river. It's not on the market yet."

Dad, quiet until then, perked up. "A river property?"

Mom nodded. "She said it's exactly what we've been looking for. If we're serious, we should check it out before it's listed."

It had always been Dad's dream to move to the country by a river. But they'd promised they wouldn't make that move until after I graduated high school—for convenience's sake, to keep things stable. So when the opportunity came earlier than expected, it caught all of us off guard.

Before he could answer, the phone rang again. Mom grabbed it and paced, phone wedged between her ear and shoulder.

Sean leaned in. "We gotta figure out how to get to Canada."

I smirked. "I know. We gotta go."

Dad set down his mug. "We'll go look at the house. You two can pitch us this Whistler thing in the car. Deal?"

Sean and I exchanged a glance—hope was alive.

About two months later, with uncanny timing, they bought the river house, sold our place in town—just minutes from the mountain—and used the extra from the sale to help fund our trip to Whistler.

The garage door creaked open like a curtain rising on the next act.

Mom stood in the doorway, arms crossed, shaking her head in disbelief. "I cannot believe we're letting them do this," she muttered.

As Sean tossed the last duffel bag into the back of the van and slid into the driver's seat, Mom's voice cut through the air one last time. "No accidents!" she shouted nervously, as if saying it out loud would make it true.

Dad just chuckled, hands in his pockets. "They'll be fine."

Would we? Sean cranked up the music and threw my parents' mini-van—generously entrusted to us—into reverse, a grin stretching across his face. "Whistler, here we come!"

I took a deep breath, watching our house shrink in the rearview mirror. *We were actually doing this. No turning back now.* I just hoped we weren't in way over our heads.

CHAPTER 5

/ No Accidents /

"NO ACCIDENTS."

That was Mom's parting instruction as we backed out of the driveway, her voice looping in my head like a mixtape stuck on repeat. And yet, here we were.

Sean had edged forward into the street, inching past a row of parked cars to make a left turn. Just as he cleared the last vehicle, we saw it—a massive truck barreling toward us, way too close and way too fast. Sean slammed it into reverse—tires squealing—just as the truck thundered past, missing us by inches. A second later, *crunch*. We'd backed straight into a Porsche.

The acrid scent of burnt rubber mingled with the salty sea air. The Porsche's front bumper was crunched. Our minivan? Barely a dent.

Sean white-knuckled the steering wheel. "Dude—didn't even see—"

I let out a nervous laugh, shaking my head. "Well, at least it's a Porsche."

Sean shot me a look, half disbelief, half frustration. "Not funny, Shan."

But it kinda was.

Before we had time to process what had just happened, the blonde-haired woman from the Porsche, dressed to the nines in heels and a foofy dress, scurried out of the car and vanished into a massive white house like a ghost. Sean and I stared at each other, completely bewildered.

"What the— Where'd she go?" Sean asked, looking around in disbelief.

"No idea..."

Moments later, a tall, middle-aged man stormed out of the house, his face twisted in anger as he marched straight to our window. We were about to find out exactly what kind of trouble we were in.

"Do you have any idea what you just did?" he yelled, his voice sharp enough to cut through our already frazzled nerves.

With a quick crank of the window, Sean leaned out. "I'm so sorry! I didn't see the car behind us—I was trying to not get crushed by a truck!"

The man wasn't having it. "Pull into my driveway, right now," he demanded, motioning with his hand as if we didn't have a choice. We had barely made it to California before we were already testing our luck. Maybe it was a bad sign. Or maybe this was just the start of the kind of wild ride we had signed up for.

Sean had made some deal to pick up a new board from a friend in Redondo Beach, California, before we headed to Whistler. Was it out of the way? Of course. Could he have probably bought a new board for the price of gas? Absolutely. Did I care? Not a bit. This was an adventure, and we were in it now.

Sean glanced at me, unsure, but we didn't feel like we had any other options. We pulled into the driveway as instructed, and before we knew it, the man had taken our keys. That's when things got weird.

He led us inside his enormous white house—white floors, white furniture, white everything. It felt more like an art gallery than a home. We weren't guests. We were inmates in a luxury jail.

Sean and I exchanged nervous glances. "Uh, should we have just let him take our keys like that?" I whispered.

"This is insane," Sean replied, fidgeting with his hands.

The man disappeared for awhile. As we sat there waiting, I glanced around the room—and that's when I noticed a few Oscars casually sitting on the shelf. I nudged Sean. "Who is this guy?"

"No idea," Sean whispered back. "But I really don't like that he took our keys."

The room felt heavy with tension. Something was off. The lady from the Porsche was nowhere to be found, and it didn't escape our notice that she looked nothing like the brunette woman in the family photos hanging on the wall.

"What if this is some Hollywood scandal we just walked into?" I half-joked, trying to break the awkwardness.

Just then, the guy reappeared, phone in hand, pacing across the room. After a few passes back and forth, he asked about our insurance.

"Call our dad," we told him. So he did—dialing up Dad to go over the details. Finally, he handed the phone to us. The second I heard Dad's voice, the weight started to lift. He wasn't nearly as upset as I'd imagined. In fact, he sounded calm—steady, like always.

"Don't worry about it, guys," he said. "These things happen. You're covered by insurance. Is the van okay?

Sean nodded, "Yeah, our bumper is barely dented."

"Well, that's good news. I'm just glad you both are okay— And make sure you've got everything sorted before you leave."

We didn't want to make it sound like we were hostages or anything, so we reassured Dad, "We're fine, really. Just a crazy situation, but we'll be back on the road soon."

Once we hung up, the man's demeanor shifted. He let us out of the house, keys in hand, without much more fuss. Maybe it was the call with Dad that softened him, or maybe he just wanted us gone. Either way, we were more than happy to get out of there. Sean and I exchanged a look of relief as we hopped back into the van.

"Dude—that was weird," Sean muttered.

"No kidding," I replied, trying to shake off the bizarre encounter.

Afterward, we picked up the snowboard Sean had come for, threw it in the back of the van, and hit the road again. Despite the strange detour and the mini heart attack from almost crashing into a truck, we were back on track.

"On our way to Canada, eh?" Sean grinned, his eyes lighting up with excitement.

We laughed it off as we drove into the evening, the road stretching ahead, wide with possibility. Our adventure was far from over—we were just getting started.

I reached for the road map to figure out our next move, but accidentally grabbed the snowboard magazine instead. *"Craig Kelly's Summer Camp"* blazed across the cover—a perfect reminder of the epic days waiting for us up North.

We crashed at a cheap motel in Oregon that night—the kind with a buzzing neon sign where the *e* had burned out, so it read *"Family Rat Hotel."*

At sunrise, we hit the road again.

Finally, we crossed into Canada. And if you've never done the drive from Vancouver to Whistler, let me tell you: it's unreal. The scenery was so lush and endless, it felt like we were driving straight into a postcard. I even made Sean pull over at Shannon Falls because I couldn't resist. Not to make it all about me, but if that wasn't Canada literally calling my name, I don't know what was. The water tumbled down in glistening sheets, the roar of it echoing through the trees like a promise: *"You're exactly where you're meant to be."*

Our condo in Whistler was everything we hoped for—right in the heart of town, with a balcony overlooking the cobblestone walkway below. We were steps from the lifts, the mountain practically breathing down our necks, daring us to ride.

Whistler wasn't just a mountain—it was a whole world. At the base sat the town, pulsing with energy. Above the town, twin giants: Whistler Mountain and Blackcomb Mountain. Both legendary, but Blackcomb held the real treasure—a glacier that stayed blanketed in snow year-round. And somewhere up there? Craig Kelly's World Snowboard Camp.

The best part? It was way cheaper to rent a condo for the whole month, buy a season pass, ride the public halfpipe on the mountain, and cook our own meals than it would've been to attend Craig's summer camp for just one week as paying campers.

We decided to stock up on groceries right away. That afternoon at the store, Sean nudged me, nodding toward a couple of guys loading beers into their cart—Canadian pros. He knew every face. I knew barely any, but I figured, if girls had been the biggest thing in snowboarding, I would've had them memorized too.

The next morning, we geared up early and made the trek: two chair-lifts, a shuttle bus, another lift. Each ride cranked our anticipation higher. And then we saw it.

The halfpipe.

Carved perfectly into the glacier, it gleamed under the summer sun like some holy shrine. We stood at the summit, staring down at the perfectly shaped walls and the T-bar lift waiting to drag us back up.

T-bars weren't glamorous. Just a metal bar placed behind your thighs, dragging you uphill while you prayed you didn't faceplant and take someone down with you.

I turned to Sean, my grin stretched so wide it hurt. "This is even better than the magazine."

We dropped down toward Craig's halfpipe, stopping at the top like kids staring into the gates of Disneyland. In my mind, the soundtrack swelled—big horns, big drums, big everything.

Doo doo da dooooo.

And there, carving through the nearly empty pipe like a king in his castle, was Craig Kelly himself.

His movements were smooth, deliberate—every carve and every tweak pure poetry. A photographer with thick, black-rimmed glasses shouted from the deck, "Yeah, Craig—that was siiick! Can you do it again, eh?"

We froze, taking it all in, watching one of the greats in his element, like we'd been given a front-row seat to snowboard history.

Sean bumped my shoulder. "Let's sneak in a few runs. The camp must be on break."

I was thinking we couldn't exactly sneak in because we were glaringly the ones who had just showed up.

"Are you sure about this?" I called out, scanning the mostly deserted pipe. But Sean was already gone, riding the pipe like he owned the place.

I hesitated at the drop-in, rocking back and forth, pressing my edges into the snow to get my board moving. My heart pounded—a surge of nerves and excitement colliding all at once. *Here goes nothin'.*

With one final shift, I committed, dropping in and setting my edge as I carved up the backside wall. My heels dug in, and as I popped off the lip for my first air, the last of my hesitation disappeared. The second I landed, the nerves vanished, replaced by pure adrenaline.

By the time I reached the bottom, Sean was already in deep conversation with a few riders. Turns out, Sean was right. The camp was in between sessions so it was the perfect time to poach the pipe. Before I knew it, he was getting invited to the local bar, called Tommy Africa's, later that night by Ken Achenbach himself. The guy was practically a walking VIP pass to Whistler. And with the drinking age in Canada set at eighteen—game on for Sean.

Ken waved us over to meet Craig Kelly, and to our surprise, he actually took a moment to greet us. He gave us both a quick handshake and a warm smile—friendly, not flashy, just cool in that effortless Craig Kelly way. He asked where we were from, nodded when we said Colorado, and said something like, "Stoked you made it up here." That was it—simple, but enough to make our day.

After that, he and Ken shifted gears, diving into a discussion about setting up the next shot. We hung back, giving them space, still a little stunned. Craig hiked up the pipe, strapped into his bindings, and gave his buckles a couple extra clicks to tighten them down.

He called out across the pipe, "Ya ready, Ken?"

Ken gave a thumbs-up and shouted back, "Ready!"

Craig nodded, then yelled, "Droppin'!"

He started by riding down the deck of the pipe—the flat section that ran along the top edge of the walls—using it to build momentum before dropping into the transition, the steep, curved section that funneled into the pipe. As he entered, he smoothly absorbed the transition and powered up the frontside wall.

Catching air, his back hand reached across his body, gripping between his bindings on the toe edge—a crail grab. The grab, a signature of stylish controlled riding, added a touch of effortless grace to an already massive air.

Ken's camera fired away like a machine gun, capturing the best angle of Craig's unmistakable style. I half-expected Ken to turn to us and say, "Don't worry, you'll see this on the cover."

Whistler was straight-up magical. Every morning, we'd hit the slopes until our legs felt like wet noodles. Snowboarding was life, and Whistler was where you went to make a name for yourself—where riders showed up to be seen, to be part of something epic. I made friends with some of the local girls. They were friendly and loved snowboarding as much as me. Occasionally, I'd catch a guy or two giving me and Sean funny looks, assuming I was just his girlfriend tagging along—gross! I quickly made sure to make a point to tell anyone I met that he was my brother. After that, guys started actually talking to me.

Meanwhile, Sean was fully embracing the scene at Tommy Africa's, partying most nights and making friends with the up-and-coming pros. I, on the other hand, usually turned in early, wanting to save every ounce of energy for the next day's riding. Each morning, he'd fill me in on all the drama and introduce me to his new friends on the hill, while I just smirked at his so-called "networking" strategies.

Time flew by. Before we knew it, we'd been in Whistler for a month—the full stretch our parents had allowed us to stay. As our last days ticked down, the OP Challenge contest loomed on the horizon, our big test. This was our final chance to see if we could hold our own with the top riders before we packed up and hit the road. So, naturally, we both signed up, ready to give it everything we had.

On competition day, the sun was blazing, turning the pipe into a slush fest. I ran through my game plan—smooth airs, a spin or two, and maybe, just maybe, the 540 I'd been working on. I'd never seen a girl pull it off, and the thought of being the first to nail it fueled my nerves and excitement. Sean and I scraped our way through to the finals, though a few shaky moments left me feeling a bit deflated. But with the "Most Stoked Air" contest coming up, I wasn't leaving without putting everything on the line for that win.

"Go big, Shan. You can go higher than any of these girls," Sean said.

This contest was all about going big with style—the kind of flair we'd practiced for hours on the trampoline back home.

I dropped in, gathering speed as I carved hard up the backside wall. As I launched out of the lip, I reached down, grabbed my toe edge near the front binding, and tucked my front knee in—a clean Japan air. Everything clicked: the tweak, the airtime, the stomp.

The second I landed, I could hear Sean cheering.

Winning "Most Stoked Air" that day was more than a title—it was my own confirmation that I could keep up with the best. The energy of that run showed me how far full commitment could take me, the kind that pushes limits and goes all in. I'd gone from tagging along with my brother to truly believing I could make this dream a reality. And our month at Whistler? Every single second was worth it, a glimpse of what was possible when I threw myself in without hesitation.

I was excited to call my parents with the big news—finally, proof that we were productive. And I figured I'd check in on Betsy, too. I knew she was still in Seattle with her boyfriend, so maybe we could swing by on the way back.

Turns out, she was more than ready to head home—she was this close to buying a plane ticket. Perfect timing. Instead of her flying, we'd pick her up, no problem. And while we were at it, Sean and I figured, why not stop at Mount Hood? It was (sort of) on the way home, and this was our only shot to check it out.

Mount Hood, just outside of Portland, was home to another rare gem—a summer glacier with a halfpipe, making it one of the only places in the U.S. where you could snowboard year-round. It had its own summer camp scene, where pros trained and up-and-comers pushed their limits. Just one day on the mountain—that's all we needed. I'd put my contest winnings up to cover it. We couldn't wait.

After a month of nonstop riding, meeting legends, and soaking up every ounce of the scene, we left Whistler feeling full—body, mind, and spirit. This place had been more than just a snow-covered playground. It was a proving ground. A launchpad. An ambition made real.

Saying goodbye was bittersweet, but we weren't leaving empty-handed. We left with new tricks, new friends, and the kind of quiet confidence that comes from hurling yourself into the unknown—and sticking the landing.

Maybe there are no accidents.

Some things just line up. Like Whistler. Like the contest. Like the road still stretching out in front of us.

And next in line? Mount Hood.

CHAPTER 6

/ Sulfuric Fart and a Sponsorship to Part /

THE SECOND WE PICKED UP BETSY, everything changed. The van went from mellow to mayhem in minutes—she and I couldn't stop talking if we tried, and poor Sean looked like he was ready to jump ship. Betsy and I were in the back, swapping out mixtapes every five minutes, rewriting lyrics to every song, and generally driving Sean to the edge of sanity.

The atlas was stretched out across the dash like we were old-timey explorers, tracing a route to Mount Hood that seemed doable in about four and a half hours.

Betsy had taken over as DJ, rifling through her endless mixtapes again, while Sean—normally the loudest one in the van—went totally silent, grinding his teeth as we belted out every song like a bad karaoke night.

About four hours into the "easy" drive, things took a turn. The gas gauge was hugging *E*, and we found ourselves on some dark, winding back road, hoping there was just enough fuel left to get us through. We'd passed a sign for Mount Hood, so we figured we had to be close.

Then, out of nowhere, this awful stench filled the van.

"Who farted?" I gagged, yanking my sweatshirt over my face as Betsy did the same. Sean threw up his hands. "Relax—it's just sulfur."

And then, right on cue, he let one rip. That did it. The tension cracked as Betsy and I doubled over, laughing so hard we could barely breathe.

"We're gonna blow!" Betsy gasped. "Sean probably ignited the fumes!"

The stench was horrific—like something had died—but we couldn't stop laughing. Turns out, Mount Hood is technically an active volcano. No wonder it stank.

But Sean's patience hit a wall about ten minutes later, right around the time Betsy and I started remixing "Love Shack" into something completely unrecognizable.

"Alright, that's it," he snapped, yanking the tape from the deck and chucking it out the window.

He rechecked the map, muttering, "We've gotta double back. We're going up the wrong side of the mountain—there's nothing up here."

We turned around, running on fumes, and somehow coasted right into a gas station in the middle of nowhere. The attendant, who had fewer teeth than directions, filled the tank and pointed us toward a little town called Government Camp.

When we finally rolled into Government Camp, we found a hotel with one bunk room available. It looked like it hadn't been updated since the '70s—avocado-green shag carpet, wood paneling, and that peculiar old motel smell. The kind of place where you expected to find a ghost haunting the halls.

But it had beds, and that was enough.

The next morning, we woke up to Mount Hood rising against a clear sky, its snow-covered peaks glowing in the early light like something out of a postcard. All the exhaustion from the drive melted away as we geared up. With perfect snow, a public halfpipe, and endless groomed runs, it was snowboard paradise. We hit the halfpipe first, taking advantage of every run. Betsy messed around with grabs, Sean worked on spins, and I was dead-set on landing my 540. Not far off, upcoming pro Todd Richards and the legendary Sims team were doing a photoshoot, adding this extra surreal layer to the day.

By early afternoon, we were sunburned, wind-burned, and running on pure stoke. Sean was ready to call it, but I wasn't ready to let go just yet.

"Just one more run," I kept saying, racing back up the hill like a kid who didn't know how to quit. I was finally nailing my stalefish grab, hitting the 540, and riding like everything had just clicked into place. Betsy and Sean sat down on their boards, burnt out and waiting for me to be done, but I was running up the pipe, riding on this crazy high, like nothing could go wrong. The whole month seemed to come together at that moment, and I couldn't get enough.

Finally, Sean looked at me and said, "Seriously, Shan, we gotta hit the road."

I sighed, feeling the pull but also knowing I had to take one last perfect run. I breathed in at the top, focused, and had a flawless ride down. As I landed at the bottom, a guy with a camera bag slung over his shoulder walked up, cool as anything.

"I'm Brad Steward," he said, handing me a business card. "Team manager for Sims." I smiled, wiped the sweat from my brow, and introduced myself, trying to play it cool. Brad started talking about sponsorship like it was the most normal thing in the world. He was relaxed, told me he had to meet up with the team, but had been watching me ride and was impressed.

"Give me a call sometime," he said with an easy grin. I nodded, probably looking like I'd just won the lottery.

As he walked away, I tucked the card into my pocket, trying to absorb what had just happened. This was the moment I'd been going after without even realizing it. It felt like the universe had pointed at me and said, "*Go.*"

The drive back was different. The van was filled with this strange silence, like we all knew something had just changed but couldn't put it into words. Sean gave me a light punch on the arm, grinning.

"You just met the Sims guy," he said, shaking his head, like he couldn't believe it either.

I nodded—exhausted, sunburnt, and dehydrated—staring out the window as the road stretched ahead of us, endless and open. All this time, I'd been chasing something—pushing, proving, trying to keep up. But now, for the first time, it felt like something was chasing me forward. *Where would it lead?*

CHAPTER 7

/ The Drop /

MY LEFT ELBOW SLID OFF THE NARROW ARMREST, jolting me awake. I'd promised myself I wouldn't fall asleep in class again, but here we were. The cafeteria iced tea was supposed to help me stay alert—instead, I was jittery and desperate for a bathroom. I rubbed my eyes, squinting through the professor's monotone voice as it droned across the packed lecture hall. The thrill of starting at CU Boulder had faded. My mind was a million miles from economics.

Instead, it was back on Mount Hood—back to that life-changing encounter with Brad Steward. My fingers traced the edge of my notebook, remembering the creased, water-stained business card he'd handed me. For weeks, I'd wondered if he'd meant it—or if I'd imagined the offer. Finally, I mustered the courage to dial the blurry number. Was it a 2 or a 7? After a few tries, Brad finally answered.

"Hi, I'm calling to speak with Brad Steward? This is Shannon Dunn," I said, trying to keep my voice steady.

A slight pause. "This is Brad!" he said, surprised but quick to take the reins. "I'm so glad you called! I'm starting something new, and I want you in on it—if you're up for it. I know you don't know me, but if you trust me, give me a call back in a couple weeks. I'll be able to share more by then."

A few weeks later, I talked to Brad again. He was now part of a start-up called Morrow Snowboards.

"We're naming it after Rob Morrow," he said casually.

I'd seen Rob at top pro competitions. He had a calm, grounded vibe, serious skills, and seemed approachable.

Brad offered me a sponsorship. I'd be the first—and only—girl on the team. The deal included free boards, photo incentives, some travel support, and real exposure. It wasn't just a hookup—it was a legitimate shot at a snowboarding career. To my surprise, my parents were on board. After some serious conversations, we decided school could wait. This opportunity couldn't. So I took off the spring semester and, with Sean, jumped into the Professional Snow Tour of America.

Brad's belief in me gave me the confidence to believe in myself. He was backing me with money and product—taking a real risk. And when someone invests in you like that, it pushes you to rise to the occasion, to become the best version of yourself. I didn't want to let him down.

Meanwhile, Sean's season was a roller coaster—lost gear, nagging injuries, and a string of tough breaks. But I was starting to find my rhythm in the halfpipe, landing on the podium at several events. I even took first place. Each result felt like another door opening, pulling me deeper into this incredible life.

/ / /

A nudge from the girl beside me snapped me out of my thoughts. I looked around, realizing the class was winding down, though my mind was already drifting again—this time to Canada, and the Gotcha photoshoot Brad had arranged.

/ / /

I stepped out of the airport shuttle and took in the view of the sprawling mountain lodge. I was just eighteen, and the weight of everything new hit me at once. My first solo trip. My first time heli boarding. I was a little shy, a little scared—but completely overwhelmed by the possibilities waiting in the unknown. And the kicker? It was all -expenses-paid.

Inside, the lobby felt like a scene from a movie set: a massive stone fireplace, thick timber beams, and wide glass windows that framed snow-covered peaks in every direction. The smell of dinner drifted through the air—rich and savory—and my stomach growled in response.

Then I spotted a familiar face.

Photographer Ken Achenbach—the godfather of Canadian snowboarding. He'd famously smuggled one of the first snowboards across the border, carving turns wherever he could, even when resorts still banned the sport outright. Sean and I had gotten to know his sarcastic wit and deep-rooted passion for snowboarding during our summer in Whistler, just nine months earlier. Now, seeing him here—amid so much unknown—felt like finding an anchor.

"Shannon!" Ken Achenbach called out, striding over, his thick-framed black glasses fogging slightly as he flashed his trademark grin. His jovial Canadian accent made me smile back instantly.

"Glad ya made it, eh? We've got some crazy stuff lined up for ya!"

"Good to see you," I said, exhaling a wave of nerves.

He threw a friendly arm around my shoulder, gave me a quick shake, and grabbed my bags as we headed deeper into the lodge. "Let me introduce ya to the crew. You're gonna have a blast."

We passed plush leather couches and a crackling fire—pure mountain luxury. It was a far cry from the cramped cabins and budget motels I was used to. Ken led me into a wide-open room where a crew of riders and guides were gathered, laughing and swapping stories over beers.

"Alright, team," Ken announced. "Meet Shannon Dunn—our newest shredder!"

A dozen heads turned. Rob Morrow—who looked uncannily like

Barney Rubble—grinned and raised his beer.

"Hey, nice to have ya here!" he said warmly. His mellow energy instantly put me at ease.

Next, Ken motioned toward Don "Schwarty" Schwartz. His face was red and raw, burn scars stretching across his entire face and neck. A clear protective mask covered it. Even without eyebrows, there was something warm in his expression. He gave me a nod, his voice muffled behind the shield.

"Welcome, Shannon," he said, eyes twinkling with a mix of mischief and resilience.

I smiled back, already curious about his story.

The introductions kept coming. Doug Lundgren—quiet and intense—carried the weight of someone who'd seen too much. He held the record for the biggest air ever landed on a snowboard in Canada. Greg "GT" Tomlinson, a sun-soaked Californian, exuded laid-back surf-bro energy. Evan Feen, the Canadian, was tall and skinny with long blond hair, part hippy and part backcountry drifter—an outdoorsman with a groovy, free-flowing style. Steve Matthews, the American backcountry guru, was a burly mountain man—steady, tough, and built for long days deep in the wilderness. Then there was Erwin, our Austrian skier guide. Thick accent. Rough-hewn look. Zero patience for BS.

And finally, Gary—the other trail guide—looked like he could vanish into the backcountry for a month and re-emerge without a scratch.

As I took my seat, a waitress appeared and set down a steaming plate in front of me—something rich and savory that smelled like heaven after a long day of travel. The crew had already eaten, but they made space and welcomed me in like I'd been there all along. That warm meal, surrounded by strangers who already felt like teammates, grounded me in the best way. As the night wore on, I found myself laughing harder than I had in ages. The crew was wild. Each one larger than life.

Later, Ken clapped Don on the shoulder.

"Schwarty's been through the ringer," Ken said. "Survived a heli crash last year with Doug—lost three friends, but the two of them made it out. And that's just the beginning."

He leaned in, animated. "Before that, he had a wipeout that nearly tore off half his nose. And then—after surviving the crash—we're doing a trampoline demo. Schwarty goes for a big backflip, misses the tramp, hits the ground, shatters both elbows, breaks his wrist...and just keeps going. Doesn't matter what gets thrown at him."

Don chuckled and shrugged. "What doesn't kill ya, right?"

We all laughed—some awkwardly, all of us a little awed. Ken caught my eye and winked. "You're in good hands, Shannon. They might look a little rough around the edges—but trust me, they're solid."

The next morning, a soft knock on the door woke me—a wake-up call at my private chalet. Scattered across the property were individual log cabins, each with a cozy, European feel. Mine had a private bedroom and bathroom, all rustic charm with exposed wooden beams and warm lighting. It was just a short walk to the main lodge, where all the action buzzed—but here, in my own quiet space, I felt like a snow princess. I pulled back the curtains. No new snow had fallen, but the sky was clear—a bright spring day, full of possibility.

But "girl reality" hit fast. I'd started my period—cramps and all. After popping two Advil and stuffing my jacket and backpack with supplies, I pulled on my gear. The Gotcha pants—men's large samples—practically swallowed me, so I rolled them up and cinched the jacket tight. I just hoped for the best, knowing I had no clue how or where I'd manage a bathroom break that day.

At breakfast, Ken tapped Don on the shoulder.

"Heya, Schwarty, how ya feelin' about today, eh?" he asked, his mouth half-full of scrambled eggs.

Schwarty grinned and gave a thumbs-up. "Good to be back," he said, though his voice carried a quiet weight. It was his first time stepping into a helicopter since the crash, and his face told the story—his eyes flickered with hesitation, the kind that comes from staring down old ghosts. The corners of his mouth hovered between forced confidence and the shadow of remembered fear.

I didn't want to stare, but I held my breath. This was a big moment, and I couldn't help watching, trying to read his body language. I'd never been in a helicopter myself, and for a flicker of a moment, the thought of a crash flashed through my mind. But I pushed it aside. This opportunity felt bigger than the fear.

When breakfast wrapped up, we made our way out to the helipad. As we approached, GT turned to Doug. "Mind if I grab the back seat?"

Doug glanced at him, eyes dark with something heavier. "That's... where my friend was sitting when he...ya know."

GT's expression softened immediately. "Oh...yeah, no worries," he said, quickly opting for a different seat. Everyone boarding the heli seemed to recognize the unspoken rule—leave that one empty. My stomach twisted at the sight, a quick, sharp pang rising inside my chest. But as I strapped myself in, pulling the harness tight, I felt something shift— like instinct taking over. My breath steadied, the roar of the heli drowning out everything else. The pilot gave the green light, and we loaded up. Across from me, Don caught my eye, giving me a quick, reassuring nod—*we got this.*

My pulse raced as the ground dropped away, mountains rising on all sides as we soared into the wild. Once we reached the peaks, the pilot dipped low, scouting our first line, and set us down in a whirl of snow— the flurry blinding us until the heli lifted off again, leaving us wrapped in the stillness of the backcountry.

Erwin took the lead, barking instructions in his thick Austrian accent. "Stay behind me, don't go ahead!" he ordered, waving us forward.

GT leaned over, muttering, "What's with the intense vibes? I thought heli boarding was supposed to be fun." He flashed me a quick grin, his sunglasses hiding any trace of a wink.

Erwin guided us toward a cliff band, barely containing his own excitement. "This is the spot," he said, pointing to the drop-off.

"Alright then, let's check it out, eh?" Ken called, already moving eagerly toward the cliffs, his voice raced with energy.

"Mind if I ride under there, Erwin?" Ken shouted—then, without waiting for a reply, he disappeared beneath the cliff band. Suddenly, his voice floated up, distant and playful: "Hey, Shannon...wanna hit this cliff? Come check it out from the top!"

Wait—was he calling me? Usually, the guys took the first big leaps. But I wasn't about to back down.

"Uh, okay, I'm coming," I called, trying to steady the nerves creeping in as I moved closer to the edge.

The guys gathered behind me, eyeing the drop-off with a mix of anticipation and caution. I overheard GT mutter, "Man, I hope we find something better than this. I came here for pow runs and massive cliff lines."

Ken shouted up, "This is a decent-sized cliff, but I can make it look massive. Think you can hit that spot over there?" He pointed to a section with a steep landing that made my stomach lurch.

I unstrapped my board and edged forward, peering over the cliff. The sun was hitting it—it looked doable, but my nerves screamed otherwise. We hadn't even taken a warm-up run yet. Fifteen feet, maybe twenty—it was hard to tell.

I spotted Ken below, lining up his camera. I started to giggle, partly from nerves, partly from the sheer disbelief that I was actually considering this.

"So...how's the landing?" I called down, trying to sound more confident than I felt.

"It's looking softer with the sun on it," Ken replied. "You're good to go."

I weighed my options. If I veered too far left, I'd drop fifty feet into a cluster of trees. Go right, and it'd be a twenty-footer with a safe landing.

My brother's cliff-jumping tips rushed back: toss a few snowballs to gauge the size and check my trajectory. Pack the takeoff so I wouldn't catch an edge. Mark a clean line in the snow, pointing exactly where I wanted to launch.

I tossed a snowball to trace the natural fall line. Ken gave me a thumbs-up, signaling he was happy with the angle. I tossed another just to double-check, then patted down the takeoff with my board and etched a clear direction using the edge of the board.

"I'm regular foot!" I called down—important so he could frame the shot to capture the front of my body.

"I'll grab melancholy, okay?" I added, locking in our plan. Good communication was key to making sure he nailed the shot.

Ken lined up his camera and gave another thumbs-up. "Alright, Shan—give me a ten-second count when you're ready."

Before I could overthink it, I was strapping into my bindings, standing five feet above the takeoff. My pulse hammered as I mentally rehearsed the sequence: hit the line, hold the grab, stick the landing.

"Ten seconds!" I called, my voice catching slightly. I pointed my board downhill, heart pounding, and gathered speed as the edge rushed closer.

In an instant, I launched off, grabbing between my bindings on the heel edge like my life depended on it. The cliff felt bigger than I'd guessed, and my stomach lurched. I held the grab, poking out my front leg as the air rushed past, my heart thundering in my chest. For a second, time stretched—the ground distant, the world silent—until suddenly, the landing rushed up to meet me.

I released the grab, braced for impact—my board slammed into the snow, legs holding firm as I skidded to a stop, laughing as adrenaline surged through my veins. I looked back at the cliff, heart pounding. It was way bigger than I'd expected.

Ken's voice echoed up: "*Yes!* That was it... That's gonna be the sickest shot ever! That was insane!"

Relieved, I collapsed back onto the snow, gazing up at the sky. A blackbird circled overhead, and I laughed—nature's little reminder of reality. I also seriously needed a bathroom break.

Ken was beaming. "I'm positive I got the shot, but just in case...

can you do it again? I can't wait to develop this film!" he asked, his face lit with eagerness.

Inside, I screamed, *"No way!"* But out loud, I called back, "Sure!" Summoning every bit of courage, I hiked back up. If anything, the drop seemed even bigger this time—but somehow, I nailed it again. Ken hyped up the guys to give it a go, and soon they were lining up at the edge, sizing up the drop. GT and Rob each hit it a few times.

GT shook his head, laughing. "Alright, I take it back—this is legit."

I shrugged, still playing it cool. "It's decent."

The guys laughed, their respect clear, and I felt a jolt of pride—I'd held my own, and Ken got the shot.

After the cliff session, we prepped to hit a new zone for the next round of shots. Erwin, ever the disciplined guide, firmly told us to hold tight and not go ahead—he wanted to scout the high ground first to see what lay below. Meanwhile, Ken packed up his camera gear, and the rest of us waited, tossing snowballs. Rob lobbed one right at my shoulder, kicking off an all-out snowball fight, though I struggled to hit him from below.

The laughter stopped abruptly when GT asked, "Dude, where'd Erwin go?"

We scanned the slope. One minute Erwin had been there—then, gone. Steve Matthews, with years of mountaineering and first-descent experience behind him, immediately took charge. Calm and deliberate, he cautiously side-slipped toward the spot where Erwin had last stood.

"Hey—there's a huge hole!" he called back, his voice tight with urgency as he searched for signs of him, calling Erwin's name into the depths. My stomach dropped, heart racing as I tried to process what just happened. *What the heck?*

Thankfully, Ken and Gary, our other guide, showed up just then, calm but focused as we filled them in.

"Hey, Erwin fell into a hole and disappeared," we explained.

Gary immediately took charge, telling us to sit tight while he radioed

Erwin. To our huge relief, Erwin responded—he was okay, though it was dark down there. He'd slid a long way, but one ski had wedged firmly into the narrow ice walls, stopping his fall and saving him from an even worse outcome.

Within minutes, a rescue team arrived—coincidentally, they'd been training nearby. From my perspective, everything unfolded incredibly fast: no panic, just quick, purposeful movements. I didn't see Erwin get hauled out, though, because Gary had already started guiding us carefully down the slope, steering us away from the rescue zone. I guessed we were the "fancy clients" they didn't want witnessing the unfolding crisis.

The weight of it all cast a shadow over the day. We left the mountain feeling shaken.

That evening, however, dinner transformed into a celebration. Erwin walked into the lodge to cheers and applause, his story already becoming legend among us. He recounted how the snow bridge had collapsed, dropping him eighty feet into darkness—and how, astonishingly, his wedged ski had caught just right, stopping his fall. His arm was sore, but incredibly, he'd escaped without broken bones or even a scrape. Erwin was basically a walking miracle.

Listening to him, I sat quietly, overwhelmed. I'd never experienced anything even close to this—it was raw, intense, and way outside my comfort zone. Honestly, if I'd known beforehand what was going to happen, I probably would've said no. But now that I'd been there, I was glad. It felt real—a glimpse into something bigger and deeper than I'd ever known life to be.

Don Schwartz was a survivor, too—though there was no way I could fully grasp what he'd endured after his helicopter crash, his third-degree burns, his shattered bones. I didn't understand how people kept going after things like that. But watching Erwin, and thinking of Don, I knew one thing for sure: I wanted to try.

Gotcha ad—cliff drop moment. Photo by Ken Achenbach.

The next day, led by Mike Wiegele himself—the legendary owner of the heli operation—we tore through hidden powder fields, breaking the day's vertical record. It was the trip of a lifetime, leaving me with a renewed gratitude for life—and for the mountains that always keep us humble.

/ / /

I snapped awake as the girl beside me stood, signaling the end of class. The professor's monotone had faded into background noise long ago. Quickly wiping the drool from my mouth, I grabbed my things and shuffled toward the exit with the rest of the crowd.

Outside the lecture hall, fat snowflakes drifted quietly through the air, brushing softly against my face. Their touch brought a rush of nostalgia. Snow had always felt magical to me—like a silent invitation to another life, one far from economics lectures and crowded auditoriums.

Walking back to my dorm, the snowflakes melted gently into my jacket as my thoughts drifted. Inside, I noticed the blinking light on the answering machine and hit play.

My dad's excited voice filled the room. "Hey, Shan, just wanted to let ya know—*Transworld Snowboard* magazine's new issue has a full-page Gotcha ad of you going off a huge cliff. It's amazing. Check it out."

His message wasn't over. "Also...someone dropped off an anonymous two thousand dollars at my office, with a note saying it's for you and Sean to compete in the World Cup in Val d'Isère, France, this December. Call me—I think one of my clients heard about your opportunity and wanted to help fund the trip. Call me soon. Love you."

I stood frozen.

France. The World Cup.

Someone out there believed in me enough to help me get there.

Even with all these doors opening, I still wanted both: the snowboarding career and the college degree. I'd read somewhere that only about one percent of athletes ever make it pro—so I knew I shouldn't put all my eggs into one basket. I wanted to prove I could chase my dreams without giving up the safety net of a diploma. It seemed doable— balancing two worlds, keeping all my options alive.

But standing there now, hearing my dad's voice echo in the room, I felt a flicker of doubt. Could I really hold onto both? I'd always placed a high value on school, but snowboarding was pulling at me in a way I couldn't ignore.

For the first time, I realized I might be standing at a crossroads—and I couldn't help but wonder how long I could keep walking both paths before one slipped away.

CHAPTER 8

/ Getting There Is Half the Battle /

JUST A FEW MONTHS AGO, I'd been half-asleep in an economics lecture, torn between college and snowboarding. In the end, I rushed through my finals, finishing early so I could squeeze in this trip. With exams behind me, I barely had time to blink before heading home to Steamboat, tossing my gear into a bag, and hopping on a flight to Europe. I'd decided to take another spring semester off to compete. College could wait; this couldn't.

Geneva Airport was in full holiday chaos mode just ten days before Christmas, with bustling crowds and luggage piled as far as the eye could see. We'd flown over in shifts—Mom and Sean first, then Dad and me— because the holiday flights had filled up fast.

When Dad and I finally cleared customs, we spotted them outside by the rental car, deep in battle with the bags. The trunk was already crammed full, and Sean was wedging a duffel into the backseat while Mom tried to reposition a suitcase to make room. Dad jumped in to help, maneuvering around fourteen bags—two snowboard bags and his endless "just in case" extras—all stuffed into a tiny red Fiat Panda 4x4, our shoebox on wheels for the next week and a half.

Mom shot Dad a look as he attempted to shove in yet another bag. "Gerald C. Dunn, what the—I think we're one suitcase short of a moving truck. What exactly did you think we'd need?"

Dad just grinned, completely unfazed. "Ya never know, Joyce! Better to have it and not need it."

Sean and I squeezed into the backseat, knees to our chins.

"Comfy back there?" Dad called, giving the hatch one last tug before tightening the rope holding it down and slapping on a final strip of duct tape for good measure.

"Like sardines!" I laughed, rolling my eyes and swiping a chocolate Toblerone from Sean. I bit into the triangle candy, the sugar hitting like a shot of adrenaline. Just as I settled in, Sean shot me a mischievous grin—then let one rip, filling our already limited air supply with a "fragrance" I hadn't signed up for.

"Seriously, Sean?" I groaned, waving a hand in front of my face.

And with that, our trip to Val d'Isère, France, for the World Cup snowboarding contest officially began—cramped, chaotic, classic Jerstyle. We'd coined that phrase after my dad, Jerry, whose trademark move was to dive headfirst into adventure and figure out the details later. Planning was optional; excitement wasn't. And though it usually led to mayhem, one thing was certain: it was bound to be unforgettable.

Dad, ever the adventurer, was determined to take the scenic route to Val d'Isère. "Look, I found a shortcut," he announced, squinting at the map and steering confidently off the main road.

Mom rolled her eyes. "Jer, we're already one pothole away from losing half our luggage. Can we just get there in one piece?"

But Dad was undeterred. "We're right by Mont Blanc—highest peak in the Alps! You don't pass that up when it's in your backyard!"

Mom sighed but gave in, and Dad triumphantly charted a course through Évian, planning a quick stop to stretch our legs. "Besides," he added, "we can grab lunch in the luxury water capital of the world!"

Sean just snorted. "Is luxury water even a thing?"

Our pit stop in Évian gave us a scenic lakeside lunch—jackets peeled off, basking in the sun, almost forgetting how tired we were. Dad knocked back a double espresso, determined to power through. Sean and I exchanged a look. This World Cup trip was already a whirlwind, and we hadn't even reached the mountain. One of Dad's clients had anonymously covered our travel expenses; we didn't know why, but we were grateful.

Back on the road, Dad tested the Fiat's limits, speeding along the Swiss highway. "Dad, slow down!" I shouted, bracing myself against the bags and Sean as the car rattled.

Mom shot him a look, clearly questioning her life choices. "Jer, I'm pretty sure I saw a sign saying 120 kilometers."

"What? This is the Autobahn, Joyce! It's European tradition to test your limits," he quipped, foot still on the gas.

Mom shot back, "We're not in Germany, Jerry—this is Switzerland, and they *do* have speed limits!"

Off the highway, we took the back roads. Then came the inevitable: Dad's "shortcut" hit a dead end. A bright red sign read, "Route Barrée." Road closed. Silence filled the car, followed by a collective groan as Dad reluctantly admitted we'd have to backtrack.

"Just taking the scenic route, everyone!" he insisted, brushing off our complaints with his usual easygoing grin.

After an almost nine-hour journey—one that should have taken three—we finally arrived in Val d'Isère. The town greeted us with festive Christmas lights and a glowing "Joyeux Noël" sign. By the time we stumbled into our condo, it was nearly midnight.

Inside hit like a walk-in freezer. My breath puffed in the dim light as I rubbed my frozen fingers together. Dad quickly found the thermostat, but no matter how high he cranked it, no warmth came. So much for the cozy retreat we'd imagined.

Determined to fix it, Dad roamed the dark building searching for the manager, but the office was locked up tight. Exhausted and jet-lagged, we gave up, layering on jackets, doubling our socks, and pulling beanies over our ears before crawling into bed. Dad joked the whole situation was "character-building," and we laughed through chattering teeth, hoping we'd wake up warm.

The next morning, the temperatures were still cold enough to see your breath. Dad finally got hold of the manager, who sheepishly admitted we were the condo's first guests of the season—hence the minor heating oversight. The heat was turned on, but in classic Euro fashion, it would take forever to warm up the entire space.

We shook off the night's mishaps, bundled up, and set out to explore.

The town of Val d'Isère felt like a fairy tale. Tall peaks framed the valley, and the stone streets echoed with the sound of church bells. In the distance, I spotted the halfpipe—a narrow stretch of white against the brown earth, like they'd scraped together every last patch of snow to make it happen. The peaks around us were capped in white, but down in town, it was all dirt. One of the best parts? Mom, Dad, and all the spectators could simply walk from town straight to the venue.

As we wandered, a shop filled with hanging sausages and hams—each with a faint, unsettling green tinge—caught our eye. Inside, a man dressed like he'd stepped out of a French film—black pants, rolled sleeves, vest, and a little scarf—calmly sliced meat behind the counter.

Mom leaned over, grinning. "It's like a French meat museum."

We'd never seen anything like it and quickly gave it a nickname: the Green Meat Shop.

As we left, the smell of fresh bread pulled us to a boulangerie-pâtisserie. We laughed, trying our best (and worst) French accents. Inside, the bakery greeted us with rich scents of caramel, butter, and cinnamon.

When Dad asked the baker about the weather, the man gave a confident nod. "Yes, it's all dirt—but many, many foots of snow will arrive soon," he promised in a thick French accent.

We burst out laughing. Many, many foots. It became our inside joke for the rest of the trip. Anytime someone slipped or pointed out the bare, patchy runs, we'd grin and chime, "Don't worry—many, many foots are coming!"

With the contest still five days away, we headed out to ride the re-sort, just to shake off the travel fog. The mountain was pure bulletproof ice—like sliding on glass. But I didn't care. Sean and I ran into Tina, her boyfriend, her brother, and a whole crew of American riders from the PSTA Tour, and it instantly felt like a reunion—a jolt of familiarity in a foreign place. We met a bunch of Euro riders too, and because we all snowboarded, we were instant friends. We laughed about the conditions, snapped goofy photos, and joked about survival mode. It wasn't about performance—not yet. It was about the sheer joy of just being there.

Back at the condo, we walked into what felt like the Sahara. The heat had finally kicked in with a vengeance. We scrambled to turn it down, only to huddle under blankets when the room plunged back to freezing. The thermostat, like all of us, was jet-lagged and confused, lurching be-tween extremes like it had hit menopause.

Then, the next morning, *bam*. Sean and I both woke up wrecked—sore throats, pounding heads, full-body aches. We felt like we'd been hit by a snowplow.

Thank God, the organizers postponed the first practice days. They were trying to preserve the halfpipe with so little snow on the ground. Honestly, I wanted nothing more than to curl up and sleep it off.

Armed with a tourist map and that unstoppable Jerry enthusiasm, Dad declared it the perfect day to explore the Olympic bobsled course in La Plagne—a nearby town set to host events for the upcoming 1992 Winter Olympics, based in Albertville and spread across the surround-ing mountains. "Come on, guys! Once in a lifetime!"

Mom lobbied hard for a rest day, but there was no winning against Dad's relentless optimism. So, we dragged our sorry, sick selves into the car, bounced around through wrong turns and mountain roads, and fi-nally arrived—standing at the base of the legendary, twisting concrete marvel. Check that one off the list.

By the time the first official halfpipe practice rolled around, I had no choice but to push through. I layered up, stuffed my pockets with cough drops, and forced my body to remember what it knew. Run by run, my energy returned. My body shook off the rust. By contest day, I wasn't at 100 percent, but I was close enough.

The field was stacked—the best riders in the world.

But here's the part I hadn't fully prepared for: the mental war.

Even surrounded by these world-class athletes, I didn't feel like one of them yet. Every time I coughed or felt my legs wobble during practice, the doubts crept in.

What if I wasn't ready? What if I blew this chance?

I made it through the qualifiers—a bit shaky, but in. Sean, on the other hand, hadn't made the finals, and I could tell it crushed him. All that effort, all this way, and no reward. But instead of sinking into disappointment, he channeled his frustration into lifting me up, and in that moment, that meant everything.

The crowd packed into the contest area, banners snapping wildly in the rising storm winds, announcers booming over the speakers. Anticipation crackled through the air.

Beside me, Tina grinned and punched me playfully on the arm. "Come on, Shan. You've *got* this!"

Her energy was contagious. Just having her beside me on this massive stage made everything feel lighter—like we were in it together, pushing ourselves, adding laughter, and turning what could've been crushing pressure into something fun.

The format was two runs, with the top combined score winning. No room for major mistakes. I figured most of the girls would play it safe. But I had something else in mind.

Over the summer at High Cascade Snowboard Camp on Mount Hood, I'd pushed my riding hard—sticking 540s and even landing photos in *Transworld Snowboarding* magazine. Brad from Morrow had lined me up as a guest coach for a couple of weeks, which gave me the perfect setup: coaching by day, and training in the halfpipe during every spare moment. It was the kind of opportunity that kept me progressing and showed I was earning my place in the scene.

Now, this was my shot to do something no girl had ever landed in a contest before: a frontside 540. I had to take the risk, set myself apart.

The mental apprehension I'd felt earlier in my contest runs was real, but enough was enough. I had a shift in mindset, a sharp realization: you don't get chances like this every day.

It could cost me everything—but deep down, I believed I could pull it off.

It was now or never. Sure, I probably should've practiced it more here, under these conditions, but it was finals, and a fire lit inside me. I needed to do this, like my life depended on it. Failing wasn't an option.

As the wind picked up and snow began to fall, it didn't shake me—it fueled me. The pressure felt mischievous, even thrilling, like when Betsy and I used to pull off pranks back home. Being the first girl to land this trick? It was edgy, daring—and I loved the rush.

At the top of the pipe, my heart pounded so hard I could feel it in my fingertips. My legs jittered, adrenaline crackling under my skin. My breathing tightened, but I forced one slow, steady inhale.

Drop in.

I hit my straight airs, but the fresh snowfall slowed me slightly. My mind raced: push through or adjust?

In a split second, I made the call: sub in an easier trick, stay on my feet, and save the big move for round two.

One more chance.

Above the halfpipe, the sky darkened. Thick clouds rolled in, wind gusting hard enough to snap sponsor banners sideways. A tent down the slope broke free, tumbling across the snow. The storm was coming, fast.

I inhaled deep. Centered myself. Blocked out the noise.

The second I dropped in, everything clicked. The first half of my run flowed perfectly, and I had just one more trick to finish it. I had to go for it.

The world narrowed. I carved up the frontside wall—just me, the pipe, and in that moment, I committed. A complete spin through the air, all the way around.

Time slowed—weightless, infinite.

Then touchdown. My board struck the snow.

Clean. Solid.

I rode away, heart thundering. I'd done it. I'd just landed the first-ever 540—not just for myself, but for women.

I came to a stop at the bottom, chest heaving, adrenaline roaring in my ears. Snowflakes drifted down—soft at first, then thicker, faster, swirling under the storm clouds gathering overhead. There was no digital scoreboard flashing instant results. Instead, we had to wait for the old-school method: hand-calculated scores posted on a physical board near the judges' tent.

Mom, Dad, and I walked over together, weaving through the crowd, every step making my nerves jump. I held my breath as the numbers were finally pinned up.

The final scores went up—and my heart sank.

Fourth. Just off the podium.

I swallowed hard, forcing a smile I didn't feel. Tina stood in third, Michelle Taggart in second, and Nicole Angelrath—the undefeated world champion—at the top. I told myself I should be proud just to stand among the best, but the sting of missing the podium ached deeper than I expected.

I gave Tina a hug, congratulating her, even as disappointment tugged at my chest.

But Mom wasn't convinced. She narrowed her eyes at the posted numbers, her finger darting between lines, mentally adding the scores. Then she grabbed Dad's arm. "Jerry—look at this. I think they added it wrong."

Dad leaned in, studying the sheet. "Oh yeah...and," he said slowly, pointing, "you got the highest score of the day with your last run."

Without missing a beat, he hustled to the judges' tent—rule book in hand, determination blazing across his face.

The storm picked up, howling through the halfpipe. Just then, an Olympic flag tore loose from its pole, tumbling end over end—landing right at Dad's feet. He bent down, scooped it up, and stuffed it into his pocket with a proud grin, like the whole universe had just handed him a personal souvenir.

We waited. Minutes stretched like hours.

Then, over the loudspeakers, the announcer's voice crackled: "A recalculation has been made..."

My stomach flipped.

"...And third place goes to—Shannon Dunn!"

Tina ran over, pulling me into a giant hug. "You earned this." She grinned.

And there I was: snow falling thick around us, clutching an oversized giant check—the kind they handed to all the top three finishers, along with a trophy. Mine, however, was still made out to Tina Basich in Sharpie for $400. They promised they'd fix it later and fill in my name. A gust of wind hit, nearly sailing us all away.

My family jumped up and down in the crowd, cheering like mad, while my dad proudly tucked the Olympic flag he'd scooped off the snow deeper into his coat, grinning like he'd won something himself.

I had done it.

I'd made the podium at the World Cup—and to me, that meant I had a real shot at becoming world champion.

Three events total—here, one in Aspen, Colorado, and the finale in Japan—and the overall winner would be crowned world champ.

And that title? It meant you were a legit, respected pro snowboarder.

Craig Kelly was a world champ.

Nicole Angelrath was a world champ.

I proved I could hang with the best. Now, I wanted to be the next world champ.

CHAPTER 9

/ Many, Many Foots of Snow /

MOM PULLED BACK THE CURTAINS AND GASPED. "Whoa, you guys... You have to see this."

I squinted one eye open from bed, shielding myself from the sudden burst of light. "Gosh, Ma—it's so bright. What time is it?"

I glanced at my watch. 7 a.m. Too early. Always one to sleep in, I silently begged this moment to be worth it.

Between the endless travel, getting sick, and competing, I was wiped. But curiosity stirred me. Groaning as my sore muscles protested, I swung my legs over the side of the bed and shuffled to the window.

"It's like the storm of the century," Mom whispered, nearly breathless. "Oh my gosh—the cars are completely buried!"

Outside, it was a total whiteout. Only a lone snowplow carved a narrow path down the street, its blinking lights flickering against towering drifts. The parking lot was packed with cars, now swallowed under a thick, heavy blanket of snow, their shapes poking up like lumpy moguls. It was December 23.

"Think we'll make it home by Christmas?" I asked, staring at the sheer amount of snow. Our flight was supposed to leave the next evening, but looking at this, it felt like wishful thinking. Not that I minded—we were all together anyway.

Sean peeked out the window and smirked. "Many, many foots!" he declared—a callback to the baker's promise from a few days earlier.

He grabbed the remote, flipping through channels. "I'll see if I can find some weather on the news."

BBC News flickered onto the screen, an emergency banner scrolling across the bottom.

"Turn it up," I said.

Outside, the plow beeped and groaned, backing up again and again, barely making a dent. The English reporter announced that nearly six feet of snow had fallen overnight—and the storm wasn't done yet.

Dad burst back into the condo, brushing snow off his jacket. "Whew, the whole town's shut down. I tried to get coffee, but I could barely make it down the steps, let alone to the café. I found a shovel, but it's practically useless. The snow's over my head!"

An hour later, the temperature rose, and it started pouring rain.

Suddenly, breaking news flashed across the TV: a massive avalanche in La Plagne had buried a chalet next to the Olympic bobsled course. Rescue teams had already recovered two bodies and were still searching for others.

My heart stopped. We had been there just days earlier, laughing, teasing Dad over his "once-in-a-lifetime" detour. Now, that same place was gone, buried under tons of snow. The weight of it hit like a punch in the chest. How fragile everything was, how quickly the world could shift, turning familiar places into scenes of heartbreak.

I watched the footage in stunned silence, my throat tightening. My heart ached for the families waiting for news, for the lives forever altered.

Dad shook his head. "No one's getting out of town anytime soon. Let's go see what's happening, maybe find out when they plan to open the pass. We might be here another night."

Mom's eyes widened. "I don't think you should go. Aren't avalanches still a risk?"

She had a good point, but I shrugged into my jacket. "Mom, come on. We'll stick to the main streets."

"Yeah," Sean added, "we're just taking a look."

Mom hesitated, eyeing the thick snowfall, but finally sighed and pulled on her coat. "Fine. But if I even think I see that snow shift, we're turning right back."

Our condo sat at the far end of town, so we trudged through deep, sloppy footpaths toward Main Street. Past the Green Meat Shop, past the church, we reached a chaotic scene. A hotel restaurant had been blown open—windows shattered, snow piled high inside. Parked cars along the street were half-buried, only a few side mirrors and antennas poking through.

"There's Tina," I said, spotting her unmistakable red ponytail whipping in the wind. She was shouting, "No one in this car—let's check the next!" as she dug furiously, knee-deep in the wreckage.

Sean nodded. "Yeah, Mikey and Andy too."

Mikey, Tina's younger brother, was calm and methodical, shoveling with steady precision—the kind of guy you wanted in a crisis. Andy, Tina's longtime boyfriend and a pro rider, worked with fierce, silent determination, his focus razor-sharp.

Dad immediately approached a man nearby, miming a digging motion. The man, struggling with English, shook his head. "No, no *pelles*," he said, gesturing helplessly—no shovels left.

I ran up to Tina. "Hey, T, you okay?"

"Hey, Shan, yeah! We're helping check if anyone's trapped. So far, no one. These are the last two cars. No one was in the restaurant, thank God."

Dad asked how they'd gotten there so fast—we'd only just heard about the avalanche on TV.

Tina laughed, shaking her head. "We didn't even know! Our front door was buried, so we jumped off the balcony to get out. We just happened to walk by, and guys were yelling. They handed us shovels—it was crazy."

Police were scoping everything out, and it seemed no one had been caught or buried. After staying to check things out, we all decided to head back and dry off at the condo.

By late afternoon, the roads were finally getting plowed. Sean and I wandered outside, meeting up with other competitors clustered together, swapping updates and rumors, trying to figure out if we'd be able to leave. The air crackled with nervous energy, a buzz of anxious chatter and half-laughs, like we were all stuck in a waiting game we couldn't control.

Meanwhile, Sean and a few other riders started "skitching"—grabbing onto the bumper of a slow-moving bus and sliding behind it on their boots. It was the ultimate mountain kid move, a free winter ride no one could resist. Back home in Steamboat, bus drivers hated it, but here, the driver didn't even seem to notice. I watched, laughing, as Sean carved smooth arcs behind the bus, grinning like a kid at recess.

The next morning, Dad checked with the police for updates. An officer, speaking in broken English, advised us to line up our car early—clearing the pass would take all day. So we packed up, somehow forced the hatchback shut, and by 9 a.m., we were second in line. With nothing to do but wait, we made the most of it: snowball fights with other riders, salami and cheese snacks, and one last round of skitching for Sean.

Finally, the police waved us forward, and we crept down the winding, steep mountain road, flanked by towering walls of snow—another humbling reminder of nature's raw power. It was a slow, careful journey, but the kind that makes you feel alive.

As we settled into the drive, my foot bumped something crumpled on the floor. Curious, I reached down and tugged at it. "Uh, Dad..." I unfolded a piece of white fabric. "You didn't return this flag?"

Dad grinned, eyes twinkling. "Hey, it landed right in front of me. Who was I supposed to leave it with? It's our souvenir, a reminder of everything we went through here." He winked. "And who knows? Maybe it's a sign."

"A sign that you stole it?" I teased.

The Olympic flag had tumbled straight from its pole, skimming the snow until it landed at Dad's feet—like it had chosen him. No wonder he saw it as a sign. My dad always loved the Olympics. To him, they were the pinnacle of sport, where lifelong dedication, skill, and passion collided on the world stage.

I used to envision following in the footsteps of Olympic gymnast Mary Lou Retton. I loved the balance of athleticism and creativity, that perfect mix of strength and grace. But snowboarding wasn't an Olympic sport, and maybe that's what made it so special. It was raw, untamed, something we did purely for the love of it. Snowboarding wasn't meant to fit inside a rulebook. It thrived on freedom.

We wound down through the valleys until we reached the lower town of Bourg-Saint-Maurice. Soldiers with machine guns waved us through the slushy streets. Sean rolled down his window as we passed a group of Japanese tourists struggling with heavy bags in the muck, their holiday starting off a little soggier than planned.

Soon enough, we hit the main highway, and it was smooth sailing to Geneva. We made it home just in time for Christmas—carrying stories, a giant check, and one unforgettable flag.

Could I keep the momentum going? Could I really take it all the way?

There was only one way to find out—I had to keep going.

CHAPTER 10
/ Mind Over Mountain /

I DIDN'T WANT A PODIUM. I wanted the title.

Standing under the lights, trophy in hand, I knew it wasn't enough. And honestly, part of me wondered if that was greedy. Shouldn't I just be grateful to be a pro snowboarder, grateful for top results?

But how could I settle when my own potential was staring me in the face? If I was going to become world champion, I couldn't just ride harder. I had to think sharper. Because here was the brutal truth: my biggest competitor wasn't any rider next to me. It was the voice in my own head.

One morning over coffee, as we talked through my goals and plans for the season, Dad cut to the heart of it.

"Shannon," he said, looking me straight in the eye, "winning a major event isn't about showing off. It's about beating the toughest competition out there—yourself."

His words confirmed what I'd already been analyzing, and he made it sound simple. But the truth was, every contest felt like a battle between the part of me that knew I had the skills and the part that doubted I could deliver. If I wanted that title, I had to believe in myself with the same intensity I brought to training.

The World Cup title hinged on points across three major events: Val d'Isère, where I'd taken third, Aspen, and the final in Japan. How I'd even afford to get to Japan, I had no clue. But I pushed that worry aside. First, I had to focus on riding.

Back home, I didn't even have access to a halfpipe, so I had to get creative. Maybe if I started visualizing every run in my mind—the sound of the snow under my board, the thump of the contest music, the rush of cold air, the lift of each hit—I could trick my brain. I figured, if I could land the tricks in my head, I'd be one step closer to landing them under real pressure.

The first time I visualized my competition run, I crashed—I actually fell in my own mental run. I couldn't believe it. If I couldn't even land a clean run in my head, how was I supposed to stick it for real?

Houston, we have a problem. And I'd just identified it. This wasn't just physical. I had to master my mindset.

Before the next World Cup, I had two less consequential contests— two chances to sharpen my mental game where the stakes were lower, the pressure lighter.

Brad from Morrow, my sponsor, offered me a spot to travel to contests and photo shoots with the Morrow pro snowboard team—four guys: Todd Richards, Noah Brandon, Tucker Fransen, and Rob Morrow. It was a huge opportunity, especially as the only girl on the team.

But taking it also meant leaving Sean behind. Sean was already questioning his place in competition, trying to figure out where he fit. And then, after France, disaster struck—an electrical fire tore through his home, destroying everything: his boards, his gear, his space. Gone overnight. I can still see him standing there in the wreckage, silent, just shaking his head. While I was strategizing contest runs, he was sifting through ashes. It felt cruel. Why was everything lining up for me while his world was falling apart?

"Take the opportunities," my parents told me.

Even Sean, despite everything, said it too. "Don't let anything stop you."

So, with a knot of excitement and guilt in my chest, I joined the Morrow crew.

We hit the road, rode the slopes together, and shot photos. Bea Morrow, Rob's mom, became our unofficial "team mom"—hilarious, warm, always cooking, always cheering. Right away, Bea could tell: I might have been one of the crew, but I was still a girl. From the moment she met me, she was trying to set me up with a "nice, cute guy." Maybe she sensed I needed a break from being buried in guy talk, fart jokes, and endless trick debates. Maybe she figured I wanted to feel like a princess for once.

She had the perfect match: a cute pro skateboarder from San Diego. We were competing at Snow Summit, and he even made the three-hour drive, leaving a dozen roses at the house we were renting. I missed him completely—out riding, out at dinner, with no way to communicate, I never even knew he'd come. But honestly, I barely had time to think about missed connections or bouquets. My focus was locked on the halfpipe.

At the event, there was no room for distractions—only the runs ahead. Unless it was a unique format, most competitions, including this one, came down to qualifying the top eight women, followed by two final runs, with the combined score deciding the winner. My practice felt solid; I was landing my 540s with clean confidence. I sailed through qualifiers and into finals—but that's when my nerves usually kicked in.

In those crucial moments, my first run wobbled, and on the second, I over-rotated. I placed third, but I knew it wasn't enough. It wasn't just about the podium anymore—I needed to conquer the part of me still trapped in my own head. And for me, that meant this contest was a fail.

At the next event in Squaw Valley, I was determined to break the pattern. But sometimes, determination isn't enough. I didn't even make finals. One solid run, and one fall on my 540, landing on my tailbone so hard it knocked the wind out of me.

At the bottom of the halfpipe, frustration slammed into me—hard enough to bring tears to my eyes that I blinked away fast. *How ridiculous*, I thought. Everyone else was laughing, throwing snowballs, soaking up the moment, and here I was, crushed under the weight of my own expectations.

I knew exactly what was happening: I was holding myself back. My heart pounded, not from exhaustion, but from sheer frustration. Why couldn't I just believe in myself? No one else was doubting me—only me. I was the one letting hesitation hijack my focus when it mattered most. It felt like a battle no one else could see: the part of me that had put in the work, and the part that still whispered, "*Maybe you're not enough.*"

Michelle Taggart took first, Crystal Aldana second, and Tina third. I came in ninth. This was supposed to be my last shot to figure myself out before the next World Cup. And I'd failed. Again. That was *not* the plan.

Bea, trying to lift my spirits, had a plan: the pro skater she'd been championing had driven eight hours just to see me. Maybe, she said, he'd cheer me up.

So I met up with him. He really had made the long drive, which was sweet—and that's exactly why I felt the pressure. He'd come all this way; I felt like I had to like him, just to make his effort worth it. But the whole thing felt more like an interview than a date.

I'd never been the sit-across-the-table type. I connected with people by doing things: riding, laughing, moving. Sitting there, smiling and nodding, I just wanted the night to end. We even gambled at a Nevada casino, where I lost twenty bucks—maybe I was just frustrated, maybe it was all bad timing, or maybe it was just never going to click. I hugged him goodbye, telling him I'd had the best time ever—a line that felt as forced as the whole evening.

"Maybe we'll meet up again soon," I added, even though we both knew we wouldn't.

Back home in Steamboat, January storms rolled in, dumping non-stop snow. I trained hard, practicing halfpipe tricks on the banks and side hits, savoring every powder lap, squeezing in every minute before Aspen. Sometimes I rode with Toby—a cute, no-ego skater and snowboarder, easy to be around. We'd smooched a few times, and sure, it was fun—but even as we laughed and lapped the mountain, I felt it deep down: I wasn't here to settle. I had things to achieve, and no cute guy was going to hold me back.

The big moment arrived. The second stop of the World Cup tour—Aspen, Colorado.

The three-hour drive from Steamboat gave me nothing but time—time to visualize, rehearse, and replace each detail of my run over and over again, again and again, until it burned into my brain. By the time I rolled into town, I'd already ridden that pipe a hundred times in my head.

Two solid practice days followed, each one sharpening the timing, tightening every move, pushing me closer to perfect.

Fast-forward to contest day.

By the time I stood at the top of the halfpipe, something inside me snapped into place. This wasn't nerves. It wasn't excitement. It was something fiercer—pure, unrelenting determination. My doubts, hesitations and holdbacks—they all fueled me now.

If fear wanted a fight today, it was going to lose. I wasn't just a competitor, I was a warrior. And warriors don't tiptoe into battle. They charge.

Outwardly, I kept it cool—laughing, joking, keeping it light. No one needed to see what was really happening inside. Because this wasn't about anyone else. It was me versus me.

The crowd's energy pulsed through the air, banners rippling in the breeze. Sean was there, having decided to step away from competing to get his realtor's license. My parents were there—even Mom didn't want to miss this one.

I'd fought through qualifiers, landing in the final eight. Now it was time—two runs to decide the winners. Gripping my board, I felt the ground vibrate with the roar of the crowd. I shut out the past—the failures, the doubts. I'd run this in my head a hundred times. This was the moment I'd been chasing.

I lined up according to the start list—third to last. I could feel the weight of it: knowing exactly what the others had thrown down, knowing what I needed to deliver. But I didn't flinch. I stood on my board, tightened my bindings, closed my eyes, and ran through my line twice more in my head.

This was my shot...

The starter called, "Shan, you're up. Drop in when you're ready."

I pointed my board downhill. Everything else disappeared—the noise, the crowd, the pressure—gone. My body took over, muscle memory carrying me like I'd been born for this. I hit the first air, soaring so high it felt like I could touch the sky. Landed clean. My momentum built, every move flowing into the next, like a perfectly choreographed rhythm. Then came the 540—the trick I'd obsessed over for months.

Time slowed. I didn't think. I knew. I spun, smooth and controlled, and hit the landing solid.

For a second, the world held still. Then the noise crashed back—cheers, shouts, my name echoing across the mountain.

I'd done it.

After all the riders finished their first runs, the scores came in—I was sitting in first. But I wasn't done yet. I dropped in for my second run, landing a clean, smooth line, identical to the first.

And then came the words I'd been waiting for: "Your winner—Shannon Dunn!"

A sob broke loose before I could stop it. I had won—not just the contest, but the war against my own doubt.

At the bottom, I threw my arms up, breathless, as the crowd erupted around me. I scanned the faces. My parents and Sean—the ones who had believed in me before I fully believed in myself. My friends, the competitors who had become part of my journey. The Morrow crew.

This wasn't just a win. It was a shift. A door flung wide open—not just to being a champion, but to discovering who I was becoming.

As I stepped off the podium, still riding the high, Tina wrapped me in a hug, grinning ear to ear. "You killed it out there!" She beamed.

I laughed, my heart still pounding.

"Hey, I might head to California for another contest, to get practice before Japan," she added. "You should come with me. Let's keep the momentum going!"

California. Then Japan. One last stop on the World Cup tour. One final shot at the title.

This wasn't just about contests anymore. This was about proving—to myself most of all—that I was the kind of person who didn't settle. The kind who rose above. The kind stepping fully into who I was meant to be.

CHAPTER 11
/ There's No Place Like Home /

I JOLTED AWAKE IN THE RENTAL HOUSE in Big Bear, California—heart hammering, walls shaking—as death metal blasted from downstairs. *What the—?*

I squinted at the digital clock: 3:23 a.m., the red numbers glowing faintly in the dark. A thin slice of light leaked up from downstairs.

Groaning, I thought, *Maybe they'll burn themselves out soon.*

Crash.

A thunderous clatter echoed up, followed by drunken laughter and then stomping. Heavy boots pounded up the stairs like a freight train. Seconds later, every single light blazed on. I winced. And just like that, the storm arrived.

I was curled in the far corner of the open-room loft, yanking the floral bedspread over my head, peeking out just enough in case I had to make a sudden dodge for survival. Frozen in place, pulse racing, I prayed I wouldn't become some accidental sideline casualty.

Two guys burst in, caught in a booze-fueled hurricane. One—scruffy, gap-toothed, grinning like a lunatic—grabbed a folding table and hurled it right past my bed, smashing it into the wall just a few feet away.

Boom. Plaster rained down.

The guy in the black beanie barely dodged the flying furniture. They doubled over laughing, staggering backward into the coffee table.

Snap. One of its legs snapped clean off, and the guys toppled to the floor in a tangled heap. It should've hurt—but they were way too wasted to notice, let alone care.

I shrank even further under the covers. *Nobody see me. Please, nobody see me.*

Then—a third guy barreled in. Bleached, spiked hair, pupils blown wide. "Whatcha doing', mofoes?!"

Added chaos.

He lunged at Scruffy. Scruffy countered, grabbed Spiked-Hair, and body-slammed him onto the couch. Beanie guy jumped in—elbows, kicks, limbs flying like some demented WWE match.

They crashed into the TV.

It toppled. Smashed. Exploded into a mess of broken plastic, glass, and static.

That's when Tina's bedroom door, connected to the loft, burst open. "Are you kidding me?!" She marched into the carnage, eyes blazing. "What are you idiots doing? This place is *trashed!*"

The guys froze mid-scuffle. Like deer in headlights.

Tina pointed at the stairs. "Downstairs. *Now.*"

And that's when Andy showed up next to Tina—broad shoulders, messy dark hair, that don't-even-think-about-it energy that silenced a room.

He was Tina's boyfriend, and someone you really didn't want to piss off. The kind of guy who didn't need to yell to command a room—his presence did the work. He'd been at Val d'Isère, where I'd met him, but even then, he had that same stern, no-BS energy. But if you were in his circle? He was the guy you wanted as a bodyguard.

"You heard her," he said, voice low but sharp. He grabbed Beanie and Scruffy by their sweatshirts and shoved them toward the stairs.

Spiked-Hair slipped away, bolting down ahead of them. Andy's jaw clenched as he surveyed the damage—the wrecked coffee table, the hole in the wall, the obliterated TV. Finally, his gaze flicked to me, still half-buried in my blanket cocoon. "You good, Shan?"

"Yeah...fine," I muttered, adjusting the covers, suddenly very aware of my bra-less state.

Andy muttered something low, almost like an apology, before slipping into his bedroom and slamming the door behind him. I stared at the ceiling, still feeling the vibration through the walls. *What the heck am I doing here?*

Tina flopped onto the end of my bed, looking as exhausted as the destroyed room. "Those idiots. I'm so sorry. Matty's a disaster—but last trip? Way worse. He left the entire condo looking like a bomb went off, not just the upstairs."

She eyed the mess, letting out a low whistle. "Lisa's gonna flip. She's not even here, and now she's stuck with the bill."

Lisa Hudson—Airwalk's legendary team manager, and the one footing the bill for this wrecked rental house packed with team riders. Tina had hyped her up before: Lisa spotted talent. She made things happen.

After Tina made sure that I was okay, and the noise downstairs finally died down, she slipped back to her room. But my body was still wired from the chaos. I needed to calm down, to shut it all out.

I shoved on my headphones, cranked up Ziggy Marley, and let the reggae rhythms wash over me. Between the bass and sheer exhaustion, I finally drifted off.

Morning slapped us awake too soon. Tina and I scarfed down instant oatmeal, eyeing the condo like a crime scene. We debriefed the night's chaos, shook our heads, and slipped out before the guys—we had a contest to ride.

On the mountain, we warmed up with practice runs, our energy building with each lap. There wasn't even time for a bathroom break before the contest kicked off, so we ducked into the trees.

"Hey, T, keep an eye out!" I called, crouching behind a pine. "And... got a tampon? Of course, today's the day." I rolled my eyes.

Tina dug through her pack and tossed one over. "Just started too. Need Advil?"

"Yeah—and toilet paper?"

She laughed, rummaging deeper. "Uh...here, Kleenex."

I caught the mini pack, grinning. *Lifesaver.*

We fueled up on snacks and water, then I paused just long enough to center myself before the start. I powered through qualifiers, laid down solid final runs, and by day's end, I landed in second place—Tina right behind me in third, with Michelle snagging first.

But honestly? I didn't sweat the results. This was one of those contests where the riding, the laughter, and just surviving the chaos mattered as much as the podium. And for once, I let myself enjoy it without overthinking. I gave myself a little grace—and it felt good.

The next day brought a whole new kind of competition—the first-ever obstacle course event. Unlike halfpipe or slopestyle, this was a head-to-head race—a motocross on snow. Six riders lined up side by side in the start gate, strapped in, knuckles tight on the bars.

The gates dropped—full send. First one down wins. No judges. No style points. Just raw speed, strategy, and survival. The course was a gauntlet: jumps, rollers, banked turns. Riders carving inches apart, elbows flying, boards clashing.

On my first run, midway down, I collided with another rider. We tumbled over the berm and slammed into the fence—total wipeout. Thankfully, no injuries. We scrambled up, untangled our gear, and raced to the finish anyway. I crossed the line laughing, shaking my head at the chaos. But her? She was livid. At the bottom of the course, the second we stopped, she ripped off her goggles, eyes blazing. "You cut me off! You ruined my line!"

I blinked, caught off guard. *What?*

I wasn't used to this. Contests were usually all camaraderie, not this kind of heat. And honestly? I hadn't cut her off. She came up from be-hind, clipped my board, and took us both down.

I just shrugged it off. I didn't even know her. *What a weirdo.* No point wasting energy on it—the day was already moving on.

Tina and I had hitched a ride up to the event with cab of the mag-azine editors, figuring we'd sort the rest out later. But after the halfpipe event the day before, the guy took off, leaving us stranded—no car, no ride, no plan.

After the obstacle course, Tina asked around, trying to find someone heading toward the airport.

Luckily, one of the Airwalk riders who'd been staying at our house (and, more importantly, hadn't wrecked it), Dana Nicholson, was still around. He had that unmistakable Cali surf drawl—laid-back, drawn-out, every word slow and deliberate, like he had all the time in the world.

"I'll give you guys a ride," he offered, half-yawning as he nodded to-ward his truck.

Dana was heading straight to Huntington—just a block from Da-mian Sanders, the original snowboard rock star, famous for going huge, backflipping off cliffs, and shaping the sport's wild, rebellious image. He'd even married Brandy, the *Penthouse* Pet of the year.

It was an easy choice because Tina was already dialing Lisa, figuring we could meet her too. She had it all mapped out: hit Damian's party, then connect with Lisa. We quickly switched our flights to make it hap-pen. Andy hitched a ride, too. He was headed to the airport, which was right on the way.

Soon enough, we were crammed into the back of Dana's pickup shell, inching through weekend traffic. Suddenly, a black car from behind us barreled down the wrong side of the road, flying past us, skimming over the double yellow line like it didn't exist.

"Whoa—" I pointed.

Up front, Dana threw his arms up.

"What the heck?" His voice was muffled through the cab, but I caught the edge of his frustration.

A few minutes later, we rounded a bend—

And there it was. The same black sedan, crumpled against the hillside, hazard lights blinking.

Dana slammed on the brakes and jumped out, already shouting. "Are you kidding me, dude? You could've killed someone!"

The driver—a heavyset guy in his thirties, wide-eyed, shaken—held up his hands in surrender.

"No, no...no brakes," he stammered, his voice a mix of English and Spanish.

Dana's whole stance shifted. He glanced at the wreck, then back at the guy, exhaling hard. "No brakes?"

The guy nodded fast. For a second, Dana just stood there, staring. Then, with a shake of his head, he muttered, "That's rough."

Seeing everyone unharmed, Dana climbed back into the truck, the weight of the moment still hanging heavy.

"Sketchy," Andy said, shaking his head.

I let out a breath I hadn't realized I was holding.

By the time we hit Huntington, the only thing on our minds was the night ahead—and whatever insanity Damian had in store.

Damian Sanders's house was already vibrating by the time we pulled up—bass pounding, voices shouting, the unmistakable crack of glass breaking somewhere inside. The second we stepped into the yard, I could tell—this wasn't just a party. It was a full-blown spectacle.

Flames shot up from some pyrotechnic madness at the pool's edge, casting eerie shadows on the walls. Go-go dancers, barely dressed in glitter and leather, twisted on platforms, their skin flashing like living disco balls.

Inside? It was like stepping into another dimension—or maybe, more accurately, into some wild version of hell. Black lights drenched the space in an eerie glow, reflecting off artwork: naked women tangled in metal, snakes slithering through warped paintings. And in the corner? A massive snake tank, its glass fogged with condensation.

I shivered. Not a fan of snakes.

The place was packed inside and outside—pro snowboarders, skateboarders, surfers, industry reps, models, randoms who had just shown up. The kind of crowd where you could spot someone from a magazine cover one second and a guy passed out on the couch the next.

Tina elbowed me. "This is next level."

I grinned. She wasn't wrong.

Then—Damian himself appeared.

If I hadn't already known who he was, I would've known just by looking at him. He looked like he had walked straight off a metal album cover—spiked mohawk, vampire-filed canines, the kind of energy that didn't just walk into a room but took it over.

But the second he saw us, his whole face lit up.

"Tina! Heck yeah, you made it!" He pulled her into a massive hug, then turned to me, clapping me on the back with the warmth of an old friend. "Welcome to the jungle!"

I laughed. I had half-expected him to be intimidating, maybe even a little terrifying with his whole bloodsucker vibe. Instead, he was genuine, animated, and totally welcoming.

"This is gonna be epic," he promised. "You ready for some madness?"

Before I could answer, a roar erupted from outside. We followed the noise to find a group gathered near the pool. A guy in snowboard boots—fully geared up, goggles and all—was standing on the diving board. Chugging a beer.

Tina squinted. "Is he about to—"

He launched. Midair, he tried to throw a backflip. Didn't even come close. He belly-flopped so hard I felt it in my chest. The entire party exploded. Cheers. Laughter. People pounding on tables.

Damian just shook his head, grinning. "Happens all the time."

The sound of a helicopter suddenly sliced through the noise. The party froze. A blinding spotlight swept over the yard.

Then—the booming voice of the police.

"This is the police! Leave immediately!"

Tina grabbed my arm. People started scrambling, pushing toward the exits, shoving out windows, running. Someone launched themselves off the roof into the pool. Others tried to act casual, like they weren't just at a party that now had SWAT involvement. We ducked out, slipping past a cluster of people who looked way too calm about the whole thing.

The next morning, the party was all over the news. $5,000 in fines. Neighbors had called the cops.

"Anyone actually go to jail?" I asked.

Tina shrugged. "Rumors, but who knows."

After everything, the beach felt like a whole different planet. The sun was warm. A surf contest was in full swing. And for the first time in days, there was no chaos—just ocean air and endless waves.

We were lounging near the surf, letting the day settle when Lisa Hudson arrived—blonde hair flowing, bright blue eyes sharp with purpose. She didn't just walk up. She arrived. Her presence filled the space before she even said a word.

"So glad you're here, babe!" Lisa's voice rang out as she pulled Tina into a hug—tight, full of energy, like they'd known each other forever.

Then she turned to me. Tina made the intro, and Lisa didn't miss a beat—wrapping me in the same warm embrace.

"So nice to meet you, babe!" she said, flashing a big, knowing grin.

She leaned back, still holding onto Tina's arm. "Okay, T...so what the heck happened at the house?"

Tina shook her head, "Typical."

"I just got off the phone with the property manager. Three thousand dollars in damages." She exhaled, shaking her head. "Seriously?"

Tina winced. "Matty and his crew. Full chaos—tables flying, holes in the walls, TV smashed. They were beyond wasted."

Lisa rubbed her temples. "Of course it was Matty—sounds about right." She shook her head, but there was no anger in her voice, just exasperation. "Well, lesson learned. Next time, I'm putting the damage deposit on Matty's credit card."

She sighed one last time, then flashed a grin like she was already moving on. "Alright, whatever. Tell me about the contest. Did you girls have fun?"

We swapped stories, laughing over the details. Tina didn't miss a beat bragging about my World Cup finishes, nudging Lisa. "You've got to get Shan on board for an Airwalk sponsorship."

Lisa smiled, no hesitation.

"Let's get you signed! If you're in, Shan?" She added, "We'll get you set up with boots for the Japan World Cup, and I'll send over a contract."

Lisa Hudson wasn't just another industry marketing person. She was one of the few women calling the shots.

This was huge.

Airwalk dominated skateboarding, breaking through to the mainstream. And now? They were making moves in snowboarding, backing riders who could help shape the sport's future. Just like that, Airwalk was my new sponsor, alongside Morrow.

I could tell—Lisa was a force. One of those rare people who could change the course of your career just by standing in your corner. And now, she was in mine.

With a grin, Lisa pulled out a pair of ruby-red patent skate shoes from her beach bag. They gleamed in the sun.

"Consider these a little extra welcome gift," she said, handing them over.

I turned them in my hands—perfect, my exact size. I raised an eyebrow. "How'd you know?"

Lisa shot a glance at Tina. Tina just smirked, letting out a sneaky laugh.

I brushed the sand from my feet, slipped them on, and clicked my heels together, grinning. "There's no place like home."

But standing there, watching the waves, feeling the shift in my career—I wasn't sure where home even was anymore. One path led back to the familiar. The other? Straight into the unknown.

And I wasn't afraid. I was ready.

CHAPTER 12

/ My Turning Point /

I NEVER THOUGHT I'D SEE JAPAN, let alone ride there—not at twenty, not on someone else's dime. But suddenly, the impossible was real: Morrow was paying my way to the final World Cup stop, and I was packing my bags for the biggest contest of my life. A shot at the world champion title was within reach.

Tokyo pulsed with neon energy, vending machines lining every street, offering hot drinks, cold drinks, toys—even underwear.

The people were unbelievably friendly, eager to meet the pro snowboarders, their curiosity and excitement totally contagious. Everywhere we went, they stopped to ask questions, flashing shy smiles that were honestly so adorable.

We had just left the city behind, winding our way toward the mountains, when I had my first encounter with a TOTO toilet at a roadside rest stop. The control panel attached to the seat looked like something off a spaceship, covered in mysterious symbols. I took a deep breath and pressed a button, half-expecting liftoff.

Nothing happened. So I stood up, eyeing it warily—and suddenly, a skinny white tube shot out and sprayed me square in the face. I shrieked, slapping buttons in a full-blown panic as water sprayed everywhere. Just when I thought the chaos was over, a cool breeze hit me from behind. I'd activated the butt fan. Drenched, stunned, and officially humbled, I stumbled out, questioning everything I knew about toilets.

Just beyond the city, the mountains were the true gem—quiet, pristine, blanketed in snow so thick it hushed the world. Every gully, every powder-draped ridge looked impossibly perfect, like the landscape had been designed just for snowboarders to slash and surf the banks of snow.

Then came the contest—a blur of nerves, excitement, and pure adrenaline. The final stop of the World Cup Tour—the event that would crown the overall world champion, based on the highest combined points across all three stops. This was the pinnacle of our sport, the stage for international acclaim. Crowds packed the venue, watching us like we were rock stars.

And here I was again—familiar setting, high-stakes contest—but this time in Japan, where everything felt playful, almost fantasy-like. My biggest worry? That I wouldn't take it seriously enough. So I stuck to my plan: visualizing my runs over and over, keeping my focus sharp—but not forgetting to laugh, stay light, and enjoy the moment.

Nicole Angelrath—known as the Swiss Miss—was a force to reckon with, in the nicest way. Petite and enthusiastic, with a blonde ponytail flying as she landed her tricks with style and ease, she made winning look effortless. Nicole was probably my biggest competition—a role model, a champion. She was genuinely kind and brought an infectious energy to the mountain. But I reminded myself: I wasn't here to beat Nicole or anyone else. I was here to beat myself—and not beat myself up.

The World Cup format was two final runs, combined score wins. My first run? Flawless. This last one, my final run, was all I needed to lock in the title.

I took a deep breath, dropped in, and let it all flow. Trick after trick, every move solid, every landing clean.

Then came the final moment—my 540. My mind went perfectly

still—no second-guessing, no panic. Just muscle memory, pure focus.

I reached the top of the halfpipe wall, snapped into the rotation, spotted my landing...and touched down clean. My board hit the snow, and I rode away strong, adrenaline surging. I lifted my arms in relief, grinning as the weight of it all hit me.

A wave of emotion crashed over me: deep joy, fierce pride, and a rush of gratitude for everyone who had ever helped me reach this point—my family, my sponsors, my friends. I wasn't just proud because I'd rode my best; I was proud because I'd pushed through every doubt, every setback, every hard-fought moment that led here.

Before I could even unstrap my bindings, a Japanese commentator rushed up for an on-snow TV interview.

"Howah, are you feeling, to be snowboarding's women's world champion?" he asked in charmingly accented English, holding the mic to my face.

I laughed, almost breathless. "I really can't believe it! Thank you to Morrow Snowboards, my sponsor, and Airwalk. Thank you to all the sponsors at this event. I love Japan! Arigato!"

He smiled wide. "Oh, well, your fans *ruv* you too!"

Fans? I blinked. *Fans?* This was so surreal.

Soon, I was signing autographs, feeling awkward but trying to embrace the excitement. I let myself roll with it, soaking in the moment, knowing this was a once-in-a-lifetime high.

And yet, even in that triumph, I understood the sting of those who didn't win—their frustration, their grace, their good sportsmanship. It was all there, flooding through me at once.

Something had clicked in Japan—a mental switch I hadn't fully unlocked before. After that event, I felt unstoppable, like I couldn't lose. Each contest fed this wild, rising confidence, a momentum that surged with every win. The victories were huge, but the real breakthrough wasn't on the scoreboard—it was in my head. I had finally mastered my mental game.

I had momentum. I had sponsors. I had a team that felt like family.

But just when everything seemed solid, everything shifted.

Brad pulled the whole Morrow team together after another contest at the end of the season. His usual easy-going demeanor was replaced by something serious. He looked at each of us before breaking the news: he was leaving Morrow to start his own clothing brand. He didn't go into details, but I could feel it in the air—that delicate thread holding us together was about to snap. He explained that we'd each have to make a choice: stay with a changing Morrow or strike out on our own. The future wasn't clear. Morrow was going through changes on the business side, and he couldn't say exactly what might shift. There were legal details he couldn't talk about, but the uncertainty hung heavy.

Brad's news felt like the floor had been ripped out from under me. He wasn't just Morrow's visionary or my team director—he was the reason I had a career at all. He saw something in me before I ever saw it in myself. He didn't just believe—he made me believe.

In snowboarding, talent alone was never enough. You needed someone opening doors, making calls, pulling you into the rooms where decisions got made. Brad had that power—and because of him, I had a shot at something bigger. He didn't just give me opportunities, he opened a world I never could've reached on my own.

But now, without him, everything felt uncertain. Sure, the contests and sponsors were still there—but would they still be there for me? How much of my momentum had been mine, and how much had been Brad working behind the scenes?

His absence wasn't just a shift. It was a test. Could I keep pushing forward without the person who'd always had my back?

In the pit of my stomach, I knew things would never be the same. This felt like the last page of a chapter that had shaped me, and as I looked around at my teammates, I realized we were all on the edge of something unknown.

I tried to hide the disappointment, but it was written all over my face. When I got home, I spilled everything to my dad—every detail, every frustration. Even he, usually steady and all-business, could see how rattled I was.

I had built momentum, and it had worked. The right people, the right timing, everything had fallen into place.

But what now?

As we talked, Dad was matter-of-fact: "Welcome to pro sports. This is a business. It's rare to have a team that feels like family. Snowboarding's growing, but most athletics are cutthroat. No handshakes. You just move on. Keep doing what you're doing—and don't take it so personally."

It felt a little harsh. I loved being part of something small, special, personal. But he was right—it was just the truth. And hearing his words gave me some strength, like, *Toughen up, kid. You've got this.*

When I asked Sean for advice, he didn't sugarcoat it either: "Toughen up."

It made me chuckle—even as the disappointment still sat heavy in my chest.

I'd always seen snowboarding as my passion, my lifestyle. But they were right—if I wanted to keep going, keep winning, keep progressing, I had to start seeing it the way everyone else in the industry did: as a business. Even Mom agreed. After that, Dad and I sat down for some real talks about what changing sponsors could mean. Snowboarding was blowing up—huge exposure, rapid growth, the industry moving at warp speed. So, we started reaching out, feeling out options.

But here's what became clear fast: companies weren't just looking for talent. They wanted riders who made waves, turned heads, and sold gear. It wasn't enough to land tricks—you had to have that elusive it-factor. Girls were part of the scene, for sure, but not many companies were putting money behind them. Luckily, I was in a strong spot—World Champion, winning most events that season.

Dad made a lot of calls, and eventually Sims Snowboards came into the picture. They were looking for a top female rider, and the timing couldn't have been better. With a woman in the marketing director role, they *wanted* a girl on the team. The salary offer wasn't huge, but they promised solid contest and photo incentives—and that's where the real hustle lived.

In snowboarding, contests paid, but getting published was where you stacked bonuses. Sponsors shelled out for magazine features: half-page, full-page, double-page spreads, and the holy grail—the cover. The bigger the photo, the bigger the check. TV coverage and video parts worked the same way—if you repped your sponsor's product on screen, you got paid. But even so, girls weren't getting much media exposure. That made one thing painfully clear: if I wanted to stay valuable to sponsors—if I wanted to build a real career in this sport—I had to chase visibility.

So I decided: instead of sticking with Morrow, where I wasn't getting a clear sense of the company's direction, I signed with Sims, a long-established brand with a major presence. What really excited me wasn't just Sims itself. It was Gaylene Nagel, their marketing director.

Gaylene knew Brad from Morrow, and after I consulted with him, he was the one who convinced me: working with her would be the smart move. More than just the Sims name, Gaylene herself would be a career-defining ally.

She was Canadian, petite, with dark hair and a power-packed presence that could command a room. Coming from a background in windsurfing and figure skating, she knew exactly what it meant to fight for space in a male-dominated world. She was the driving force behind Sims even bringing on a top female rider in the first place.

The second we started talking, Gaylene lit up—practically overflowing with ideas about what we could accomplish together. She saw huge potential in adding a woman to the team, and her excitement was contagious. I couldn't help but feel like I was stepping into something big, with real momentum behind it. Most importantly, Gaylene seemed to get what mattered to me. She knew relationships, trust, and camaraderie weren't just nice extras—they were the foundation of a solid team. She got it. She wasn't just about business; she understood that loyalty and connection could shape a rider's entire career.

Signing with Sims wasn't just a contract—it was a fresh start. With Gaylene in my corner, I felt fired up, motivated, and ready to push my riding to the next level. I wasn't just joining a new team; I was stepping into a new phase of my career, with someone who believed in what we could build together.

CHAPTER 13

/ Highs to Lows /

THE NEXT WINTER WAS THE BIGGEST SEASON OF MY LIFE. I was winning nearly every contest—U.S., Canada, Europe, Japan—stacking podiums and World Cup points, riding a wave of momentum. I was on track to claim my second World Champion title.

But then the International Snowboard Federation threw in a curveball: they added a last-minute European event I couldn't attend—a move that felt political, tailor-made to tip the scales toward European riders.

How do you just add another contest at the end of the season? I wasn't even sure it was technically legal according to the rule book.

I was frustrated, no doubt. After all those wins, to miss out on the overall title because of a last-minute European event I couldn't even get to? It stung. I vented to Gaylene, called Dad, and ran through every "what if" in my head. But both of them gently nudged me toward the same truth: Let it go. Skip it. Focus forward.

And they were right—because something bigger was waiting.

The Burton U.S. Open wasn't just another contest on the calendar—it was *the* contest. This was the one that put you face-to-face with the people who could shape your future: the sponsors, the brands, the industry decision-makers who held the keys to doors I didn't even know existed. And best of all? Every top rider from around the world showed up.

The U.S. Open was snowboarding at its rawest—iconic, a little chaotic, and fully alive. The crowd went all out; it was so packed, fans climbed trees just to catch a glimpse. Competitors poached the pipe mid-contest, dropping in whenever they felt like showing off. Try that at a World Cup, and you'd be reprimanded or disqualified, no question. But at the Open, that rebellious, free spirit was the whole point—a place where amateurs could qualify earlier in the week and end up riding alongside the pros. The energy on the mountain was electric—fans lining the halfpipe, shouting your name as you hiked back up between runs, their cheers echoing off the scattered beer cans.

I'll never forget my first-ever U.S. Open win that season. 1993. It was a sunny, slushy spring day, and I was riding my Sims Mini Palmer—the top-selling board in their line. The graphic? A cartoon of Shaun Palmer as a pimp, cruising a Cadillac with a lingerie-clad girl at his side, boobs practically spilling out. Guys loved that graphic. Me? Not so much. But hey—I was grateful for the sponsorship, so at the awards ceremony, I grabbed the mic and gave Sims a solid shoutout: "Thanks to my sponsors. I couldn't have done it without the Mini Palmer."

Standing on that podium, it hit me hard—being a girl at the U.S. Open felt good. Like we truly belonged. Women had been earning equal prize money for podium spots since the Open's inception, and that mattered. But I thought: the overall purse prize should be equal also. I hoped that someday the women's field would grow big enough, gain enough value and recognition, that we'd see full equality in payouts across the board. To me, that wasn't just about matching numbers—it was about matching respect.

After I won, both major snowboard magazine publishers and their editors came up to introduce themselves. *Transworld Snowboarding* even asked to interview me, so I shot a headshot with their main photographer, Jon Foster. I was thrilled—it felt like a big step forward. At the time, there were two powerhouse publications: *Snowboarder* magazine and *Transworld Snowboarding*. Someday, I hoped to land one of those coveted invites on an editorial trip. Meeting the editors opened my eyes to just how much more there was to being a pro than I'd realized. Connections mattered. And honestly, it made the whole scene more fun—seeing familiar faces at every event, people who loved the sport as much as I did. Everyone had their role in promoting snowboarding, and in the end, we were all just trying to make enough to keep doing the thing we loved most.

But when the U.S. Open broadcast finally aired on TV, my excitement turned to frustration. I sat at home watching, eager—only to see the girls got two minutes of airtime. Two minutes in a one-hour show. And they didn't even show our best runs—just the wipeouts, the shaky landings, the screwups. It was embarrassing. Later, I found out it wasn't Burton's fault; it was the network's call.

If we—if I—wanted change, we were going to have to make it happen ourselves.

I grabbed the phone and dialed Tina. The second she picked up, I blurted out, "Did you see the U.S. Open coverage?"

She sighed, already knowing where I was going. "Yeah...they barely showed us."

"Not only that, but they aired our *worst* runs. It's like they don't even care." I paused, frustration tightening my chest. "This is ridiculous. If they won't show us, we'll show ourselves."

She didn't even hesitate. "Let's do this!"

Within hours, Tina was on the phone—dialing photographers, lining up photo shoots, and calling in every favor we had. We weren't going to wait for the industry to catch up; we were going to force it to pay attention. Together, we mapped out a plan, targeting magazine coverage. Meanwhile, we took our push straight to Lisa and Gaylene—our strongest advocates for advancing women's snowboarding. They backed us all the way, carrying our pitch directly to Doug Palladini, the publisher at *Snowboarder* magazine.

A Freeriding Story Starring...

Snowboarder Magazine, photo by John Kelly. The first-ever girls' article. Girls being girls—glamming it up in a sport that rarely saw us that way.

Doug didn't just like the idea—he *loved* it. He gave us the green light for the magazine's first-ever multipage spread dedicated solely to female riders. No more one-page token features shoved between gear ads. This was our moment to own. And the lineup was a powerhouse: Tina Basich, Michelle Taggart, Circe Wallace, and me.

We had to navigate a lightning storm, but we didn't let it stop us. Instead, we worked shoulder-to-shoulder with the photographer, adjusting on the fly, chasing pockets of light to capture the shots we envisioned. The results? Action photos that were bold, unique, and impossible to ignore.

Doug's story about our trip didn't just showcase the riding—it built up each of us as individual athletes, giving weight to what we were doing and proving that women's snowboarding wasn't just a side feature; it was a movement.

And we had fun with the lifestyle side of the story. Why not throw in something completely unexpected? The week before the shoot, Tina and I raided a thrift store and came out with enough '70s glam to outfit the whole crew. We showed up looking like a full-blown disco revival, and the photographer's jaw practically hit the floor. He'd been expecting the usual hoodies and beanies—not a glam rock takeover.

Doug was all in. He laughed, shaking his head. "You're gonna be the most stylish pages we've ever printed."

I came home that spring riding high—full of momentum, full of ideas, full of everything I thought was ahead. And then, just when I thought things couldn't get better, the call came.

"Shannon," Gaylene said, her voice practically vibrating through the phone, "how would you feel about designing your own pro model snowboard?"

I froze. *A pro model? My own board?*

Of course, I wanted one. In snowboarding, only the legendary guys had pro models. It wasn't just a cool bonus; it was the highest honor. A pro model was the ultimate stamp of respect, a sign you'd earned your place among the best. And more than that, it meant the company believed you could sell—that you had the rare power to move product, inspire fans, and shape the sport.

Gaylene laid it out: for the first time ever, a board designed for girls who wanted to rip, tired of riding their boyfriend's hand-me-downs. She believed I was the rider to make it happen.

"Ya know," she added, "Lisa Vinciguerra—our Canadian friend—had the very first women's pro model with Checker Pig in Europe a few years back. It was a great board, solid and well-designed. But barely anyone here in the U.S. knew about it. Checker Pig fumbled the timing, totally missed the mark, and the board slipped under the radar."

She shook her head, her voice tight with determination. "It was such a wasted opportunity. They didn't understand what they had. That's why I'm so fired up about this, Shannon. The timing is perfect now, and we're going to do it right. Just keep this idea top secret, okay? I don't want it getting out into the industry."

When I hung up, I was stoked—heart racing with a million ideas. To even be considered for a pro model meant one thing: I had truly arrived.

But dreams have a way of shattering fast.

A few days later, back in Steamboat, the spring sun dipped low over the slushy slopes. I'd spent the whole day laughing and lapping runs with Betsy—a rare treat, since we didn't get as much time together anymore.

Betsy needed to leave, but I stayed behind for one last run. Just me, the mountain, and a challenge I couldn't shake: a 360 with a stylish grab off a ledge I'd been wanting to land. I hadn't seen other girls throw that trick off any bigger features yet, and today, I was determined to nail it— to progress my riding, and to be ready for the next photo shoot.

As I glided to my spot, I felt the snow was a bit icy under my board. It was late in the day. The sun was low now, casting long shadows over the run. And just as I leaned forward, ready to drop in, it came.

A voice. Sharp. Undeniable. Loud inside my head. "Don't go."

It landed like a weight in my chest. I hesitated. Then I pushed it aside.

"No. I'm good," I spoke back to the voice.

Without wasting another second, I rode toward the cat track, picking up more speed than I'd planned. I launched off the ledge, twisting into the spin—but instantly, I knew something was wrong. I had too much speed, and instead of landing on a downhill slope that could help absorb any mistakes, I flew straight past it. The run was flattening out, and a flat landing was like jumping off a two-story building onto concrete. My heart lurched as I spun through the air, rocketing toward the flats, completely powerless to control what was coming.

My legs were extended as I hit—and then came the gut-wrenching *pop* in my knee. I crumpled instantly, folding into the snow as the pain tore through me.

The world went silent.

I lay there, the snow cold under me, breath ragged, pain searing through my leg. That voice echoed in my mind. *Why hadn't I listened?*

A skier zipped past, shouting, "Get outta the way, you freakin' idiot snowboarder!"

He'd come off the cat track just like me, but hadn't seen me sprawled in the blind spot. Luckily, he didn't hit me—but he didn't stop to check on me. Tears blurred my vision as I scooted aside, clutching my knee. *No, please—let it be okay. It has to be okay.*

But no one was coming to help me. The lifts were shutting down; the mountain was nearly empty.

I had no choice. Gritting my teeth, I forced myself upright—shaky, breathless—and began the painful, lonely ride to the bottom.

Rock bottom.

Barely holding it together, I couldn't stop hearing that voice. *Don't go.*

CHAPTER 14

/ There's Hope on the Horizon /

LIFE DOESN'T HIT PAUSE FOR ANYONE'S PLANS—not mine, not anyone's. One moment, everything was lining up: the season of my life, new sponsors, a pro model board on the horizon. Then, in a blink, I was sitting across from a doctor saying,

"The MRI shows a complete ACL tear. Recovery will take about a year."

A year? That wasn't going to work for me.

Outside, thunder cracked as Dad and I trudged toward the car. My knee throbbed, swollen and stiff—no broken bones, but for an athlete, no ACL meant no stability. No riding at full strength.

Dad gave me a half-smile, trying to lift the mood. "You'll be fine. But yeah—that doctor didn't impress me at all."

I let out a bitter laugh. "Yeah, I do *not* like that guy. At all. I told him I'm planning a miraculous recovery—I need to be back on snow by November, contest in January!"

Dad raised an eyebrow, waiting.

I threw up my hands. "He just rolled his eyes! Total 'whatever' attitude. Thanks for the motivation, dude."

In the car, I wiped at the tears that had mixed with the rain on my face.

I wasn't ready to let this injury define me. I'd be back—faster than anyone expected.

I slumped onto the green leather couch at home, a bag of ice strapped to my knee, the big-screen TV flickering in front of me. The smell of pot roast drifted from the kitchen, warm and familiar.

Scarlet, my dog, rested her head on my lap, licking my hand.

"Scarlet," I mumbled, stroking her fur, "you bounced back from your ACL surgery, right?" She wagged her tail, and I gave a soft laugh. "Guess I'll have to, too."

From the kitchen, Mom called out, "You've always been stubborn, you know. Remember when you insisted on ditching your training wheels at two and a half?"

I smiled faintly, the memory flashing back—skinned knees, scraped elbows, pushing past the tears, getting back on that little bike.

I'd always been a fighter.

After my initial visit with the doctor, my dad jumped into action. He tracked down one of the top orthopedic surgeons in Vail, known for working with elite athletes. The surgeon was confident: with surgery in early May, I could be fully recovered in nine months—and maybe even back on snow by six, if I hit rehab hard.

That plan was solid, and I held onto it as everything else swirled with uncertainty.

A message waited on the answering machine—Gaylene, Sims's marketing director, her voice bright with urgency. "Call me back ASAP!"

I could almost feel her positivity radiating through the message. She had no idea about my knee injury. I braced myself as I dialed her back, nerves pounding. But before I could even tell her about my knee, she blurted, "Shannon! How would you feel about doing the art for your pro model board? We can bring in a graphic artist, but I thought you'd want to be hands-on."

Umm...she wants me to design it? She had no idea how much I loved art, how it was my calm, my creative escape. This wasn't just about a board; this was about putting *my* stamp on something that mattered.

But then the weight hit. I swallowed hard. "Gaylene...I have to tell you something. I just tore my ACL."

There was a beat of silence. Then, her voice softened. "Shan, I'm so sorry. But you'll bounce back. You've got time before winter—I know you can do this."

Her belief felt like a lifeline.

Then, a few days later, Gaylene called again: the team was heading to Austria at the end of May, only a few weeks post-surgery. Could I go?

"I'll make it," I promised, heart pounding. I had no idea how, but I wasn't about to miss this shot. With Gaylene's excitement still echoing in my head and my pro model taking shape, I zeroed in on the next step: surgery.

On the operating table, wired up and surrendered to the unknown, doubt crept in. I'd chosen an epidural, curious enough to stay awake, but my mind spun. Should I just walk away from snowboarding? This injury exposed the brutal reality—professional sports were risky. Maybe kinesiology, my college major, was the smarter path. Physical therapy, a steady career. Respectable. Safe.

But snowboarding had always been my passion. *Am I about to lose it?*

"This is beautiful!" Dr. Gottlieb's voice sliced through my spiral. "Everything looks amazing here, Shannon. Now...I'm getting the drill out."

Classical music floated softly through the operating room, oddly calming. The anesthesiologist hovered. "Need a little something extra to take the edge off?"

I smirked. "No thanks. I'm already getting drilled."

After surgery, in the recovery room, the nurses helped me up to walk the hall, my knee locked in a brace. They offered crutches, but I waved them off—too much like admitting defeat.

One nurse casually mentioned Monica Seles—yes, *the* Monica Seles, tennis superstar recently stabbed by a crazed fan—was recovering down the hall. I joked, "Think I could swing by for a quick hello?"

Flat reply: "No." Tough crowd.

Then my parents arrived with the perfect gift: colored pencils and a notepad.

"Thought you might want to start on that pro model graphic," Dad grinned.

I shoved aside the sad hospital food. "Why is hospital food always the worst?" I muttered, flipping open the notebook. A memory popped up—just a few weeks earlier, Betsy and I had been home on her spring break, sitting on the floor embroidering sunflowers onto our jeans. I'd casually asked, "What do you think would make a cool graphic for my board?" She gave me a look like, *obviously*. "Sunflowers."

Smiling at the memory, I sketched: giant sunflowers at the tip and tail, their stems intertwined through the center, framed by a bold red backdrop. For the base, I pulled inspiration from a funky sun face I'd seen in *Sports Illustrated*, weaving the whole design together.

"Done," I whispered. Even from a hospital bed, I was taking back control—shaping my future.

Two weeks later, I was deep in rehab. Dr. Gottlieb had warned: push through the pain to get your range of motion back ASAP or risk locking up with scar tissue. So I built a checklist: stretching, massage, PT, icing, visualization, even speaking my goals aloud. Every day I hit that list, I marked an *X* on the calendar.

Those *X*s became my private trophies.

If only I'd listened to that voice on the mountain, I'd think during long rehab stretches. The memory gnawed at me. *Maybe I could have avoided this pain.*

But here I was, facing it head-on, determined to beat it.

Three weeks post-surgery, I flew to Austria with the Sims team, refusing to miss out. While they snowboarded on the glacier, a local photographer led me to a stunning yellow flower field—the perfect backdrop, a burst of inspiration for the *Sunflower* graphic.

But after days stuck on the sidelines, restlessness took over. I grabbed a beat-up hotel bike and cruised down the mountain pass, savoring the rush of the descent.

Then the wild idea struck: I needed to ride back up to the hotel—but what if I kept going, all the way to the glacier? Seventeen miles of switchbacks, straight uphill.

At a roadside map, I met Freddy, a local cyclist in full kit—matching jersey, padded shorts, mirrored shades, the works. We struck up a conversation—his broken English and sharp German accent paired with a contagious, positive energy. We teamed up, grinding uphill, breathless but determined, the jagged Alps towering around us. My knee brace grew unbearable, so I tore it off and strapped it to the frame. Freddy kept me going with cheerful calls like "We go slow, but we go strong!"—making me laugh even as my legs screamed. He shared his water and snacks, and after more than four grueling hours, we reached the top—sweaty, exhausted, triumphant.

At the parking lot, we ran into the Sims crew packing up their gear. They froze when they saw me—jaws dropping, eyes wide. Their shock made me laugh out loud.

Coasting down was pure joy—wind in my face, legs burning, heart full.

Yeah, I'd done it. Swollen knee, exhausted legs—but I'd done it.

After Austria, it felt good to be home and focus on recovery. The slower pace threw me—no team dinners, no nonstop laughter—but with extra time, I drifted into the self-help aisle at the bookstore, stacking up books that promised to help me figure out life. If there was ever a time to focus inward, to figure out who I was and what I wanted, this was it. Personal fulfillment and success? Yes, please. A blend of spirituality and practical wisdom? Sign me up! Consider me coachable and ready to dive in.

The big question hung over me: stay in college, following the safe, mapped-out path? Or throw myself fully into snowboarding—risky, unpredictable, but thrilling. I was torn, waiting for a sign. With none appearing, I stuck to the plan and signed up for another fall semester at the University of Colorado.

One late summer evening, as I packed for Boulder, the phone rang.

"Hey, Shannon, it's Gaylene." Her voice bubbled with energy. "So... about the graphics. The guys at the office think your design is too bold. They're calling it 'way too feminine.' They had someone draft something more muted. I told them you'd at least look, but I'm on your side."

The next day, a FedEx tube arrived. I unrolled the design and froze: a washed-out mauve hummingbird on a drab teal background. I called Gaylene immediately.

"No way. If that's the only choice, I don't think this pro model is for me," I said flatly. "My graphics should reflect my personality, right?"

"Yeah, I get it," she sighed. "The reps keep saying women's boards won't sell—they don't even want to try to pitch them to get them into the snowboard shops. One guy even said, 'What are you talking about, Gaylene? Snowboards are just tools to go down the hill—they can't be women's specific.'" She scoffed. "He just doesn't get it... But don't worry, Shan. I have a plan."

Her determination reignited mine. We weren't just slapping art on a board; we were trying to push the industry to see what they were missing.

Meanwhile, I was back in the chemistry lab, making aspirin and polyester as part of a college class assignment—and all I could think was, *I'd definitely rather be snowboarding.*

Weeks later, the phone rang—Gaylene, brimming with excitement.

"Good news: your *Sunflower* graphic is a go. Exactly as you drew it. It looks incredible full-size. I can't wait for you to see it," she beamed over the phone.

Then she dropped a real shocker.

"I gotta tell you—I just came out of a meeting with Tom Sims, the Japanese distributor, and some of the investors. They think a women's pro model is risky. They don't want to spend money on a new mold. But I told them that's the whole point. This board needs to be built *for* women, from the ground up. I want it for aggressive riders, for girls who want to lead, not follow."

She laughed, breathless but determined. "Anyway, you don't need all the details, but I told them flat out—if they won't cover the cost, I'll pay for the ten thousand dollar mold myself."

"Ten thousand dollars?" I blurted. "You're betting *big* on this, huh?"

"I called our top accounts and offered the boards on consignment so the shops don't feel like they're gambling. I promised to take them back if they don't sell. They all agreed. And I told them one condition: your board goes right by the front door—front and center. No way is this thing getting shoved in the back."

I nodded instinctively, forgetting she couldn't see me.

"Oh, I'm not worried," Gaylene said, her voice strong. "I know this is the right time. And since the reps haven't budged—they're making this really difficult—everyone is, really. I went ahead and had a hundred boards made early. I'm handing them out to key people. This is it, Shannon. We're gonna make it happen."

By Thanksgiving break, Gaylene called again—the *Sunflower* prototype was ready, and it looked incredible. She needed catalog photos, fast. My knee brace had just arrived, and between PT and long bike rides, I was feeling stronger. At only six months post-op, I nervously said yes, heart pounding.

She'd hired Jeff Curtes, a Colorado photographer just getting his start but already making waves in the Vail snowboard scene. When I met him at the Steamboat gondola, his easy grin and laid-back vibe immediately put me at ease. We warmed up, laughing about the "ganjala"—the gondola where locals often lit up their weed.

But it was early season, and the mountain was barely covered with snow. We needed something for me to catch air and get an action photo—anything—for the catalog, but I couldn't ignore the risk. Underneath the casual jokes, I was sharply aware of every move, knowing my knee was still in that delicate phase where the ligament was fusing to bone. I didn't say it out loud, but the worry buzzed at the edges of every decision.

Then we found a tiny cat track jump.

"Think you can get up in the air here?" Jeff asked, grinning.

I gave a nervous laugh. "This little thing? Are you sure that's gonna look good?" I smirked. "Okay...sure."

Ten jumps later, Jeff was glowing. "These are going to look awesome," he grinned.

That night, Tina called, practically bursting. "I got offered a pro model!" she squealed.

I blinked in surprise. *Wait—huh?* Gaylene had told me to keep it quiet. *Who let the cat out of the bag?* With all the pushback we'd faced from the company and reps, the timing felt *way* too coincidental. But honestly, I didn't care. Now I didn't have to keep my secret anymore. And the thought of promoting our boards together? That was going to be so much fun.

"No way—me too!" I shouted, grinning so hard my face hurt. We stayed on the phone, bubbling over with plans—contests we'd hit, tricks we'd master, goals we'd chase down. We were going to be carving out space for every girl coming up behind us.

A few days later, Jeff called. "You won't believe how good the shots came out. Want me to swing by and show you?"

"From Vail? Isn't that a long drive?" I asked, laughing.

"Nah. It's not far, plus I've got other stuff to do in Boulder anyway."

That weekend, he showed up glowing with excitement. We spread the photos across my coffee table—snowy shots of me midair, the *Sunflower* base graphic popping like a firework.

"Sheesh, that jump was tiny, but these are insane!" I laughed.

"Told you," Jeff grinned. "You killed it."

Then he dropped a surprise. "I just got invited to be the photographer for a *Transworld Snowboard* magazine shoot in Italy. Shan, you should come—it's mid-January."

I lit up. "No way! I just talked to Tina—there's a contest in Italy at the same time. If the dates line up, we could go together!"

"Perfect, invite her! It'll be epic. This is gonna be my first job for a snowboard mag."

A flurry of calls later, it was set. Tina and I scrambled to grab the only airplane seats left: last row, smoking section. I winced but shrugged—we'd deal.

Not long after, Gaylene called, raving about Jeff's shots. "These are perfect for the catalog, Shan. You're going places, girl!"

For the first time since my injury, I felt it—this wasn't the end. It was fuel. The long road ahead? I didn't need easy. I just needed this hope.

CHAPTER 15
/ Leap of Faith /

I WALKED OUT OF CU BOULDER FOR THE LAST TIME, snow crunching under my boots, knowing that door was closing for good. I'd officially unenrolled. The counselor's words still echoed: to finish my degree, I'd need spring science classes—no shortcuts, no summer options.

But school wasn't where I was meant to make an impact. Snowboarding was. It would take everything I had, especially because I was committing at my most vulnerable point. I was still recovering from ACL surgery, clinging to faith that my "miraculous" comeback would hold. But here's the brutal truth: after your first big injury, the questions never stop. Am I doing enough? Will my body hold up?

And in the end, all I needed was to know I'd given it everything. As a pro athlete, your body is your job. Strength equals survival. I stood at the crossroads, heart pounding. This wasn't just about chasing a dream now—it was about risking failure.

The voices crept in: *"What if you fail? What if they're right—the people who smirk when you say you're a pro snowboarder, the ones who think it's not a real sport, just some reckless hobby? The ones who believe you're chasing a fantasy?"*

But this was my life—my decision. What did I want out of this whole snowboard career? To fly down snow-covered peaks, slash the perfect turn, launch off a cliff into the unknown. Yes, it was thrilling. But it was more than that. It was for a purpose. It was about carving space for the women coming after me, about helping build something bigger than just myself.

Movement was my voice—my way of speaking to the world.

Now, back home, I was ready to sort through college leftovers, organize my gear, and rehab my knee. My parents were heading off to Italy for ten days, leaving me alone with Scarlet and Reese—Sean's golden retriever, on loan while he worked toward his realtor's license in Fort Collins.

Before they left, Mom paused at the kitchen table, flipping through her travel guide. "We're visiting St. Francis of Assisi's Basilica—it's supposed to be beautiful."

On impulse, I surprised even myself: "Could you bring me back a cross necklace?"

My parents smiled, nodded. It felt small, but it was something—a reach toward a faith I wasn't even sure I believed in anymore. As a kid, faith had been easy—prayers, rosaries, certainty. Now it was like trying to hold smoke. I'd stacked my shelves with self-help books, desperate for answers, but none had filled the growing void.

While they traveled, I buried myself in workouts and rehab, trying to keep moving, trying to stay sane. But the silence pressed in. Betsy was gone, old friends had drifted, and Steamboat felt familiar but no longer fully mine. I was stuck between worlds—healing, waiting, wondering where I fit in life.

I had just turned twenty-one. Most of my friends had serious boyfriends. Me? Nothing. I remembered my college roommate teasing, "You're so picky, Shan, you'll probably never get married."

Maybe she was right. My expectations were high—but they were high for everything. Meeting someone who could handle my strange mix—the drive, the discipline, the constant overthinking—felt impossible. I wasn't looking for a snowboarder; most were thrill-chasers, not exactly relationship material. My mom used to joke, "Just don't bring one of them home."

I smirked at the thought, but it faded fast.

The stillness left too much space to spiral. I replayed every choice, second-guessed every move. Injuries mess with your head. One moment, you're sure you'll come back stronger; the next, you're convinced you're finished.

I missed Sean. He'd walked away from his own snowboarding dreams, knowing—like I did—that in this sport, making it wasn't just about talent. It was timing, connections, luck.

Reese, the big golden ball of energy, was a comfort to Scarlet and to me. But some days, I wanted more. A coach. A guide. Someone steady to push me when I couldn't push myself. But that's not how snowboarding worked. You were your own coach, your own lifeline. And right now, I was barely holding on.

Over a week into my parents' trip, I was stir-crazy. *Time to get Reese out.*

That dog had tons of energy. Scarlet stayed home—I promised her a gentler stroll later.

We headed down the gravel road by the river, frost clinging to the edges. Reese's leash jingled, his tail wagging and nose to the ground.

Then he stopped cold.

I followed Reese's gaze—and my breath caught.

A hundred elk grazed quietly near the river, their bodies a rustling sea of movement against the frosted landscape. I'd never seen that many up close before; the sight was unexpectedly breathtaking.

But then—just above them, standing alone on the embankment—a coyote. Not slinking, not sneaking, not scared. It just stood there, watching. First the elk, then slowly, unnervingly, its eyes shifted to us.

It didn't flinch. It stepped forward.

"Come on, Reese, let's go." My voice was tight. I turned, pushing him back to the house.

A glance back—the coyote was closing the distance.

Suddenly, it broke into a run.

My heart jerked into my throat. Reese darted ahead instinctively, but I was slower, fumbling, glancing back over my shoulder.

The coyote was closing the distance.

I broke into a sprint, breath punching out of my lungs in sharp bursts. Gravel crunched under my boots; the road ahead seemed to stretch forever. My pulse roared in my ears as I sprinted, the cold air slicing my face.

I felt it at my heels—a nudge, a press, the cold snap of its nose against my foot. I shrieked, a sharp, piercing sound I didn't know I could make. The coyote yelped in surprise but didn't let up, pressing in closer, relentless.

God, help! He's hunting me.

Another shove at my heel. I stumbled, my ankle giving a light roll.

"Ouch," I gasped, breath catching, heart pounding so loud it thundered in my ears, like it might rip straight out of my ribcage.

And then—

I heard the low rumble of a truck engine ahead.

My arms shot up, waving frantically. "Help!" I shrieked, throat raw, heart pounding, hoping—praying—the driver would see me.

The truck roared around the corner, brakes screeching as gravel spat in every direction.

The door flew open, and out jumped a man in a cowboy hat. His voice cut clean through the chaos: "*Hey!* Get on outta here!"

The animal flinched but didn't fully retreat. It just stood there—watching.

The cowboy frowned. "You okay?"

I nodded, still catching my breath. "Yeah, I'm okay. Just...that coyote was nipping at my heels. Scared me so bad."

"That's strange. Coyotes don't usually go after people." He glanced across the river, pausing as he tried to make sense of it—and then it hit him. "Ah, you know what? Those folks over there raised one as a pet. Probably thinks you're a playmate."

My chest heaved, breath ragged. I tried to laugh, but it caught in my throat. "Yeah...he's got a weird way of showing it."

Reese was gone, of course—bolted the moment things got scary.

The cowboy's face softened. "You need a ride home?"

I shook my head, forcing a shaky smile. "I'm okay. Thanks."

He gave a slow nod, then climbed back into his truck and rumbled off, dust swirling behind him.

My ankle was throbbing, knee pulsing with a warning ache. And when I glanced back, the coyote was still there—lingering, watching. I walked slow, forcing every step. Finally, the animal slipped back into the trees.

When I reached the house, Reese was already sprawled on the porch, panting like nothing had happened. I slipped inside, shut the door behind me, and crumpled to the floor—heart still pounding, hands trembling, every muscle wired tight. The dogs rushed over, licking my face and hands like I'd been gone for days, their tails wagging wildly.

I forced myself up, shaky on my feet, and grabbed the frozen peas and corn from the freezer, thinking I'd ice my ankle and knee. But when I reached my room, the bags slipped from my hands. I collapsed face-first onto the bed. The room tilted slightly, then steadied.

And the tears came—hard, fast, unstoppable. I didn't even try to stop them.

Maybe the adrenaline brought it all on, but I felt overwhelmed. All the fear, the loneliness—the *what-if-I-never-make-it-back* terror, the *what the heck am I doing with my life*, the *what's my purpose in all of this*—came crashing down, pulling every last shred of strength out of me. I buried my face in the pillow, sobbing until my body shook, until there was nothing left but aching emptiness. I rolled onto my back and squeezed my eyes shut, chest heaving, heart cracked wide open.

God, I need to know who you are. I need help. I believe you made the trees, the earth, everything around me...so why don't I know you? Why do you feel like a stranger?

And then—a memory surged up, sharp and undeniable. That voice on the mountain: "Don't go." I'd heard it, clear as day, before I hit the jump, before I tore my ACL. I'd argued with it, pushed through, gone anyway—and ended up hurt.

The realization hit like a gut punch. *That was you, wasn't it, God?*

I didn't know how I knew—I just knew, as sure as if someone familiar had nodded silently beside me. The floodgates opened, and the sobs came hard, unstoppable, full of raw regret. I gasped the words out loud, fierce and unfiltered. "I'm so sorry. I'm so sorry. I heard your warning, but I talked back to you."

I shook my head, mind racing back to that moment—God had been trying to protect me, and I wouldn't listen. "God, who are you—for real? I need truth. I need real. I need *you* to show me who you are!"

My voice cracked, caught somewhere between a plea and a demand, stripped bare but purehearted. I paused, breathless, vulnerable—and then, softer, steadier: "And...if it's okay...could I meet my husband? Not just some guy—someone for me. Someone I don't have to pretend around. God, if it's ok with you...I think I'm ready to meet him."

The words hung in the air. And then the shame rushed in.

Who am I to ask for this? I'm such a mess.

The tears kept coming, hot and relentless. Suddenly, the phone rang, jolting me so hard I nearly fell off the bed. Scarlet barked. Reese leapt up. I fumbled for the receiver.

"Hello?" My voice cracked.

"Hey, Shan," Sean said, calm and familiar. "You alright?"

I hesitated. How did he always know? It was like something had nudged him to call, right when I was at the edge. I pulled my knees up, curling tight, the phone cold against my cheek.

"Uh-huh," I tried to fake it, but my voice gave me away.

"You sound...bummed."

That was it. The dam burst. The sobs came back, shaking me all over again.

"I just...I feel lame," I choked. "I'm sick of being injured. I'm stuck. I don't know what I'm doing with my life."

Sean let the silence stretch, steady and grounding.

"Hey," he said gently. "You're not alone. You've got me. You've got a lot of people who love you. You might not feel it right now, but you've got this."

I squeezed my eyes shut, holding onto his voice like a lifeline. "What if I never get back to where I was?"

"You will," he said without hesitation. "You've always figured it out, Shan. Even when it sucked. Even when you doubted. You kept going. That's who you are."

A shaky breath escaped me. "Yeah, but what if this time...I don't?"

"Then we figure it out together," he said firmly. "You're not in this alone."

The tightness in my chest eased just a little. "You really think I can do this?"

"I know you can."

A small laugh broke through my tears. "Thanks. I feel better...really."

"Good. But I mean it—if you need me, I'll come over."

For the first time all day, I felt a shift inside—like I wasn't just barely clinging on anymore.

"I'm okay," I whispered. "I'm so glad you called."

We hung up, and I sat there for a moment, the phone still warm in my hand. Across the room, the self-help books stared back at me—rows and rows of advice I'd spent hours devouring, hoping for clarity, and all they'd given me was...nothing.

Without overthinking it, I stood up, swept them off the shelf, and dumped them in the trash.

My knee and ankle—surprisingly—weren't throbbing. They felt steady, maybe even a little stronger.

In the bathroom, I splashed cold water on my face, watched the droplets trail down, and met my own eyes in the mirror.

I didn't have a perfect plan. I didn't know exactly how I'd make it back. One day at a time, I was going to keep plugging away.

CHAPTER 16

/ European Road Rallying /

FIRST, WE WERE IN—**HEADING TO EUROPE** for an epic photoshoot with Jeff. Then, we were out—dropped, just like that. The magazine editor, Jamie, already had a lineup that didn't include Tina and me. And then, three days before takeoff, the call came: we were back in. In snowboarding, plans could change in a blink, but this was the ultimate last-minute rally—a whirlwind of high hopes and a second chance we weren't about to miss.

It all started just after New Year's. I'd spent Christmas at home, nine months post-op and feeling stronger than ever. My surgeon had just given me the green light—I was healed, solid. Meanwhile, Utah's snow reports were lighting up with headlines about a record-breaking storm. For most people, that meant stocking up on canned goods and hunkering down. For snowboarders? It meant one thing: go time.

I booked a flight to Utah to meet up with Tina, ready to chase champagne powder and log some much-needed turns. The plan was simple— shred Utah's best, then fly Europe for a *Transworld Snowboarding* magazine photoshoot Jeff had lined up, followed by the first contest of the season.

At least, that was the plan...until it wasn't.

Not long after I'd arrived, Jeff called Tina's place, his voice carrying a tone of apology I'd never heard from him before.

"Hey, I've got some bad news," he started, and I could sense the let-down coming.

"What's up?" I asked, sharing a look with Tina.

"Circe's already been booked for the *Transworld* shoot," he said, sighing. "They only budgeted for one girl, so...it's a no-go for you two this time."

With the change in plans, Tina and I called the airline to cancel our flights to Europe and stay in Utah to bask in the storm's aftermath. The powder was calling. But when we checked, the fees to change our flights were astronomical, so we exchanged a look, shrugged it off, and decided to stick to the original plan. "Guess going early to Europe is still on," I said with a grin, the thrill of the unknown starting to creep back in. Wing it, ride, and make the most of whatever came our way.

Three days before our flight, the phone rang. Jeff's voice crackled through the line with excitement. "Guess what? You're in! Can you and Tina still make it for the Euro shoot?"

My jaw dropped. My pulse kicked up. This magazine trip was happening after all?

"Wait, seriously? Explain, explain!"

"Circe blew her knee out—ACL. She's out. It's rough for her, but the editor, Jamie, wants to know if you guys still have your tickets. *Transworld* will cover everything once you're there."

My stomach dropped. I knew that pain too well. But the opportunity was right in front of us, and I couldn't deny the excitement bubbling up.

"Alright then, count us in!" I practically shouted, the plot twist sending a surge of adrenaline through me. I didn't even think to ask any other questions—but Jeff had me covered.

Jeff shot back a quick reply. "Sick, we're gonna have so much fun! I'm so glad it worked out with you guys. I felt so bad when Jamie told me you couldn't come." Then he added, "By the way, Jamie Meiselman—*Trans-*

world's editor and the guy in charge—will call you with all the details: where we're staying, addresses, everything."

When the day finally came, Tina and I boarded the plane to Zurich, feeling like we were ready for anything—except maybe the last row in the smoking section. The woman next to me promptly lit up, surrounding us in a fog of cigarette smoke. Tina and I exchanged tortured looks, pulling blankets over our heads as we choked on the fumes.

Hours later, we stepped off the plane and into the crisp European air like a slap and a kiss all at once—cold, clean, a total reset after the suffocating torture-flight cabin. Snowflakes floated through the air, and suddenly it sank in: we were really here.

We wrestled our bags to the rental car counter, only to hit another snag. The agent frowned at the screen. "Sorry, no more four-wheel drive SUVs available. Only a compact sedan."

Tina shot me a sharp look. I shot one right back. *Seriously?*

She turned to the agent, her voice sweet but edged with steel. "That's not going to work. We're heading up to the mountains, and it just snowed a *lot*. Could you check again?"

Fifteen minutes, a lot of hand gestures, and one miracle manager override later, we were tossing our bags into the back of a scratched-up four-wheel drive SUV. I slid behind the wheel (I was usually the driver on these kinds of missions) while Tina unfolded the paper map across her lap, tracing routes with her finger like a seasoned rally navigator. I cranked up the heat as I pulled out of the parking garage.

"Alright, let's do this!" Tina said, scanning the map, sitting shotgun. "We're taking...Butts-in-bull-ring—A-51?"

I laughed as she stumbled over the German street name, and soon we were hitting the highway with Lenny Kravitz blasting through the speakers. Jet lag caught up with me fast, and I let out a huge yawn, making Tina crank up the volume and shout, "No sleeping, Shan! Let's go!"

After checking the map, Tina said, "Looks like we've got about a four-hour drive."

I raised my eyebrows, pressing the gas pedal a little harder. "Bet we can make it in two."

We rolled down the windows, letting the cool air rush in. Tina poked her head out and yelled, "Whoo-hoo! Europe, here we come!" Her excitement was contagious, and just like that, any lingering fatigue vanished.

An hour later, we pulled into a small mountain town gas station to grab snacks. As we climbed higher, the snowbanks grew taller, so I switched the car into four-wheel drive. "I guess I was a little ambitious with that ETA," I admitted, rubbing my eyes.

Tina popped in the Beastie Boys CD, cranked the volume, and our car morphed into a full-on private concert. She threw her hands up as "So What'cha Want" kicked off, and I steered with my knee, hands in the air like we were rock stars playing to an imaginary crowd. We were both singing loud enough to make the car shake, our voices blending with the bass and adrenaline.

As the song wrapped, I turned the volume down, catching my breath. "Hey, remind me, how'd you meet Adam Yauch? You were in Australia, right?"

Tina grinned, her eyes lighting up.

"Yeah, Adam." She sang out dramatically, "The Beastie Boysss," mimicking the start of one of their infamous songs, laughing. "I met him last summer in Australia. I was there for a Kemper photoshoot, riding with the team. The weather was foggy, really bad visibility, and I didn't feel like keeping up with the guys, so I went solo.

"I kept bumping into this random dude on the lift—we ended up riding together all day. He was super nice, soft-spoken, and all bundled up—so I had no clue who he was. I even invited him to lunch, but he was like, 'Nah, I'm good,' and kept riding."

"When I met everyone at the restaurant, they were all buzzing about Adam from the Beastie Boys—green hair, supposedly on the mountain somewhere." She paused, laughing to herself. "After lunch, I went back to the lift, and sure enough, there he was. We rode together the rest of the day. But it wasn't until we hit the bar afterward, when he took off his goggles, that I realized—green hair! It was Adam Yauch, right there, just chillin' like a regular dude."

I shook my head, grinning. "That's insane. How cool is that?"

Then, out of nowhere, the car jerked, tires slipping on a slick patch. My hands gripped the wheel.

"Oh, man!" I muttered, easing off the gas as we skidded into the opposite lane. My heart leapt into my throat as the wheels caught, snapping us back just in time—barely ten feet from an oncoming car.

"Whoa, that was close, Shan!" Tina said, wide-eyed.

"Black ice—didn't see that coming. Slowing down for sure," I said, my pulse pounding. I shifted into a lower gear, feeling the lingering shiver of adrenaline. "Sorry about that...but yeah, keep going. What about Adam?"

She shot me a knowing look. "Alright, but seriously, be careful! Ice is no joke." She settled back in her seat, still riding the high. "So, he actually hit me up before this trip, asking if I knew of a place to rent for the winter in Utah. I told him I had a spare room in my condo, and he's moving in soon. Crazy, right?"

With Beastie Boys still pounding through the speakers, she skipped to another track, the beats driving out the fatigue from our bones. Just as we hit our groove, a road sign flashed by, pointing toward Bormio, and then—out of nowhere—a dark mouth in the mountainside: a narrow, ominous tunnel looming ahead.

Tina grinned, cranking the volume even louder. "Let's do this!"

I couldn't resist. I pressed down on the gas, the car surging forward into the tunnel, the beat from the Beastie Boys reverberating off the stone walls. She laughed, singing, "The BEASTIE BOOOYS, when are they coming hooome..."

My voice rose over the music. "This tunnel's super narrow—what if we meet another car?"

I don't think Tina even heard me—she was too busy unzipping her bag, pulling out her camera. "I *have* to get a shot of this!" she shouted, leaning forward as the lights streaked past in a crazy, kaleidoscopic blur.

I glanced at the speedometer and let out a yell. "A hundred sixty kilometers! Whoo-hoo!"

She laughed, her eyes wide with exhilaration. "These shots are gonna be epic!"

As we sped toward the tunnel's end, I eased off the gas, bracing for any icy patches outside. Just then, Tina glanced over her shoulder, counting cars out loud.

"One, two, three, four... Oh my gosh, Shan."

My stomach dropped. "Did you see a stoplight at the tunnel entrance?"

She blinked, realization dawning on her face. "No... Did you?"

I exhaled, the weight of what we'd just done sinking in. "We could've just died in there."

Tina's face went pale for a moment before she broke into a nervous laugh. "That was definitely a one-way tunnel. Talk about living on the edge."

We hadn't even thought to check for a light at the entrance—no red, no green, nothing. It hit me: all it takes is one missed sign. It was late, we were giddy from jet lag, and only now did I realize: if another car had come from the opposite side, we would've been trapped head-on, with nowhere to go. A chill ran through me. Just a little slower, just a green light from the other side—and we would've slammed straight into oncoming traffic inside that narrow, one-lane tunnel.

Tina and I shared a wide-eyed look—and then burst into laughter, the kind that spills out when you realize you either had angels watching over you or just got ridiculously lucky. Our European adventure was only just beginning, and already, we were hurtling headfirst into the unknown.

CHAPTER 17

/ Powder Posse /

I STEPPED INTO THE BREAKFAST ROOM. The smell of espresso and warm pastries wrapped around me like a promise of comfort. But my stomach clenched. This wasn't just breakfast; it was my first real moment sizing up the *Transworld* crew—and silently wondering if I belonged at the table. But as the morning unfolded, the tension began to ease. We started bonding quickly, connecting through shared travel chaos and a mutual love for snowboarding.

Jamie Meiselman, *Transworld's* sharp-eyed editor, known for catching every detail and keeping things on track, steered the conversation, laying out the plan for the shoot. Jeff Curtes, camera always within reach, was already capturing candid moments. Eric Kotch, Burton's serious team manager, sat beside Brian Thien—baby-faced, fresh out of Big Bear, with a smooth style that hinted at serious potential. Jake Blattner lounged nearby, easygoing and grinning beneath a mop of short dreadlocks.

But it was Dave who held my attention. Something about him made me skeptical. With his chiseled jaw, broad shoulders, and quiet, in-control presence, he read the room effortlessly. Was he trying too hard—too polished, too proper, maybe even a little nerdy? Or was he actually just himself? I wasn't sure yet.

Over cappuccinos, tea, and plates of bread and cheese, the conversation turned to their wild journey from Munich—an autobahn crash, two snowed-in mountain passes, and two flat tires. We related and chimed in about our crazy drive, swapping stories like old friends. At some point, they even ended up drinking Lucifer beer in a random bar—fitting for the hell they'd gone through.

As the laughter faded, the talk shifted to gear: who was riding what, which brands were dropping new products, and the latest sponsorship rumors floating through the scene.

That's when Dave turned to me. "Oh, by the way," he said casually, "the Oakley rep sent something for you—a pair of their new sunglasses."

I raised an eyebrow. *Oakley?* That was unexpected—but not totally out of nowhere. I had just been in contact with their team manager, who mentioned they wanted to sponsor me.

"I have them in my car if you want to check 'em out," he offered, flashing a smile.

Curiosity piqued, I followed him outside into the crisp, cool morning. The snowy mountains framed the horizon, each peak a reminder of the day's promise. Dave popped open the trunk and pulled out the Oakley sunglasses, his easygoing smile never fading.

"Here they are," he said, handing them over with a look that was equal parts friendly and teasing. "Latest style—hot off the press."

"Thanks!" I grinned, opening the case. I slipped the sunglasses on and caught my reflection in the car's side mirror, stifling a laugh. "Whoa—I look like a space creature!" I said, turning my head to catch the light. The Oakley Sub Zeros were ultra-sleek and wraparound, narrowing my eyes, the lenses curving sharply across my face like some futuristic bug or alien. "Seriously, am I supposed to wear these?"

Dave chuckled. "That's the idea. Scott, the marketing guy, was hoping for a photo op. Just one shot?" he added, raising an eyebrow.

Just then, Tina strolled up. "Whoa, Shan—those are something else. Stylin'!" She laughed, and I laughed along with her.

"Think they'll work for a photoshoot?" I asked, striking a ridiculous pose—hands on hips, chin lifted, lips puckered.

Dave gave a serious nod. "Perfect."

"Alright, that's settled," I said, slipping the sunglasses into my jacket.

Tina stretched. "I could go for a snack run. What do you think?"

"Oh yeah," I agreed.

"The hotel lady said there's a little market up the street." She turned to Dave. "You in?"

He shut the trunk with a thud. "Sure, why not?"

A few minutes later, we were wandering cobblestone streets, the town's old-world charm wrapping around us—shuttered windows, espresso drifting from cafés, everything feeling a little unreal.

At the *supermercato* checkout, I watched Dave quietly step in, grabbing the grocery bag from my hands without a second thought.

"Here, I got it," he said, flashing an easy smile.

"Thanks," I said, surprised. I'd never met a snowboarder who offered. Chivalry? I thought that was long gone—but clearly, not with him. Maybe I'd been too quick to judge. Maybe he wasn't trying to be anyone but himself. And yeah...I had to admit, he was cute—with that rugged, outdoorsy charm, the kind of guy who could pull off both Cali surfer and mountain cabin woodchopper. Eric had mentioned offhand that Dave used to surf professionally—just for a bit. It tracked—the way he moved with casual confidence made total sense now.

As we walked back, he shared how surreal the whole trip felt. "I got my first passport just days ago—stood in line at the LA passport office to get it expedited," he said, shaking his head. "One minute I'm in California, the next, I'm flying to Italy."

I laughed. "Tina and I ended up here last-minute too—invited, uninvited, then re-invited at the last second."

He grinned. "So none of us were supposed to be here."

I smiled. "I think it's more like we were all actually supposed to be here."

Once back at the hotel, we met our local guide from the nearby town of Santa Caterina—a lanky guy we called "Lurch." He told us the area had been buried under a record ten feet of snow in just two weeks. But then came the gut punch: just two weeks ago, his brother had died here in an avalanche. We all exchanged uneasy glances and quickly agreed—no pushing limits. We'd stick to the safer, lower trails.

Afterward, we headed up to our room to get ready for the day, trying to shake off the heaviness of the conversation. We pulled out our over-sized outerwear and started layering up, swimming in sleeves and pant legs. Lisa Hudson had hooked us up with fresh gear. She was the former Airwalk team manager and had just taken on a new role as Swag Outerwear's marketing director. The catch? Swag only made men's snowboard outerwear. Lisa promised gear in our size soon, but for now, we were stuck with next year's men's large samples. We rolled up the cuffs, laughing and I cracked, "I swear, I'm not wearing my dad's stuff!"

Since magazines ran their photos and stories a year ahead, it was crucial that pros were seen riding in the latest gear—even if it meant drowning in jackets five sizes too big. Looking oversized was a small price to pay for getting the shot.

Our first day on the mountain turned out to be one of those rare days where everything just clicked—floating through untracked powder like it was a dream. Between runs, we laughed, swapped stories, and built the kind of connection you only get when sharing untouched lines.

That night, a fresh layer of powder blanketed the hotel grounds. Our crew was growing—Tina's brother, Mikey, had just arrived to join us for a few days—but it was the easygoing kind of vibe where adding one more just made it better.

By morning, the sky stretched out in full bluebird glory, crisp and cloudless—the kind of day that practically begged you to ride. It was time to chase another round of powder. With Tina riding shotgun, I followed the caravan up the winding mountain road toward Livigno, a sprawling resort town tucked deep in the Italian Alps. Snowbanks rose like frozen walls on either side, narrowing the road into a tunnel of white. We blasted the Smashing Pumpkins, windows fogged, voices loud, the lyrics echoing through the car as we shouted, "Today is the greatest..."

By the time we rolled into the base area, our crew was buzzing. We piled into the gondola together, high on anticipation, swapping stories and shaking off the chill as we climbed toward the ridgeline. The sun lit up a wide, untouched snowfield below, shimmering like it had been waiting just for us. Lurch and the locals dropped in first, boards pointed downhill, and we followed—floating through deep, dry powder, light and fast, leaving plumes behind us. Tina yelled, "Today is the greatest—" and we all joined in, hollering the rest of the line in unison: "—day I've ever known!"

I could feel my knee holding strong beneath me—a reminder of all the hard work that had brought me to this moment. Riding through the rolling terrain, we dropped into a natural powder halfpipe, the snowbanks on either side shaping perfect transitions. Each turn felt effortless, each dip a rush of pure freedom.

We kept going, weaving over a cat track, threading through the trees, and plunging into another gully, the terrain unfolding like an endless playground. By the time we reached the bottom—breathless, legs burning, adrenaline still pumping—we couldn't help but cheer. This was snowboarding at its purest, and we were living it. Our anthem, the Smashing Pumpkins' "Today," stayed on repeat the rest of our trip.

We'd been snapping photos every day, but by the third morning, everything aligned in a way that felt different—the light, the snow, the sheer stoke of the group. It was the kind of day that defined the trip, the one that truly captured its spirit: raw energy, untouched powder, and the pure joy of riding together in a place that felt almost too perfect to be real.

Jeff focused on taking photos of Tina and me, the untouched powder below us sparkling in the early light. The guys tore past, whooping and slashing deep turns, their energy full-throttle. Jeff pointed out a cornice—a wind-sculpted overhang of snow that jutted from the ridge, creating a natural jump with a steep landing. It was the kind of feature that, when hit just right, launched you into flight.

"Tina, if you go off that to the left—there are fresh landings over there. Then Shan—I'll direct you based on Tina's landing track after she goes," Jeff called out. As we gave him the okay, he pointed to where he'd be shooting from—well within view. "Just give me the signal."

We knew what that meant—both arms above your head, forming a circle.

"Alright, ready for takeoff!" Tina shouted, flashing me a grin before launching off the edge. Midair, she grabbed her board and tweaked her front foot out for extra style points, then vanished into the white abyss below.

When my turn came, I lined up my board and took a deep breath. One small wiggle to set my momentum, then I pointed it off the cornice and launched—soaring higher than I'd expected. Instinct took over. I grabbed a method, tweaking it for style, holding the moment in midair before floating down into a soft, bottomless bed of powder. Jeff's voice rang out, full of excitement. "That's a keeper, cover shot potential!"

The day carried on with more powder, more laughter, and more unforgettable turns. By late afternoon, our legs were spent, our faces sore from grinning, and the last rays of golden light were dipping behind the peaks.

"I don't know about you guys, but I think we earned some hot tub time," Jake said, shaking snow from his hair as we rode the last lift down.

No one disagreed. That night, we all piled into the hotel's tiny hot tub—way too many of us squeezed into a four-person Jacuzzi, laughing, retelling the day's highlights, and soaking in the high of it all. I was smushed between the curved fiberglass wall and Dave, our bare arms brushing every time someone shifted.

"I like your cross," Dave said, nodding toward the necklace my parents had brought back from Italy—ironically, I'd later learn, from a town just a fifteen-minute drive from where we were staying.

Something about the way he said it made me pause. He wasn't just making small talk. And I definitely noticed—his eyes never drifted to my boobs, where most guys' eyes would go, especially impressive since I was in a bathing suit.

I felt myself drawn to him. He definitely had the looks—tan, six-pack, sculpted muscles, a little more manly-hairy-chested than boyish—but there was something else. A quiet confidence. A grounded, thoughtful vibe. He wasn't trying too hard, wasn't putting on a show like some guys did. It was effortless. Refreshing. And, if I was being honest...really attractive.

As I smiled and told him thanks, something shifted. For a heartbeat, time froze. His gaze held mine—steady, intense—and for a split second, I wondered, *What more is there to him? And maybe... Could there be something more with us? Whoa—too much, too soon.* I quickly shoved those thoughts aside. No need to read into things. Everyone else kept laughing, joking, swapping stories from the day—oblivious to the little electric moment Dave and I had just shared. We snapped back into the group conversation, like nothing had happened.

The next day, we all rode through Livigno's endless fields of powder again. At dinner, Brian, ever the goofball, bit into an olive and spat it out, groaning about a hard bit.

"That's called a pit," Eric laughed. "You're not in Cali anymore, dude."

The night carried a bittersweet sense of finality. We'd just lived some of the best days of our lives, and none of us was ready to let it end. Tina, Mikey, and I had to shift gears for the grind of competition, but the others weren't eager to head home either. Jamie offered to postpone their flights—they could keep the magazine story rolling, with expenses still covered.

So, we hatched a plan: the three of us would head to the World Cup, while the rest of the crew chased more powder in Cortina—a world-class mountain not far from the contest venue. They'd meet us for the finals to watch us compete, and afterward, we'd squeeze in one last day of riding together, keeping the good vibes alive just a little longer.

With the plan set, we packed up and hit the road, leaving behind the snow-covered dreamland for a new kind of adventure—the unpredictable, high-stakes journey to the World Cup.

As we caravanned toward Geezerville—or whatever that impossible-to-pronounce Italian town was—Mikey, a few cars ahead of us, gunned his engine and swung out to pass a car on the narrow mountain road. But he must not have seen the oncoming vehicle. My heart shot into my throat as Tina let out a sharp gasp, her arm instinctively bracing against the dash.

Mikey swerved back just in time, the oncoming car jerking wildly and skidding into a ditch in a spray of snow and gravel.

I hit the brakes, slowing to a stop as the chaos unfolded right in front of us. The road narrowed, boxed in by snowbanks—nowhere to turn off. Tina and I sat frozen, eyes wide, rattled, my pulse pounding in my ears.

Mikey eased his car toward the shoulder, probably to check if they were okay. But before his door even cracked open, four burly Italians in matching red sweatsuits exploded out of the other car, charging toward him like an avalanche of fists and fury, their faces twisted with rage.

Tina and I froze, breath locked in our chests, bracing for impact. And then—without a second's hesitation—Mikey floored it. His engine roared, tires shrieking as they fought for grip, kicking up a cloud of slush and ice shards in his wake. He bolted forward, disappearing around the bend, leaving the furious Italians shrinking in the distance, arms flailing, shouts echoing faintly behind.

We exhaled all at once, nerves crackling in the silence. Tina let out a shaky laugh. "That was a close one."

When we finally pulled up to the World Cup venue, I just stared—a muddy halfpipe, one lonely snowy lane, and cows. Literal cows. And the worst part? Their stench hit my nostrils hard—manure wafting in every warm breeze, thick and toxic. After a week of untouched powder, it felt like we'd landed on another planet.

I couldn't help but wonder: were contests even worth it? We'd just lived some of the best days of our lives—pure, unscripted joy. No rules, no scores, just friends pushing each other, run after run. But contests paid the bills. They kept us in the game.

Some riders were already breaking away, finding new paths. Snowboard films were blowing up, giving kids an inside look at what was possible—and what was cool—on a snowboard. You didn't have to be at the mountain to feel it. You could sit in the comfort of your living room, pop in a VHS, and get a front-row seat to the revolution. We'd watch every new part on repeat, soaking in the progression, imagining what could be next.

As the contest kicked off, riders grumbled—soft halfpipe, slow speed. Tina and I just laughed it off. I was riding high—my knee still felt strong, and this crew gave me a kind of confidence I hadn't felt in a long time. They weren't the party-hearty type; they rode hard, laughed harder, and helped keep things light when it counted.

Honestly, I wasn't stressed about this contest, even though it was a World Cup. I just wanted to finish and get back to chasing pow with our crew. Making the finals felt like a piece of cake—and the format was familiar: two runs, top combined score takes the win.

I nailed my first run and lined up for one more. As I dropped in, that focus switch flipped—muscle memory took over, flow kicked in, and everything else just fell away.

At the bottom of the halfpipe, Dave was waiting, grinning, cheering me on. I wasn't sure if he was just caught up in our crew's stoke or if there was something more, but when he wrapped me in a hug, I felt it—a spark. Subtle, but real.

Then the announcer called my name over the loudspeaker—for the win. All the rehab, the discipline, the late-night doubts—it all came crashing over me in a flood. Hard work had paid off, no doubt. But the bigger reminder? Stop wasting time on fear. Keep the faith. Hope for the best.

I stepped toward the podium—but before I could hop up, Jake launched himself onto it, arms raised like he'd just won the Olympics.

We all cracked up as he struck an exaggerated pose, hamming it up for the crowd.

The event coordinator, though, was stone-faced. He quickly hustled Jake off, shaking his head like it was the most unprofessional thing he'd ever seen. But for us? It was perfect. It wasn't just my win—it felt like a win for all of us.

When I finally stepped up, they handed me my medal, an oversized check, and a bottle of champagne. Without a second's thought, I shook it up, popped the cork, and sprayed it all over the crew, dousing them as they cheered.

We weren't just celebrating a contest—we were celebrating the kind of trip that felt like it could never be topped. But it wasn't over yet. We still had one more day to make the most of it.

True to their word, the boys showed us Cortina, charging through untouched powder with jagged cliffs and sprawling mountain peaks.

The contest was behind us, and now, it was just about the ride—another awesome day that reminded us why we did this in the first place. We rode the gondola up and were greeted by mountain goats, casually perched on the rocky ledges as if they owned the place.

The powder didn't disappoint. We spent the day riding endless untracked snow, dropping into steep, untouched faces that felt like they'd been waiting just for us.

As the sun began to dip behind the mountains, casting everything in a golden glow, Tina and I lagged behind the guys and stopped at the top of a steep face on our final run. We looked up to see a staggering 600-foot cliff towering above us, rugged and raw against the sky. Below, the town looked like a miniature model, and in that moment, the sheer magnitude of it all hit me. Every ounce of grit, sacrifice, and relentless passion that had led me here swelled up inside, filling my chest with an ache so deep it spilled over into tears. It was as if I were standing in the middle of something far greater than myself.

And then it washed over me. My life—this wasn't random, this wasn't just luck. There was an undeniable orchestration in every twist and turn, every high and low, that had led me here. I could feel it, this presence so much bigger than me. God was here with me.

CHAPTER 18
/ First Kiss /

I WAS ON A WINNING STREAK—Italy, the last two contests, and here I was again.

First place at Squaw Valley, second for Tina. My knee wasn't even a thought anymore—I felt 100%. My confidence was high. For the first time in a long while, everything felt like it was falling into place. We were bouncing from contest to contest, juggling packed schedules and sponsor demands—but underneath it all, one thing pulsed louder than the rest.

Dave.

The night after the Squaw Valley contest, Tina and I collapsed onto our rented condo's worn-out couch, laughing as we replayed memories from Italy. I leaned back, letting the warmth of those moments settle over me. And then—there he was again in my mind. Dave. I kept thinking about the way he'd taken my grocery bag without hesitation, like it was second nature. I smiled without meaning to.

"Dave is so cute and nice," I said, almost to myself.

Tina's eyes sparkled knowingly. "He is super cute. I think he likes you."

"Really? How can you tell?" I tried to sound casual, but my curiosity was anything but.

"I dunno—I just can." Tina grinned, then nudged me. "We should invite Jeff, Eric, and Dave to my condo in Utah before the Vegas trade show. You should call him now, get it started."

My heart sped up.

"No way—I can't call him," I said, instantly nervous.

Tina raised an eyebrow. "Why not?"

"Because I'd be so nervous I'd freeze. I'd feel like such an idiot. What would I even say?"

Tina gave me an exasperated look, walked over to the phone, and started dialing his number. "Just tell him we're inviting everyone to come ride. There's a huge storm rolling in, and the powder's gonna be epic."

I blinked. "Wait—how do you even have his number?"

She smirked. "Oh, I got everyone's number in Italy before we left. Thought it might come in handy. You're welcome."

Before I could protest, she pressed the phone into my hand. "There. Now you have to talk to him."

Butterflies erupted in my stomach as I clutched the receiver. The line rang once. Twice. Then, a woman's voice answered, warm and friendly.

"Hello?"

"Uh, hi," I said, my voice suddenly three octaves higher. "I'm calling for Dave. Is he around?"

"Oh yeah! This is Janey. How ya doing? Who can I tell him is calling?"

Janey? My brain scrambled. *Who was Janey? His girlfriend? A random roommate?* I hesitated before finally saying, "Uh...it's Shannon."

"Awesome! Hang on a sec."

I shot a panicked look at Tina, mouthing, "Who's Janey?"

She shrugged dramatically.

A few seconds later, Dave picked up. "Hey, Shan! What's up?" His voice was casual, warm—like we talked all the time. "That was Janey—she's the Burton rep. I rent a room from her so I can stay up here a couple days at a time. Otherwise, I'd be driving back and forth from Redondo Beach to Big Bear."

Relief washed over me. *Not a girlfriend. Cool.*

"Oh, gotcha," I said, my brain catching up. Then, before I could over-think it, I powered through. "So, yeah…Tina and I are getting some of the Italy crew together at her place in Utah before the Vegas show. Thought you might want to come?"

"That sounds rad," he said without hesitation. "Who all's going?"

Tina leaned in, whispering, "Jeff, Eric…obviously you."

I repeated the list, and Dave chuckled. "Sounds like trouble. I'm in."

I exhaled, tension easing. "Awesome. Maybe talk to Tina to coordinate flights after she figures it out with Eric and Jeff?"

"Sounds good," he said. Then, after a brief pause, "Hey, Shan, before I forget, what's your address?"

My stomach did a weird little flip. "Um, my address in Steamboat?"

"Yeah," he said casually.

I rattled off the details, and he repeated them back, making sure he had it right.

"Got it," he said. We caught up on everything—how the contest went, what we'd been up to—until he casually said, "I bet you won, huh?"

I smiled. "Yeah, I did."

"Dang, that's awesome!" His excitement felt real. "I knew it. I can't wait to see you."

My brain short-circuited. My face went hot. *Did he just say he can't wait to see me?*

Flustered, I blurted, "Uh—Tina wants to say hi!" and practically threw the phone at her.

Tina took it with a knowing smirk, launching straight into conversation while I sat there, heart racing. When she finally hung up, she crossed her arms, looking smug. "Told you he likes you."

After the contest, I flew home to Steamboat, and the day before I was set to leave for Utah—Valentine's Day—a red envelope arrived, addressed in a guy's handwriting. Inside was a simple, sweet doodle of a stick figure holding a heart, asking, "Will you be my Valentine?" signed with a heart, "Dave."

My stomach flipped. I couldn't help but picture his warm smile, his strong, easy presence. Did he really like me? Probably. Or maybe he sent Valentine cards to all his friends.

The next day, Dave, Eric, Jeff, and I gathered at Tina's cozy three-bedroom condo in Utah, ready to ride Snowbird Resort's steep and deep powder. Something changed after Italy—like that trip had bonded us all in a way that made things feel both brand new and like we'd known each other forever.

Adam Yauch—yes, from the Beastie Boys—had moved in but was out of town, and meanwhile, Tina was quietly rethinking her relationship with her longtime boyfriend, Andy. You could feel the tension: Andy grunted a curt "hey" when we arrived, barely acknowledging Dave, Eric, or Jeff before disappearing into his room. Moments later, he emerged, cigarette in hand, stepping onto the deck to smoke, frustration practically vibrating off him.

"Whoa. Tina, are you sure it's cool we're here?" Eric whispered.

"Yeah, don't worry about Andy," Tina said. "I want you guys here. He's flying out this afternoon anyway—he won't even be around."

We went to bed early, knowing we'd need the rest for a big day ahead. The next morning, snow swirled around us as we loaded the chairlift for a deep powder day. I ended up on the three-seater with Dave, while Tina, Eric, and Jeff rode just ahead. As the chair glided up the mountain, conversation flowed easily—Italy stories, powder day laughs, all of it.

Finally, I worked up the nerve. "By the way...I loved the Valentine's card you sent," I said, my voice barely above a whisper.

"Oh, you got it?" He smiled, and in that moment, he reached an arm behind me, resting it casually on the back of the chair. My stomach fluttered, my cheeks flushed. Was he just being friendly...or was there something more? Our knees brushed, and he held my gaze, his smile lingering just long enough to leave me wondering.

That moment lingered. As the days slipped by, it buzzed quietly beneath the nerves, the excitement, the pressure—a spark I couldn't shake.

After a few more epic days on the mountain, it was time to shift gears. Our crew split off in different directions, but we'd reconnect soon—at the trade show. Powder runs would give way to convention halls, fresh tracks to fluorescent lights.

The morning of the Las Vegas show, I took my time. Sleek black bodysuit. High-waisted, belted jeans, cinched just right. White Airwalk sneakers. A swipe of pink lip gloss, a deep breath, one last look in the mirror—I was ready.

The Vegas Show, officially the Snowsports Industries America trade show, held in Las Vegas, was the heartbeat of the snowboard world. Every March, brands unveiled next season's gear, buyers placed orders, and deals were made in booths, at dinners, and over late-night cocktails. Retailers, media, athletes, designers, reps—they all showed up. And everyone was watching for what would blow up next. For riders like me, it wasn't just about product. It was about presence. About being seen, taken seriously, and, if you were lucky, launching something that could shift the culture. And this year, I was excited to be there for the launch of my *Sunflower* board.

The moment I stepped onto the trade show floor, the energy hit like a tidal wave. Cameras flashed, voices called my name, hands reached for mine. Interviews, photos, meetings—

"Shan! Quick interview?"

"Shannon, tell us about the new board!"

"One more photo!"

The hype was relentless.

I pushed through the packed aisles toward the Sims booth, heart hammering. My *Sunflower* board stood dead center—bold, vibrant, and impossible to miss. The booth swarmed with buyers, media, and onlookers, the air buzzing with curiosity. Heads turned. Conversations hushed. All eyes locked on the board.

My first Sunflower board pro model ad—crafted by Gaylene and featured in the mags. A milestone moment.

Gaylene appeared, practically glowing. "Shan! We can't take orders fast enough. Your board is selling more than all of them!" My knees nearly buckled.

It all rushed back: the design battles, the doubts, the industry shutouts, and negativity from all sides. Gaylene, especially, fought tooth and nail to make this women's pro model a reality, facing resistance at every turn:

"Is the market even big enough?"

"Do women really need different products?"

I'd hung up the phone so many times, near tears, wondering if this crazy idea would ever leave the sketchbook.

But here it was.

The *Sunflower* didn't whisper, "Girls can snowboard too." It stood in shops shouting it: "We're here. We've got our own gear. We're not just fitting in—we're making an impact. And you're going to love us, because we're not going anywhere. We'll bring you profit, joy, and an energy that will keep this sport fresh, unique, and unforgettable."

Across the floor, I spotted Tina at the Kemper booth, laughing with a group of people, her energy electric, arms waving as she told a story. I started weaving through the crowd toward her, but before I could reach her, Lisa appeared out of nowhere, grabbing my arm.

"Hey, babe!" she grinned, pulling me into a hug and steering me through the throng. Together, we cut a path toward Tina, who spotted us and lit up, waving us over.

In seconds, the three of us were huddled together, the noise and chaos of the show blurring around us—just a tight circle of excitement, big news, and even bigger dreams.

"I pitched Swag to let you two create a women's snowboarding outerwear line," Lisa grinned. "Full creative control."

Tina's jaw dropped. "You mean we won't have to keep rocking oversized men's gear?"

We all burst out laughing, because that was exactly it. Lisa had her finger on the pulse. She saw what was coming. Women weren't just dipping

FEBRUARY 14th, 1994

Shannon Dunn Pro Model

Is The Shannon the first Women's Pro model?
Yes, it is for Sims, and at the time of our release there were not any other boards on the market that were designed by women for women. In the history of the sport, however, there has been one other female signature model that I know of. In 1990/91 Lisa Vinciguerra had a signature model released by a European company, Checker Pig. The board was great, but unfortunately it wasn't distributed or marketed well in the U.S. As far as I know there have been no others.

In the past, women snowboarders have been riding sized down versions of men's boards or boards designed for entry level kids. The exciting thing about the Shannon Dunn is that the size, shape and graphics were designed by women that snowboard. The board is being marketed to women, but some of the Sims team male riders have been riding it and love it.

Female specific features are the width, lightweight core and the length, which has a longer effective edge to length ratio than you would expect. The width is almost 2cm narrower than comparitive sized boards designed for guys. Because women have smaller feet, their toes often don't sit on the edge of the board. When you put pressure on your toe to get an edge response and your toe is closer to the middle of the board than the edge, the response is weak. By having a narrower board, those with smaller feet can experience an immediate edge to edge response, which gives a whole new level of effortless control. I say effortless because on equipment that is too big or too heavy, you have to work twice as hard, but you don't even know how much better it can be. Until now, the option for most women was to ride a junior board, but these boards are too soft for an aggressive rider and the effective edge is usually too short for any kind of stability at speed. The Dunn has a very high ratio of effective edge to length, which gives the stability of a longer board, with the shorter overall length to reduce the weight and improve freestyle maneuverablity.

You don't have to be female to ride this board, but one thing is certain. If you're riding a DUNN 150 this season, be prepared to lead and not follow.

For more info, please contact Gaylene Nagel at SIMS Snowboards.
604/525/9441

Official press release announcing my first Shannon Dunn Pro Model—a defining step in shaping women's snowboarding gear.

a toe into this sport—we were taking over. And now, we had a chance to lead an untapped market.

Lisa leaned in. "Dinner tonight at seven. I'll call your room—let's make this happen."

The rush of interviews and excitement kept coming—until I hit a wall. Dry mouth. Spinning head. Empty stomach. I slipped away toward the café, weaving through the crowds. On the way, I passed the Burton booth, nerves kicking in—I was hoping to run into Dave, who was showing their line to the Southern California buyers. Instead, I ran straight into Eric.

"Shan, your board is the hottest thing at the entire show," he said, grinning.

I froze. Eric didn't hand out compliments, not without meaning them. "Seriously?"

"Dead serious. It's making a big impact—huge."

Gaylene's excitement, the media buzz—that was one thing. But hearing it from Eric? That was *confirmation*. He was with Burton—a brand at the top of the game—and his perspective carried weight. If Eric said it was a big deal, I knew it wasn't just hype. It was real.

Before I could even process it, Dave appeared, his easy smile lighting me up.

"Want to grab a bite?" I blurted, feeling bold.

Minutes later, we were sitting outside in the sun, snacking on almonds—the only thing that looked remotely edible in the café—guzzling water, laughing. Just the two of us. No cameras. No chaos. It felt easy. Unhurried. Warm.

"Want to hit the hotel pool?" I asked, half-joking, half-hoping. We headed back to my room to grab my swimsuit, but we never made it to the pool. I sank onto the bed, the weight of the day catching up with me. *Just for a second*, I thought.

Dave sat beside me. We both exhaled, the space between us humming. He grabbed the remote, flipping through channels until he landed on *Wayne's World 2*.

Before I knew it, we were shoulder to shoulder, laughing, trading funny movie lines, leaning closer and closer. And then—like magnets—we tipped toward each other.

Our lips met.

My soul, my body, my brain launched into outer space.

Fireworks. Full-color, all-consuming, no-going-back fireworks.

With just one kiss, I knew—with all of my heart.

This was the guy.

The guy I was going to marry.

CHAPTER 19

/ I'm Over the Moon /

THE SUN HOVERED LOW ON THE HORIZON, casting a golden glow as I lifted my *Sunflower* board high, feeling its weight—and everything it sym-bolized—in my hands. Another small step for women, one giant leap for womankind.

Standing atop the podium at the first-ever 55DSL Riksgränsen event in northern Sweden—an event like no other, blending snowboarding, skateboarding, and live music against a backdrop of endless snow—I felt a deeper rush than any win before.

This wasn't just another medal. Nearly every contest that winter had ended in victory, but more importantly, the fear had finally quieted. It was another win on my pro model board, capping off a season where I'd made history: back-to-back U.S. Open titles—the first woman to do it—and the first to land a backside 540 in competition. All the old doubts—leaving college, fighting through injury, second-guessing myself—felt like faint echoes.

Snowboarding had become something bigger than just a sport or a career. It was a way to open doors—not just for me, but for every girl watching, wondering if there was space for her here. I wanted them to feel the thrill of discovering strength they didn't know they had. Because if a girl from modest beginnings like me could carve her way here, they could too.

Winning had become a tool—to draw more women in, to inspire them to get outside, take risks, chase adventure, and find a community where they belonged. Thanks to Gaylene's visionary marketing, the *Sunflower* board wasn't just a product—it was a statement. And it opened the floodgates. Other brands took notice and were ready to follow. Now, there was proof.

Although this was the last contest of the season, today didn't feel like an ending. I knew I still had so much more to give. And for the first time in a long while, I wasn't just surviving the ride—I was loving it.

After the ceremony, the crowd shifted toward the skateboard ramp. We were still outside, surrounded by looming clouds and a sun that refused to disappear. This far above the Arctic Circle in May, it only skimmed below the horizon, leaving a soft twilight glow that never fully faded. It felt like we were playing on the moon.

The skate vert ramp was built right on top of the snow, just below the snowboard halfpipe. Next to it, a band tore into their set—amps cranked, drums pounding, guitars wailing through the crisp air.

Pro skateboarders dropped in one after another, wheels snarling, launching massive airs in sync with the beat. Big, fat snowflakes suddenly began to fall, coating beanies, shoulders, and the ramp itself—but no one backed off. The skaters kept going. The crowd surged. The band dug deeper, feeding off the wild, unrelenting energy.

Then John Cardiel dropped in—no pads, no helmet, no hesitation—and hurled himself into a McTwist, spinning high above the crowd and into the snow-choked sky. Hundreds of us stood packed around the ramp, heads tilted back, snow collecting on our shoulders as we watched him twist and float in a moment that felt both reckless and poetic. He landed clean on the slick, snow-dusted plywood like it was nothing.

A woman from the event staff approached me. I had no idea how she'd spotted me in the crowd. "MTV Europe's taping in the red hotel. Will you do an interview?"

It was the only hotel on the hill, nestled right at the base, so I followed her inside. I brushed the snow off my beanie, ducked into the bathroom to fix my braids and freshen up, then stepped into the interview room.

And there he was: legendary pro skater, sharp, famous, unexpectedly charming. He greeted me with an easy smile and a firm handshake. Lights, camera, rolling—I sat across from him, heart racing.

"Congrats on your win, Shannon," he opened smoothly. "What do you think about Riksgränsen and Sweden?"

I was still buzzing. "It's incredible! The halfpipe, the skate ramps, the live bands—seriously, one of the best events I've ever been to."

He nodded, leaning in. "And your board—tell me about that."

I grinned. "My pro model with Sims. One of the first women's pro models out there. I wanted the graphic to stand out, to let girls know: 'You belong in snowboarding.'"

He leaned forward. "And what did you think of the halfpipe event?"

"It was awesome," I said, heat rising in my voice, "but honestly, prize money should be equal. Equal money brings in more women, more media, more sponsors."

Then, without blinking, he shot back, "Why would girls get equal prize money? They're not even good."

I froze, stunned. "Not...good?" I repeated, sure I'd misheard.

My pulse pounded. Heat flooded my cheeks. I gave him an opening, a lifeline. "Did you mean girls aren't as good as the guys?"

He smirked, shrugged—no backpedal, no joke, just a smug certainty. My breath caught. My fists clenched around my board. The burn in my chest roared to life. He had no idea—no clue about the hours, the grit, the constant proving we had to do just to stand here. No one flat-out said we couldn't—some just made it clear we were second tier. But you show up anyway. Ride with purpose. Let your riding do the talking. Get out front—so there's space for the girls coming next.

And keep pushing, because you see a future no one else does.

And here he was, dismissing all of it with one smirk.

Before he could open his mouth again, I cut in. "First of all, that was rude." I lifted my *Sunflower* board, holding it up between us. "See this? This has outsold every guy's pro model in Sims—Shaun Palmer's, Noah Salasnek's. You know what that tells me? Girls are out there. They're riding and watching. They want their own space."

He fidgeted, eyes darting sideways, but I didn't let up.

"They want to see other girls ride. They want gear made for them. That's why you're here interviewing me. The demand is real. Time to get a clue."

I exhaled, fire still pulsing in my chest. "We're not here to be compared to the guys. We're here to do our own thing. And we definitely don't have to prove anything to you."

I bit back words that would've made my mom flinch. "Thanks for the interview. I'm done."

I pasted on a smile, got up from my chair, turned, and walked out.

I never found out if that interview aired—probably not.

CHAPTER 20

/ Summer Lovin' /

THAT SUMMER WASN'T JUST ABOUT SURFING, lipstick, or playful photo-shoots by the pool. I was standing at a crossroads—launching a wom-en's outerwear brand, riding the high of a new relationship, and quietly wondering where all this momentum would take me. But today, instead of powder turns or podiums, Tina and I were at a backyard pool in Cardiff, California, dressed in full vintage glam, trying not to burst into laughter for the camera.

"Think fierce and fabulous," Tina giggled, cracking up mid-pose. I couldn't help but join her, and soon we were both doubled over, laughing like teenagers. I puckered dramatically, careful not to smudge my bright red lipstick as I struck a playful pose.

We stood back-to-back by the pool's edge, our hair teased and hair-sprayed into 1950s perfection—my sun-bleached curls overdue for a root touch-up, Tina's red beehive rock-solid.

"You ladies look fantastic. Can you shift a little to the right?" the photographer called, refocusing us.

Lisa, our marketing director, stood to the side, arms crossed, beaming. She'd gone all in—makeup artist, hair stylist, bold lipstick.

The Prom ad. Me and Tina, doing what we do best: shaking things up.

At first, Tina and I had imagined this photoshoot to be low-key, but Lisa had a vision. And she knew exactly what she was doing.

"You two just rewrote the rules," Lisa said, grinning wide.

We'd brainstormed dozens of names for our brand, scribbling ideas on scraps of yellow paper, tossing out everything from cliché to downright bizarre. Nothing landed—until, out of nowhere, Tina blurted, "Prom."

That was it.

My mind flashed to high school, dressing up in my mom's vintage gowns with Betsy—feeling fun, girly, maybe a little over-the-top, but completely unstoppable. *Prom.* That was it.

Prom was our declaration that we could embrace femininity—something snowboarding hadn't really made room for yet—and still send it off a cliff and stomp the landing. We weren't here to copy the guys. We were ready to create something entirely our own.

But part of me wondered: *would people take us seriously, or just think we were playing dress-up?*

To catch the industry off guard, we had to be unapologetically feminine—loud, over-the-top, impossible to ignore. We weren't here to blend in. We were here to stand out.

As the shutter clicked and the sun illuminated our curls, I felt it deep in my gut: we were going to change the industry.

Just then, two guys peeked over the backyard fence, curious about the commotion—Selema Masekela and Tim Swart, both early in their snowboard careers. I couldn't tell if they were impressed, confused, or just intrigued—but either way, we had their attention.

"Hey, whatcha guys doing?" Selema called, grinning.

The photographer climbed the ladder for a top-down shot. Tina rocked a strapless vintage pink prom dress with lace and ruffles; I wore a baby blue organza number with its own lacy overlay. These thrift-store dresses, paired with our attitudes, captured everything *Prom* stood for: playful but fierce, glamorous but edgy.

Buzzing from the shoot and excited to dive into outerwear designs,

Tina headed home while I settled into Cardiff for the summer, renting a room from one of Lisa's friends to be closer to Dave. He was living with his parents in Laguna Niguel, just forty-five minutes north. We were inseparable, surfing every break along North County San Diego and spending every free moment together.

One sunny morning, we decided to surf Cardiff Reef. I paddled out on Big Bluey, a 7-foot longboard and a gift from Dave, feeling the rush of the open ocean. Surfing was freedom—like snowboarding on a perfect powder day—but rawer, wilder, and more unpredictable.

We sat just outside the lineup, past where the waves were breaking. I balanced on my board, trying to center myself, and glanced down at my board shorts. Lisa Andersen, the pro surfer, had just launched the first board shorts made for girls—and I was wearing them. She was inspiring girls around the world, including me. I wanted to do the same for snowboarding. Not just with my *Sunflower* board, but with *Prom* too. I wanted to give other girls what snowboarding had given me: confidence, inspiration, and a sense of style all their own.

A shadow darted beneath the water just in front of me. My heart leaped into my throat.

"What was that?" I blurted, panic creeping into my voice as I pulled my feet onto my board.

"I don't think it was anything," Dave said, calm as ever.

He stuck by my side, unbothered. I admired his steadiness, but it did nothing to quiet the knot of fear tightening in my chest. I wasn't used to open water—not like this. I was Miss Colorado, not exactly raised for surfing. Panic squeezed my ribs as I scanned the deep blue beneath.

"I'm not down with being shark bait," I muttered, half-joking, half-terrified.

Dave laughed lightly, brushing me off. "Don't worry, I've surfed here a thousand times. Never seen a shark. Trust me."

Trusting didn't come easily. Fear had a way of creeping in through the cracks of my confidence. I'd always had to fight to overcome it—

first, fear of failure, and now, fear of whatever was lurking beneath.

I could've paddled in, but Dave said, "Here, grab my ankle. Let's get to the lineup and catch a wave."

I reached out for the "Dave Express" to get into position.

We finally reached the lineup. The water was unnervingly still—too quiet, almost like something was watching us.

"Why doesn't anyone talk out here?" I asked, my voice tight with nerves.

Dave's grin was steady. "Because you have to focus. Watch the swell. Be ready for it. You paddle toward the peak—it's not gonna come find you. Surfers surf—they're not out here to chat."

The sets were slow, long lulls between waves. I tried to distract myself, thinking of Lisa Andersen, my idol: graceful, confident, fearless. I wanted to surf like her. Be like her.

"How long until I'm good enough to surf like Lisa Andersen?" I joked, hoping to shake off the nerves still clinging to my chest.

Dave shot me a smirk. "At least seven years. And that's just to surf like...mediocre."

"Whatever, Dave. I'm goin' pro!" I laughed, grabbing his ankle again. Then, out of nowhere, the wave started to rise. Clean. Powerful. It was perfect.

"Alright, here it comes," Dave said. "Spin around, start paddling, and look toward the peak—I got you."

I paddled hard, arms slicing through the water. Dave gave me a small push, and I felt the wave lift beneath me. I popped up sideways, and for a second, it was like flying.

Then I saw it again—a shadow, large and dark, moving just ahead of me. Panic ripped through my chest, cold and sudden. *Is it a shark? Is it circling me? Don't fall!*

But then, the shape shifted. Sleek. Smooth. A dorsal fin curved out of the water.

A dolphin.

I gasped, almost forgetting I was surfing. The dolphin surfed along the same wave, just inches from me. I could feel its power, its calmness in the chaos of the ocean. What kind of sign was this?

"Oh my gosh!" I shrieked, breathless, barely able to speak as it darted away. Dave paddled over beside me, grinning like a kid. "Did you see that?"

I laughed in disbelief. "I did! The dolphin—he was right there, next to me!"

"Totally insane," Dave said, still shaking his head. "He popped up on my wave too. You don't see that every day."

"Best day ever," I murmured, the adrenaline still rushing through my veins. This Colorado girl was hooked. The ocean, the waves, the dolphins—it was an entirely new world.

Later, over lunch at Honey's Café on the 101 in downtown Encinitas, the beach town pulsed with energy—classic woody cars rolled by, surfers strolled past, and a woman on a beach cruiser pedaled along with a little dog wearing goggles in her basket.

"Only in California," I chuckled, taking in the scene.

As we ate, Dave mentioned, "Hey, Eric invited us to dinner with the Burton reps tonight at the Chart House. You can meet Janey—the lady who answered the phone when you called me at Big Bear."

"Sounds great! That was funny when I called you—I was like, 'Who's Janey?' I didn't know if she was your girlfriend or something," I said, savoring a bite of my breakfast scramble. "I still can't believe how things worked out in Italy. It was so random…except it felt like it wasn't random at all. Like, a miracle trip."

Dave grinned. "That trip changed everything. It led to me filming with both Mikes, which basically started my whole career. It's been a whirlwind since."

I laughed. "Yeah, Gaylene set me up to film with Mike 'Mack Dawg,' the legendary snowboard filmmaker, and I asked if my boyfriend could tag along. Mike was super skeptical, like, 'Um…really? Who's your boyfriend?'"

Dave laughed, "Totally! I was so nervous. They stuck me with the backup crew, and I'd never filmed before."

"Meanwhile, I was just trying to keep up with Jim Rippey—the guy doing insane backflips off forty-foot cliffs—and I'd barely hit any jumps before that trip. We were on this wind-blown, rocky slope, and even he couldn't get a shot. I felt totally out of my league." I paused, smiling at Dave. "But then you showed up and nailed every clip. They couldn't stop talking about you. Next thing we know, we're invited to Tahoe to film with Mike and Dave Hatchett—total legends."

We both laughed, remembering how surreal it all was. Meeting our group in Italy had opened unexpected doors—for Dave, and for me too. Opportunities neither of us could've seen coming.

Dave got quiet for a second. "Yeah, I feel like God took me from just a normal life as a California surfer kid, working at a surf shop, working as a Burton rep, and then I meet you...and everything starts to unfold. My whole life changed."

I'd asked God for something real. Was this it? Was Dave really the answer—or just what I wanted to believe? I didn't know for sure, but something inside me kept leaning in because it felt like home with him.

"I've never told you this, but...before Italy, I was in a rough place. Frustrated. A little lost. I'd asked God to show me the real deal—and to bring someone special into my life. And then, a month later, I met you. I really feel like...we're meant to be together."

Dave reached for my hand, covering it with his. "I feel it too. I love you, Shan. It's crazy, but it feels like I've known you forever."

Warmth filled my chest. He'd said the big word—but somehow, it felt normal. Good. Not overwhelming or scary.

"I know God put you in my life." I stared into his eyes.

"I know he did," he said quietly.

That evening, dressed in a sundress with Dave by my side, I felt grateful for the unexpected path life had taken. Dinner was full of laughter and good energy. We reunited with Brian Thien—still as hilarious as ever—

and cracked up all over again about the olive pit comment he'd made on our Italy trip. It felt like family around that table, everyone sharing stories, teasing, and catching up.

I was mid-bite of warm bread—content, relaxed—when Eric's gaze landed on me.

"Hey, Shan...what would you think about riding for Burton?"

The table fell silent. All eyes were on me.

I nearly choked. Grabbing my water, I took a long sip and wiped my mouth, trying to process what he'd just said.

"Wait...seriously?" I asked, still stunned.

"I'm dead serious," Eric said, his tone steady. "I'd like to offer you a sponsorship with Burton. Would you consider it?"

My blood rushed to my cheeks as my stomach did a flip. A second ago, we were laughing about olive pits, and now I was being handed a golden ticket.

Burton.

The pinnacle. The godfather brand of snowboarding. Jake and Donna Burton had built the company from the ground up. They legitimized the sport, getting snowboarding into the biggest resorts and paving the way for all of us. Being on Burton's team meant access to the best tech, travel, support—and more than anything, it meant being taken seriously. Worldwide. A million thoughts fired through my mind.

"Honestly...I'm honored. I mean—wow," I said, still trying to catch my breath. "But...I just got my pro model with Sims. It's not even in stores yet..." Then it hit me again. "Plus, I have a contract. It's up for renewal this month—but after everything Gaylene did for my board...that would be hard."

Eric nodded, his expression easy. "Don't worry about your contract—we can work that out."

I turned to Dave, searching his face. He gave a small nod, his eyes steady.

"Did you know about this?" I asked, half-accusing, but smiling.

He shrugged, grinning. "Yeah...Eric and I talked. Burton would be next level for you, Shan. Better board design. Full travel support. They'd give you everything you need to go even further."

My mind reeled. There was no way I could walk away from my pro model—it was a milestone I'd worked so hard for. But the idea of being the first woman with a Burton pro model? That's what I'd want. It was almost too big to imagine.

"Oh geez, Eric, I'm stoked. Seriously honored," I said, the words tumbling out. "I'd love to ride for Burton. But...I don't know. I just got my Sims board, and like I said—it's not even on shelves yet. I'd need time. I'd need to really think it through."

Eric's tone softened. "Of course. No rush. Let me know if you have any questions."

As the conversation picked back up around the table, I sat back, letting the moment sink in. I glanced at Dave. Somehow, without words, we both knew—this was bigger than Burton or Sims, or any single brand. This was the unfolding of something bigger. And in that quiet, shared knowing, I felt peace. But still—

If God is writing my story...
What comes next?

CHAPTER 21
/ I Surrender /

"IT'S A SIGN," I SAID WITH A CHUCKLE, pointing at the church marquee up
ahead. "Take a right, Dave."

He grinned and turned The Toaster—his silver Mitsubishi van that
looked exactly like a giant toaster—into the lot. That van was big enough
to hold everything he owned. His life was simple, and as he liked to say,
I was just enough chaos to keep life interesting.

Going to church wasn't some big, premeditated decision. A few days
earlier, I'd noticed a Bible on the nightstand at his parents' house and
casually told him I wanted one. He got me an easy-to-read version, complete with notes that explained what everything meant—and we started
reading it together. Then, almost without thinking, I asked him to take
me to church. I didn't analyze it. It just felt right.

Dave mentioned his sister knew of a church nearby—nothing stiff
or traditional, just good music and down-to-earth people. That sounded
like exactly what I was craving. I'd grown up Catholic, but the services
always felt rigid and disconnected from real life. I was ready for something different.

I wanted to figure out who God really was—outside the rules and rituals.

As we pulled into a plain parking lot with a sign that read "Calvary Chapel Encinitas," I wrinkled my nose.

"This is a church?" I asked.

"Looks like it," Dave replied, just as curious. "I've never been to a church in an office building."

I was used to steeples and stained glass—the kind of churches that felt almost otherworldly. We'd attend on holidays or when I stayed with my grandma during the summer. She'd offer us gum to keep Sean and me quiet in the pews. A simple nudge from her was all it took to remind us to behave. Afterward, we'd help her make her famous pancakes.

I watched as a few casually dressed people walked by, Bibles in hand. One guy wore shorts and a T-shirt, and a woman passed by in a jean skirt and flip-flops.

"I didn't bring my Bible," I muttered, suddenly feeling a little unprepared.

"Don't worry—they probably have extras," Dave said, parking The Toaster at the far end of the lot. "Besides, my sister said this place is super chill. Not like the Presbyterian church I grew up in—suits, silence, everything formal."

He wasn't wrong. It already felt different.

"This is my Sunday best right here," I said, gesturing to my jean shorts, plain pink tee, and flip-flops. "But seriously, why are we parking way back here?"

Dave laughed. "I just don't like crowded parking lots. It's easier to get out from the back."

"Oh, so you're one of those people," I teased.

"Those people?" He shot me a look.

"Yeah, one of those people who plays it safe. You park in the back so you don't have to risk going for the front row and getting shut down." I grinned, playfully nudging him.

Dave shrugged, unbothered. "I don't know about that. I just wanted to park my car. What's risky about that?" He paused, a playful glint in his eye. "Hey, I took a risk on you, didn't I?"

I raised an eyebrow, trying to hide my smile. "Oh, really? I'm *risky* now?" I threw up a pair of dramatic jazz hands. "I'll take that as a compliment. But seriously—I think you're just afraid of disappointment. My dad raised me with a front-rower mindset."

He rolled his eyes, pulling me close and planting a quick kiss on my cheek. "Next time, I'll go to the front row just for you."

At the entrance, a man and woman greeted us, handing out bulletins. "Hi, welcome!"

I thanked them and we made our way inside. A band was already on stage, guitars, drums, and singers blending smoothly as people filed in, some singing, others with hands raised in worship. We chose seats near the back, by the exit.

As the first song started, a trickle of sweat ran down my back. My nerves were catching up to me despite the cool air. I watched as some people sang with their eyes closed, hands lifted in a posture of surrender. It reminded me of the Green Day concert I'd gone to at Mount Hood— crowds jumping, arms up, voices loud. But here, it was quieter, reverent. The energy wasn't directed at a band but at something unseen, something I couldn't quite explain.

This place felt different. There was none of the fancy-schmancy, polished church atmosphere I was used to—no grand building, nothing beautiful to speak of, no hushed echo of rituals repeated by rote. Instead, here in an office building with people who looked like they just stepped off a surfboard, God didn't seem as far away.

The lyrics to "Amazing Grace" appeared on a screen at the front. Church karaoke, I thought, smiling at the memory of the karaoke bar in Japan where Tina and I had belted out Pat Benatar's "Hit Me With Your Best Shot." I shook off the distraction and joined in, singing softly. The words settled deeper than before. I dropped my head, letting my hair hide the tears gathering in my eyes. I felt Dave's arm brush against me, and I instinctively hooked my arm into his.

The next song's lyrics spoke of grace, mercy, and love—God's love, my

Father's love, a love that felt bigger and more overwhelming than I'd ever considered. Something started to shift inside me. As we sat down after the music, I noticed the padded seats, a far cry from the hard pews I was used to. I tried not to get caught up in the details, but they stood out to me.

Growing up, I knew the story of Jesus, but I'd always felt like God was distant—detached. And what's the point of a detached God? This pastor spoke about something I hadn't considered: having an actual relationship with God, not just going through motions or rituals. It was like he was speaking directly to me, filling in gaps in my faith I hadn't even realized were there. I started to understand that my drift from God in the past was because I'd never seen him as personal, as near.

At that moment, something clicked. I didn't see God as some distant figure anymore; instead, he felt like a real, loving Father who actually cared about me, flaws and all. It wasn't about following rules or getting everything right. This wasn't religion—it was personal, like I could actually know him.

The pastor explained the gospel in a way that finally made sense: God created everything perfect, but people chose to go their own way, sinning and separating themselves from him. To bridge that gap, God sent Jesus, who sacrificed himself to pay for our sins. Jesus took all that weight, died a shameful death, and then God brought him back to life. Because of that, we get a fresh start—a chance for a real relationship with God through Jesus, who communicates with us through the Holy Spirit. Eternal life was a gift, not something we have to earn by being "good." If we follow him, he changes us from the inside out.

I felt like a literal light switched on inside me, like a "no duh" moment. How did I not get this before?

As the service wrapped up, the pastor invited us to close our eyes and told us to raise our hands if we wanted to follow Jesus. I figured everyone would do it—*why else would you come here?* So, without thinking, I raised my hand, peeking out, expecting to see others doing the same. To my surprise, my hand was the only one up. Embarrassed, I quickly lowered it. Doubts raced through my mind. *Do I truly believe this? Am I ready to accept Jesus fully? And what does that mean for me? Will I have to wear long skirts and go hut to hut in Zimbabwe?*

I took a deep breath, pushing aside my nerves. Yes, I believed. I raised my hand again—this time steady and sure—locking eyes with the pastor. *Today, I'm all in, God. I believe. I'm ready.*

The pastor smiled and gave a small nod, acknowledging my decision. Then he invited all of us to pray silently along with him. I repeated the words in my mind: *Jesus...I know that I need your forgiveness. I believe you died for me, and I want to live my life for you. Please come into my heart and guide me. I trust you. In Jesus's name, Amen.*

Warmth flooded me from head to toe, a tingling sensation that made me feel wrapped in love. This sensation was mind-boggling. What was happening to me? I'd never felt anything like it, this inexplicable mix of peace, relief, and pure joy.

Tears streamed down my face, surprising me with their intensity, as though years of pent-up emotions were finally breaking free. I couldn't hold them back even if I wanted to; it was as if a dam had burst inside me, releasing everything I didn't even know I was carrying. I closed my eyes, letting the feeling wash over me. It was raw and powerful, filling me with a sense of acceptance I hadn't realized I'd been missing. Dave pulled me close, his hand resting on my back, comforting me as I silently wept. Then I rested my head on his shoulder, my body still trembling as wave after wave of emotion swept through me, and I surrendered to it fully, feeling more at peace than I'd ever felt in my life.

The band played on, and we stayed until the last note. Walking back to the car, Dave stayed silent, sensing I needed space to process. As soon as we reached our parking spot, he wrapped his arms around me, letting me cry tears of joy and release. He didn't need to ask or probe—he just held me as I let the tears come, his quiet presence saying more than any words could. The car, the parking lot, the whole world had transformed—ordinary spaces had become sacred ground.

CHAPTER 22
/ The Burton Showdown /

AS I GAZED OUT THE WINDOW of Jake Burton Carpenter's private jet, the lights of Manhattan stretched below like a galaxy. The city pulsed with possibility, and tonight, I was right at the center of it. Burton Snowboards had flown me out to discuss a potential sponsorship, with a surprise, whirlwind detour to Saturday Night Live, of all things. Seal was the musical guest—another snowboarding enthusiast—which only made the whole experience that much sweeter. It was flashy, yes—but intentional. This wasn't just a night out in New York. It was a signal—as bright and undeniable as the city lights—that Burton saw something in me.

But even as I soaked in the glitz and adrenaline, one thing kept tugging at the back of my mind: the call from Tom Sims's wife.

It had been exactly three months since Eric first offered me a Burton sponsorship. At the time, I hadn't taken it seriously. I'd toyed with the idea, but always snapped back to loyalty—to what felt like reality. Then suddenly, everything shifted. The Sims accounting office wouldn't return my calls about renewing my contract. Gaylene had gone to bat for me, warning them that I had another offer—and if they didn't act, they'd lose me.

Still, nothing. I finally told her I was done chasing them. If Sims didn't care, why should I keep waiting? I reached out to Eric and told him I was interested in exploring the Burton offer.

Then, out of nowhere, the phone rang.

I didn't recognize the voice. I'd never met Tom Sims's wife, but there she was, calling me out of the blue. Her tone was casual—almost too casual—as she dropped the bomb: "Tom had a heart attack when he heard you were leaving us."

For a split second, I pictured him in a hospital bed, hooked up to machines, and felt a pang of guilt. "Seriously? Is he going to be okay?"

She quickly brushed that aside. "Well, no...not really. He didn't have a heart attack, he's just upset you're leaving Sims, especially after all the success of the *Sunflower* board."

Something inside me snapped. A rush of frustration flooded my chest—not just because of the drama, but because Tom hadn't even bothered to call me himself. He sent his wife, as if she could somehow change my mind, like it was some "woman to woman" conversation. It felt manipulative. Weak. And it made my skin crawl.

"Wait a minute," I snapped. "First of all, no one called me back about my contract. I reached out multiple times. Gaylene also warned them, and still, no one contacted me. So I decided to move on."

She apologized, but there was no real defense.

"This isn't personal, okay?" I said, my voice more firm than I felt. "This is business."

When the call ended, a heavy stillness settled in. I stared at the floor, and the weight of my decision crashed over me. Each breath felt heavier than the last. I took a long inhale, trying to steady myself against the rush of emotions. The sting behind my eyes came too quickly to stop. Tears fell—quietly, steadily—releasing the pressure I hadn't even realized I'd been carrying.

I was starting to tear up on the plane, just thinking about it. *Get it together,* I told myself, wiping my face. *You're exactly where you need to be.*

Stepping off the plane in Manhattan felt surreal—like I'd just flown straight into a future I wasn't sure I was ready for.

The SNL studio buzzed with energy as we settled into our VIP front-row balcony seats, perfectly positioned above the stage. The crowd's excitement was electric—a pulsing beat in the air as the set crew scrambled to get everything just right. Lights blazed, and for a moment, I let myself get lost in it all, forgetting about contracts, negotiations, and the pressures waiting back at Burton. Adam Sandler and John Travolta had us laughing until we couldn't breathe.

And yeah—the schmoozing? It was totally working on me.

Then, a new feeling began to build—a pulse of purpose, of possibility. Was this what Burton was really offering? Not just a sponsorship, but a chance to step into real influence and lasting impact?

As the lights dimmed and the grand stage came to life, I leaned into the unknown, heart racing. This was about more than snowboarding—it was about stepping into the future I wanted to help shape.

Later, back in my hotel room, the weight of it landed. The idea of leaving Sims hadn't just been a business move—it was a turning point. The *Sunflower* board's success confirmed what Gaylene and I had believed: women's gear wasn't just profitable—it was powerful. It invited more girls into the sport, helped them feel seen, and fueled a new wave of progression.

We weren't just building boards. We were building belief—in what women could do, and in the future we were carving for ourselves. This wasn't just about snowboarding anymore. It was about reshaping culture and demanding visibility where it had been ignored for too long.

And none of it would've happened without Gaylene. She didn't just launch a product—she lit a fire. One that spread far beyond anything we could've imagined.

When I confided in Gaylene about the lack of support from Sims—the unanswered calls, the stalled contract renewal, the unpaid royalties—she wasn't surprised. I hadn't wanted to believe they were brushing me off, but the missing checks were hard to ignore. Gaylene had pushed them as hard as she could, warning that I had other offers if they didn't step up. Still, they didn't care enough to take the bait. She hinted that the company might be going through internal changes, but she didn't have the full story.

Unlike the rest, Gaylene treated me like a friend—not just another name on a roster.

When I shared Eric's proposal with her, I wasn't sure how she'd respond—but I trusted and respected her deeply.

"It's about more than snowboarding, Shan," she said gently, fully understanding the weight of my decision. "You're building a life—and with Dave already at Burton, it makes sense. Sims's loss for sure, and I'm going to miss you like crazy...but I want what's best for you."

Her words felt like a steady hand on my shoulder—grounding me, reassuring me, giving me the clarity I needed.

It was about taking a leap, not playing it safe.

With the whirlwind of New York still buzzing in my chest—and Seal's "Kiss from a Rose" looping in my head—I felt newly bonded with the Burton marketing crew. We'd connected, laughed, and shared a night that felt unforgettable. I was hopeful—genuinely excited—to hammer out my contract and take the next step.

But as thrilling as New York had been, the mood was about to shift—fast.

Monday morning, I walked through the doors of Burton's headquarters, awe washing over me. Craig Kelly's original board hung on the wall like a relic, welcoming us. Burton wasn't just a company; it was the heartbeat of snowboarding. And being there lit me up.

At the front desk, the receptionist looked surprised to see me. Eric just flashed a conspiratorial smirk.

"Secret mission," he whispered as we continued down the hall—like I was about to be inducted into something far bigger than just a contract.

Eric led me through the building, my nerves twisting into excitement as we made our way to meet DJ, the vice president of marketing. I'd heard the stories—how tough he was, how relentless in negotiations—and I mentally braced myself, riding that strange blend of anticipation and resolve. As we navigated the halls, it felt like I was slipping into some kind of secret lair—a place where the real deals went down, where handshake agreements turned into magazine covers and product launches. Eric nodded at a few passing faces, tossing out casual hellos that didn't do much to hide the mild confusion on everyone's faces. It was clear no one knew I was supposed to be there, and somehow, that only added to the rush.

Finally, we reached DJ's office—where I instantly felt his no-nonsense energy. As soon as Eric introduced me, DJ didn't just size me up—he cut straight through me with a look that said, "You're already losing." His handshake was strong, bordering on intimidating, his gaze evaluating me as if he'd already seen every angle of my pitch before I'd even opened my mouth.

Stay cool, I told myself, *don't let him see you sweat.* But it was like trying to keep calm while holding a live grenade. My palms were slick—I wiped them on my jeans.

As soon as Eric's introductions were through, he stepped back, his role over until after the meeting. I felt a flash of betrayal. *Way to just lead me into the lion's den and then leave as I get eaten alive.* But instead of panicking, I decided to rise to the challenge. I put on my best "screw you" face, a mask I'd perfected for anytime I felt even a subtle hint of psychological warfare vibes from competitors. If DJ thought this was some kind of game, then fine. I'd play too.

I locked eyes with him, feeling every bit of competitor's grit kick in. *Bring it on.* My parents' advice for negotiations floated through my mind: never give the first number. DJ, though, was clearly no rookie. He leaned forward, the shift in his tone almost cinematic—from warm and welcoming to all business in a heartbeat.

"So, what kind of number are you thinking about for a salary?"

I was stunned. *Well, no small talk, huh?* I refused to flinch.

"Well...you tell me, DJ," I replied, channeling my best New York mafia voice. "I'm here for an offer I can't refuse."

A nervous laugh escaped me, but I held his gaze, calm and steady. DJ nodded, quick to respond.

"Yes, let's talk about that. We want you to design the first Burton women's pro model from start to finish. You'll have our best designers working with you."

This was it—the validation I'd been searching for. A quiet ease settled in. Maybe this wasn't going to be so hard after all.

"What about the other girls on the team?" I asked carefully, testing the waters. "Are they going to be cool with me coming in?"

"If they could pull off a pro model, they'd already have one. You've earned it, Shannon."

I nodded, but Gaylene's dedication to my Sims pro model was fresh in my mind. "I did my part—winning contests, promoting it—but Gaylene was the heart of that project. She got it into stores, made it the success it is. If we're doing this, Burton has to commit fully. Ads, marketing—the same level of backing the guys get."

As DJ kept talking, a whirlwind of thoughts raced through my mind. I was barely processing half of what he was saying, more absorbed in the way he carried himself—his tone, the unyielding stare, the razor-sharp edge in his words. Where was the warmth that had always set the snowboarding world apart? Suddenly, this felt more like an NFL negotiation, all serious and corporate, completely foreign from the camaraderie I'd known. *Is this really what I'm signing up for?*

A small laugh slipped out, but I kept my gaze steady—calm, determined.

He started by writing $20,000 on a piece of paper. The number hit like a slap—and from the look on my face, he knew it. I didn't even have to say it: *You've got to be out of your mind.*

He tried to smooth it over, claiming the rest would come from photo incentives. He scribbled down yet another insultingly low figure, pushing the paper across the table with a smug little smile, as if he was handing me the Holy Grail.

I blinked. *Was I supposed to fall over in gratitude?* I glanced at it, unimpressed. "Is this a joke?"

DJ leaned back, tapping his pen against the paper, a smirk playing on his lips. The arrogance was palpable—like he was toying with me, waiting for the moment I'd break and accept whatever crumbs he tossed my way.

"Look, Shannon," he said smoothly, "you're talented, no doubt. But this is Burton. We can make your career."

My stomach twisted with anger. "I already have a pro model that's selling more than all the guys' boards on the team. I don't need to be here, begging."

He chuckled, unfazed, and leaned in closer. "And that's great for you, but we're talking about taking things to a whole new level here. Don't you want to be a part of something big?"

"I don't think you understand," I said, leaning forward to meet his gaze, not willing to give him an inch. "I know what I'm worth. And I know what I've already accomplished. If Burton can't recognize that, then maybe this isn't the right fit."

His pen scratched across the page, tossing out another lowball like it was no big deal. "There you go. Think it over."

Thirty grand? That wasn't even in the ballpark. I shook my head, feeling both exhausted and insulted.

He raised an eyebrow, feigning innocence. "That's the best we can do—considering the circumstances." His words hung in the air, so loaded and patronizing that it took everything in me not to lose my cool right there.

"Circumstances?"

"We're getting late into the season for contracts," he said. "We're already a year out from being able to use your images."

Photos in the magazines were the rhythm of the industry: pros rode next year's gear, shot photos and filmed all season, and by the time the products hit retail, the magazine features would line up—perfectly timed for the consumer.

I took a slow, measured breath, steadying myself, refusing to let him see even a flicker of doubt.

"Well, DJ," I said, keeping my tone even, "I've already got a sponsor who's stoked with me and my pro model. If this is your 'best,' then maybe you're right—I should think it over. I'll think it over at home."

DJ leaned back, his look unapologetic. "Just remember—opportunities like this don't come around every day."

I paused, met his stare. "Neither does a rider like me."

I gave him one last look, my voice cool. "I'm not settling for this. You're gonna have to sharpen your pencil," I said, echoing my dad's signature line—one I'd watched shut down bad deals. I stood up, let my silence say the rest, and walked out—leaving his pitiful offer right where it belonged.

As I stepped out of DJ's office, Eric was there, right on cue, reading the exhaustion all over my face. He looked at me, his expression a mix of concern and something close to disbelief, as if he could feel the tension radiating from me. I glanced at my watch—I had a flight to catch. The sting of defeat hit me hard, mingling with an unsettling clarity. My stomach growled, low blood sugar was kicking in, and I really, really needed a bathroom break. *How did I get here?* I couldn't believe this wasn't going to work out after everything.

"I need to get out of here. Right now," I managed, barely keeping my voice steady. Eric threw a quick glance back toward DJ's office, his eyes flickering with a silent, "What the heck happened in there?"

Just then, DJ's voice drifted out, directed at Eric but pitched loud enough that I heard every word: "You'd better keep her here until she signs that contract."

I didn't turn back. I was done.

/ The Deal That Shaped My Future (And My Board) /

I WANTED TO RUN OUT OF BURTON'S HQ—but my feet were moving in slow motion down the hallway, dragging me toward the exit. I felt somewhere between pissed off and heartbroken. The negotiation had tanked. DJ's parting words still echoed in my head, and I felt raw.

Business was brutal. I missed the good old-fashioned handshake—the kind where people looked you in the eye and actually wanted the best for you.

The scent of coffee lingered in the air. Somewhere nearby, a couple of dogs barked—Burton lets employees bring their dogs to work. The hallway buzzed with a quiet hum of a normal work environment that I couldn't connect to.

Then Eric caught up to me, snapping me out of my spiral. His face tightened with concern—he was clearly expecting better news.

I shook my head and rolled my eyes. I didn't want to say anything while we were still inside.

"I gotta get out of here," I muttered, motioning toward the door.

Eric didn't say a word—just opened it for me. Once I stepped outside, the wind hit my face—sharp and blustery, like a reset button—but the weight in my chest didn't budge. I glanced around to make sure no one was watching. That's when I finally let it out.

"Dude, DJ sucks. What a nightmare. Seriously, Eric, what the heck?" I threw my hands up. "We didn't come to an agreement. I'm completely over it."

He stayed quiet for a beat, letting the silence stretch before he spoke.

His voice softened. "Yeah, I know. I'm sorry, Shan. He can be a total jerk, for sure. But it's his job to negotiate hard. I swear, he—and all of us—want you on this team. You have my word that I and the marketing team will be fully behind you—to promote you, support you on a whole other level. Just give it one more shot. Let me talk to him tonight. Tomorrow, we'll go in first thing, and I promise we'll get this worked out."

I gave a dry laugh, shaking my head. "If DJ wants me at Burton, he's got a pretty messed-up way of showing it."

He was trying to smooth it over. I could see that—but DJ's whole vibe had drained me.

"No way I'm staying," I snapped, sharper than I meant to. "I'm out. What—am I supposed to hang around like some hostage until I say yes? My flight's in three hours. I'm going home."

Eric blinked, stunned. He wasn't expecting that. And to be fair, he was my friend—but now he was stuck between business and loyalty. We didn't say much as we walked to his car. My bags were already packed, stashed in the backseat from earlier that day, just in case. I glanced at my watch.

"Perfect timing," I muttered, folding my arms as I sank into the passenger seat. "Just drop me at the airport. I'll think it over. If you all come up with something real, we can talk on the phone."

The car was quiet as he pulled out of the lot. His usual relaxed energy was gone, replaced by a tighter, heavier silence. I could feel him trying to find the right words, but I was too drained to help.

Finally, he exhaled. "Okay. But I need to stop by my apartment downtown first. It'll be quick."

We drove past glowing brick buildings and the cobblestone main streets where shop windows reflected the amber spill of the streetlights. Everything felt distant as I stared out the window, trying to focus. My body felt heavy—like I'd just gone a full round in a boxing ring. When we pulled up, I stretched stiffly and asked, "Hey, I need to use the bathroom. Got anything to eat? And I want to call Dave."

Inside, the apartment smelled faintly of a floral candle. A snowboard leaned in the corner by the door, and a stack of unopened mail cluttered the counter. I sank into a dining chair like I'd just finished a marathon. Eric tossed me a granola bar, and I took the cordless phone into the spare bedroom for privacy. The door clicked shut behind me, and the second I heard Dave's voice, I broke. Tears I hadn't planned on came hard and fast.

"They tried to hold me hostage," I said between sobs, pacing the room. "DJ lowballed me, over and over. Then when I tried to leave, he told Eric to keep me there until I signed."

Dave let me talk, grounding me with his calm.

"Listen," he said, steady and sure. "I know you're emotional right now—and you've got every right to be. But hey—if DJ's acting that desperate, that means they need you. You've got leverage. Go back tomorrow. If nothing changes, walk away. But this opportunity? I really believe it's worth one more shot. I truly believe it's going to open big doors. This is Burton. And you belong there."

His words hit me with the kind of clarity I didn't want—but needed. I still felt defiant, but somewhere beneath it all, a question stirred: *What if he's right? What if it actually works out?*

I wiped my face and stood there, breathing deeply. Then I walked out of the bedroom, set the phone on the table, and headed for the bathroom. I splashed cold water over my face, fixed my hair, and reached into my jacket pocket. Somehow, my mascara was still in there from a past photo shoot— I'd never taken it out. I swiped it on, a small attempt to look like I hadn't just fallen apart—to hide my puffy eyes, to pretend I hadn't been crying.

In the hallway, I heard Eric's voice. Low, sharp, and tense. He was pacing. On the phone. I paused, listening.

He didn't know I could hear him—but I could. He was talking to DJ, and he was pissed. Really pissed. I caught enough to know he was going to bat for me, calling DJ out for how he'd handled things. He wasn't just placating me—he was fighting behind the scenes.

And that softened something in me. Eric was standing up for me—not as a company guy, but as a friend. And out of that respect, I felt like I owed it to him to give this one more chance.

I stepped back into the dining room. Eric was standing there, phone still in his hand, but he wasn't on it anymore. He looked up at me, hopeful.

"C'mon, Shan. Just one more day. Go back to the office tomorrow. See how it feels. You're already here. What's one more day?"

My stubbornness pushed aside the compassion I had just felt, before logic had a chance to land—before Dave's calm words could settle in.

"No," I snapped. "DJ was a nightmare—totally unprofessional. I'm not sticking around to be treated like that."

"Look, I get it. But I just talked to him—he's serious. He wants to lock this in. If it doesn't work out tomorrow, I'll drive you to the airport myself, first flight out. No pressure. No questions."

I crossed my arms, tension rising in my chest. "My flight's tonight."

Eric nodded slowly, like he was trying not to spook me. "I can change that right now. Just say the word. Stay, have a good dinner, get some real sleep. You don't have to decide anything tonight."

I looked past him toward the window, then stepped toward the door. "I need some air."

Outside, the cold bit at my skin, but it helped. I stood in the stillness, face tilted to the sky. *God, help me with this next move.*

I was fried. Spent. Maybe what I needed wasn't a dramatic exit—but a pause. To eat. To sleep. To just *be*.

The thought of dragging myself through an eight-hour flight back to California sounded more exhausting than freeing.

So I stayed.

The next morning, I woke up still in Vermont. My head wasn't spinning—I was thinking. Steady. Clear.

I didn't feel strong walking back into Burton—I felt spent. But something in me still needed to know if today could be different. I strode into DJ's office, surrendered to the idea that whatever happened next—with him, with Burton—was meant to be.

"DJ, let's make this quick. I'm not staying unless the terms are right," I said, setting the tone. "I like what we discussed yesterday—a pro model, incentives—but the salary's gotta reflect my value."

DJ jotted down $90,000 and slid it across the table.

Here we go again. Closer, but not where it needed to be. That familiar rush of frustration simmered beneath the surface. He was still testing me. It felt like some backroom negotiation—numbers scribbled on scraps of paper, no one saying them out loud. All we needed was a cigar and a dim lamp swinging overhead.

I pushed my chair back from the table and stood up, ready to walk.

He held up a hand. "Wait, wait. What are you thinking?"

I met his gaze, steady and unblinking. "I thought we were on the same page, DJ. I'm not here to walk away from Sims for anything less than fair compensation. If Burton can't recognize my worth, then this isn't gonna work out."

He slid the paper and pen toward me. I took a breath and wrote down a highball number—fifty grand more than what I'd been willing to settle for.

His face tightened as he absorbed my words. He glanced at the figure and huffed, clearly not thrilled—but he came down halfway and added a line about board royalties.

I gave a small nod and slid back into the chair. "Now we're talking. Let's go over the royalties."

When he looked up, his tone had shifted—less ego, more sincerity. We went line by line—dissecting terms, pressing in where it counted—until it finally felt right. This wasn't just a paycheck. It was recognition. Proof that

I knew my worth—and now, they did too. Could I have pushed the salary higher? Maybe. But it felt fair. And honestly, I was done fighting.

DJ leaned back, the tension finally easing from his frame. Then he stood and extended his hand—with a demeanor that, for the first time, actually looked like respect. I had no clue what the other riders were getting paid. I assumed the guys made more. But I was my own agent—and I'd just walked through fire and come out the other side. That, in itself, made me proud.

A small smile tugged at the corner of his mouth. "Congratulations, Shannon. Welcome to the Burton team."

A surge of excitement and adrenaline washed over me as I shook DJ's hand. This felt like a major accomplishment. Just as I was mentally checking out—more than happy to head to the airport with over three hours to spare—Eric walked into DJ's office, almost like he'd been waiting for the green light.

"Congratulations," he said, pulling me into a hug. "There are two people you've gotta meet before you go."

He shifted gears quickly. "We've got a lot to figure out for your pro model. Since we're past the normal production timeline, it's going to be a late release. Most boards ship to shops in the fall, but yours will miss that window—it'll drop mid-winter instead. So we need your design locked in fast, graphics included. Ideally, within the next couple of weeks."

He led me just across from DJ's office into a sprawling, gear-strewn room with concrete floors and the faint smell of epoxy in the air. Two guys stood waiting amid stacks of snowboards, binding parts, and what looked like endless prototypes.

"Meet John Gerndt," Eric said, nodding toward an average-height guy with a chill vibe and laser-focused eyes. "Everyone calls him JG—the Yoda of board shapes and design."

Then he pointed to a taller guy leaning casually against a workbench, arms crossed, sharp-eyed. "And this is Paul Fidrych—'Fiddy.' Our hard-goods specialist."

As we shook hands, I could already sense their excitement.

JG gave me a nod, his voice easy but direct. "Alright, here's the deal—we're on a wicked tight timeline. Usually, we've got months to dial in a board. Yours? We need shape, flex, and graphics, like, yesterday." He offered a half-smile, unfazed. "But don't worry—we can pull it off." He paused, then leaned in a little. "So, what kind of shape are ya thinkin' for your board?"

I hesitated, suddenly hyperaware of both of them watching me like I knew exactly what I was doing. My eyes flicked up—these guys were expecting answers. I had to say something.

"Honestly?" I shrugged. "I have no idea where to start. I'm totally clueless when it comes to board design."

They exchanged a quick glance—surprised, but not in a judgy way. Just curious.

"I mean, I designed the graphics—did the original artwork for my Sims board—but I never got the chance to help shape the board itself."

JG and Fiddy didn't even flinch. JG nodded, calm and steady. "Alright then, let's start from the beginning. We'll walk you through board basics and build from there."

Relief flooded me. They weren't expecting me to know it all—they were ready to teach me. And I was more than ready to learn.

JG stepped up and showed me how to test a board's flex using the right technique, then handed one over for me to try. I fumbled a bit—grabbing the nose and pressing down on the center. He smiled and gently corrected me.

"If you flex it from the tip, you're only feeling the tip—not the board's core flex," he said, adjusting my stance. "Flexing it right shows you how it actually rides—how it loads up and releases when you're on snow. So yeah, it definitely matters," he said, guiding my arms with patient precision. "Hold your forearm like you're cradling a baby," he said, motioning to the board's base just below the tip. "Right where the edge would touch the snow. Then press down on the center."

I adjusted, following his lead. When I pressed down, the board pushed back—stiff, but responsive. Like a spring loaded with potential.

Right then, I knew—I was about to get a crash course in everything I'd never been taught about board design.

He dove into the nuances of shapes and materials, opening my eyes to a world I hadn't fully appreciated. With each board I flexed, I started noticing subtle differences I'd always taken for granted. JG continued, diving deeper into the technical aspects.

"Let's talk side cuts," he said, explaining how the arc carved into a board's edge impacts turning and balance. Each element, he empha-sized—length, camber, and flex—could completely transform how the board handled different types of terrain. Then he looked at me thought-fully. "So, what terrain do you envision for your board?"

"I want a board that can handle any conditions, any terrain—some-thing any girl could grab and feel instantly at home on, no matter where she's riding. It should hold up in the pipe, rip groomers, pop off side hits, and float in powder. Basically, I want it to be good for everything. Because I love to ride everything."

It sounded like a tall order, but JG didn't blink. Instead, he nodded with the same calm confidence, ready to make it happen.

Next came the questions about nose and tail shapes, board lengths, and all the specs I'd never really thought about. JG grilled me—in a good way—asking about my riding style and even how I set up my stance. Did I want a twin tip or directional?

Don't worry—I barely knew what half of that had meant either. But I was getting schooled in all the best ways. The details I used to overlook were now front and center, and I was finally learning what made a board truly ride the way it does.

Fiddy nodded thoughtfully, underscoring the tight timeline. If we wanted to get this board to market, we'd need to move quickly, aligning design, manufacturing, and marketing efforts in sync. This was a chance to create something revolutionary—something that would resonate with girls who, like me, needed a high-performance board made for them.

The next stop on my board education tour was the factory, tucked just behind the offices. Stepping inside felt like pulling back the curtain on the heart of snowboarding magic. Machines hummed, molds and presses clanked, and the scent of resin and fresh wood from the cores filled the air. Each board was built like a layered sandwich—wood core, steel edges, fiberglass, resin, and a topsheet—all pressed together in a heated mold to take its final shape.

Watching each board come to life—from raw form to graphic screened art—I could finally see the soul poured into every layer. Snowboards had always been something I just rode. But here, with my name on the line and a chance to be involved in every detail, it all felt different. Every decision mattered. They told me a board could be built start to finish in about fifteen minutes. Each one handmade. Each one flex-tested after the glue cured—every bend waking it up, making it ride-ready.

What if more girls were part of the technical side, too? Getting their hands dirty, seeing the beauty in how things are made and shaped. Honestly, I didn't think I'd be interested—but thankfully, these guys knew better. They understood how much it matters. Because it *does*.

It changes how products get built—for women, by women. Girls need to see themselves not just in the ride, but in every wrench twist, every graphic choice, every flex test. The outcome is better when we're part of the process. I could already feel it. Burton's decision to bring me in at this level was a first—and it meant everything. I felt genuinely honored that they took the time to teach me, to open my eyes. And now that I'd seen behind the curtain, I knew I'd never ride the same way again.

JG laid it out simply: "Before we finalize anything, we need to know this board rides the way it should. We can only do so much in here—the real test is on snow."

Mount Hood was the go-to spot for testing prototypes, and the second he mentioned it, my heart jumped. That glacier was where my pro snowboarding journey had started. Full circle. How cool was that? I didn't hesitate.

"For sure," I said, already picturing it.

He smiled, nodding. "We'll create several prototypes based on what we talked about today. Fiddy and I will work with the engineers, and I'll send you some notes on exactly what to feel for and how to give feedback."

According to Dave, Burton took this part seriously—they never put out a board that hadn't been tested and perfected.

Then Fiddy chimed in. "And once we dial in the shape and flex, we'll layer in the details to make it truly yours. You'll be working with JDK—the design firm. They'll oversee and help get your graphics just right. And we can talk about adding signature touches—like metal tip protectors, custom materials, anything that makes it stand out. We'll use top-of-the-line construction—everything about this board will be next level. It's gonna be something totally unique. Something no one's seen before. That's what makes it cool."

Excitement was building, and I couldn't help but feel a bit like royalty. Burton was putting everything into this board—no shortcuts, no holding back. I felt a wave of gratitude for sticking around, for pushing past that frustration. What if I'd left over a rough negotiation? I wouldn't be here, about to be part of something this big, this personal. I could see now that this partnership was going to be worth it. And I couldn't wait to get out there and ride—to feel what we'd created in action.

On the flight home, I started brainstorming graphics for my board. Ideas swirled, but nothing really clicked—until I was finally relaxed, drifting toward sleep. Suddenly, a memory surfaced: that incredible moment surfing alongside a dolphin. *Yes—a big, bold dolphin on the base of my board.*

When I landed in Chicago for a quick layover before heading back to San Diego, I used the time to call Gaylene and give her the final word—I was leaving Sims. We'd talked through this transition so much that I wasn't nervous. She was expecting it.

Our conversation quickly shifted to Tina. Kemper, her sponsor, was on shaky ground—financially unstable, maybe even done for—so she was open to new options. Within a week—literally—Tina met with Gaylene, signed with Sims, designed her board graphics, and had her pro model heading into production. Fastest turnaround ever. Total win-win.

My negotiation wasn't easy, but maybe life was about building character. And if that was true, then I had just been forged in the fire.

CHAPTER 24
/ Boots on the Ground /

YOU WOULDN'T EXPECT A BEASTIE BOY to be your friend's mellow room-mate who gave bass guitar lessons between powder days—but that was Adam Yauch.

Tina had just sold her condo in Utah and upgraded to a cozy subur-ban house near the Wasatch Mountains—a perfect launchpad for moun-tain missions. The place had a warm, lived-in feel: snow gear piled by the door, the faint scent of pine in the air. Dave rented a room there, and so did Adam of the Beastie Boys. His random, low-key presence became a steady fixture in our lives.

Adam was more than a rock star to us—he was the quiet, ground-ed friend who'd sometimes give Tina and me bass lessons in the living room or walk us through his favorite songs from legendary jazz artists. His passion for snowboarding easily matched ours. Offstage, he was soft-spoken, never carrying the loud energy you'd expect from someone all over MTV. He was just Adam. But there was an aura about him—like he carried a powerful, quiet secret.

One afternoon, Adam and I settled in for a chat while Tina took a phone call. I confided in him about some new team drama—one of my

Burton teammates wasn't thrilled that I had a pro model, and rumors were swirling that she might leave the team because of it. I felt like I was the problem.

"I never wanted to bring that kind of negativity into the team," I admitted, the exhaustion slipping into my voice.

Adam listened with his usual calm, his steady gaze grounding me. When he finally spoke, his voice was warm and reassuring.

"Shan, you're gonna face challenges like this whenever you're pushing forward," he said. "Stay true to yourself, keep doing your best, and let go of the rest. Jealousy and backstabbing come with success—don't let anyone else's issues hold you back from what you're here to do."

His words sank deep, and I felt a rush of emotion rise. Just as I looked down to steady myself, Tina walked over, concern clouding her face.

"Monica's not doing well," Tina said quietly. "Lisa just called."

Lisa, our *Prom* marketing director, was close friends with Monica Steward, who had co-founded Bonfire Outerwear with her nephew, Brad Steward—who had also been my marketing director at Morrow.

In an industry where few women held roles on the business side, Monica was one of the pillars. She, along with the rest of us, had worked to push and support one another at every stage. With her dark hair, striking eyes, and infectious smile, she radiated warmth and strength. She'd been battling breast cancer for over a year—since she was just twenty-six. When she first found a lump, her doctor brushed it off, and Monica followed his advice to ignore it. By the time she had a mammogram, it was too late—she discovered it was late-stage cancer. At that time, most of us still saw breast cancer as something distant—something that affected only older women, like our grandmothers. Monica's battle shattered that misconception.

Tina's voice cracked slightly as she continued, "Can you call Lisa in the next couple of days, Shan? Monica is urging us to use our platform to raise awareness about breast cancer. She and Lisa have this idea—to start a snowboarding and music festival for breast cancer awareness. They're thinking of calling it 'Boarding for Breast Cancer.' She wants us as athlete ambassadors...maybe help bring in a few bands as sponsors, too."

She turned to Adam, eyes searching. "Adam, do you think the Beastie Boys might want to be part of it?"

Adam nodded without hesitation. "Let's discuss it with my manager," he said.

For a moment, we sat in silence, letting the weight of it all settle in. Tina began flipping through the stack of action-sports magazines on her coffee table, each one highlighting women breaking barriers in the sport. She was clearly looking for something specific—her fingers pausing on covers that caught her eye.

There was Lisa Andersen on *Surfer*, with the bold tagline "Lisa Andersen Surfs Better Than You," and Cara-Beth Burnside on the cover of *Thrasher*—the first woman ever to land that honor on a skateboarding magazine back in 1989. Then, Tina lingered on the preview cover of *Fresh and Tasty*, the first all-women's snowboard magazine, where I was featured, and on her own cover of *Japanese Snow Style* magazine. 1995 marked the dawn of a new era for women's sports. Monica had been a driving force in that movement, helping to pave the way for all of us.

Finally, Tina pulled out *WIG—Women in General* magazine—the one she'd been searching for.

"Here," she said softly, holding it up to show Adam and me. "Monica's piece is in this one."

As Tina flipped through the article, her eyes scanned the page until they settled on a section that made her pause. She began reading aloud, and Monica's words cut through the room with clarity and emotion. Monica had written about her fears and the lessons she'd learned—her message full of gratitude and resilience. Then Tina read the passage that struck us all: "Why do we need a near-death experience to live life the way we're supposed to? Every day, I get out of bed, set my feet on the floor and start the day. Have you ever done the same? Ever set your feet on the floor and thought how wonderful it is to have feet? Feet that have no pain and do exactly what you tell them? We never realize how good something is until it's in pain...or gone."

The room fell silent.

Everything I was complaining about earlier? I'm all good, I thought, humbled.

Monica's words were a stark reminder, echoing what my mom always told me: "The hardest times shape our character and leave us with lessons we carry forever." It's so easy to get caught up in life's small battles and forget to appreciate the simple things.

CHAPTER 25

/ We Came for the Podium, Left with a Bill /

WE WEREN'T JUST FLYING TO AUSTRIA—we were about to make history. Tina and I were set to launch *Prom*, the first-ever women's outerwear brand, and I was about to ride my brand-new Burton *Dolphin* pro model—the first-ever Burton women's pro model—for the first time. From the first sketch to the finished snowboard in just a few months—that was a feat in itself. A sprint that showed just how hard the Burton crew, especially the production team, worked.

The first World Cup contest of the season was set for Ischgl, Austria, in January 1995. Tina and I had a plan to set us apart: arrive a week early, dial in our tricks on the halfpipe, and shake off any jet lag before the contest.

After booking the airline tickets, Tina hung up the phone with a big smile. "Boom."

"Boom—going over early for the win!" I shot back, picturing myself on the podium, proudly holding my new Burton *Dolphin* pro model.

Burton was shipping me the *Dolphin* board just in time for Europe, and I could hardly wait to ride it. The board came in four colors, but my heart was set on the bold pink base—a dolphin leaping through stylized waves—paired with a shimmering silver topsheet. The topsheet was pure artistry: a dreamscape of moon and stars woven into ribbon-like waves, finished with a glow-in-the-dark layer Burton was experimenting with for the first time. It wouldn't hit shops until the following season, but I had to ride it now to get photos for next year's catalogs.

They'd also introduced a custom wave-shaped metal tip protector—next-level design. Every detail was crafted with intention, from the glowing topsheet to the precise shape we fine-tuned together. This wasn't just another board; Burton treated it like a masterpiece, and I was beyond grateful. I knew it would resonate with girls—a piece of art and performance reflecting their strength, creativity, and individuality.

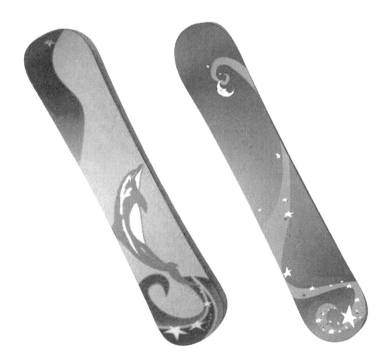

Top and bottom graphics of Burton's first women's pro model—the Dolphin, my Burton pro model. A milestone moment for women's gear.

Despite a few solid seasons under my belt, I felt a wave of nerves heading into that contest year. This was my first season with Burton, and I carried the weight of my own expectations. Even after winning almost every event in the past two years, one question still lingered: was I worthy to be on the Burton team?

There's a difference between someone spotting your potential and offering you an opportunity—and having to fight to prove your worth. Ironically, both happened to me at Burton. Eric saw the potential, but I still had to fight to negotiate my contract. The pressure was real. Honestly, I wished I'd had an agent to handle it, because fighting for yourself as an athlete can feel too bold. It puts you in a vulnerable position and chips away at your confidence. Most athletes just want to perform. We want to feel wanted—needed—to rise to the occasion.

Still, snowboarding was my passion, and I was driven by a mission— to show girls how life-changing this sport could be. Burton was my platform to spread that message, so I was all in—even if my confidence needed a little boost.

That past summer, I had bought a small condo near the Salt Lake City canyons—perfect for soaking up Utah's unbeatable snow and living close to Dave and Tina. It was an ideal setup, especially since Dave was on the same program. We split our time between riding powder in the winter and surfing in San Diego during the summer. Each place aligned perfectly with the activities we loved.

With the season goals in mind, Tina and I settled onto her dark purple velvet couch. True to form, Tina—the list master—handed me a yellow notepad and pen.

"Here," she said, "Let's get this down."

Making lists was her thing. She made one nearly every day: goals, gear, groceries, life stuff. If it wasn't written down, it didn't exist. We were deep in discussion when Dave, who was renting a room from Tina, walked in with tuning gear in hand.

"Hey girls, how's it going? Want me to wax your boards?"

"Go for it—mine's in the garage. Thanks, Dave!" Tina replied.

"My board's in my car. Wanna grab it for me?" I asked. Dave always found it funny that I never messed with my gear. I was more than happy to let him handle it.

Outside, big snowflakes had started falling. I was feeling pulled to stay home and ride the incoming powder—why leave a good situation for a dumb contest?

"Are we sure about heading to Europe early?" I asked, watching the flakes pile up. "We could do photo shoots here and just pull up for the contest."

"Yeah, maybe..." Tina shrugged, glancing out the window where thick snowflakes were accumulating—already an inch on the railing. The mountains in the distance stood cloaked in white, promising fresh turns.

"Then again, I guess if we hadn't taken those flights the last time, we wouldn't have gone on the best trip of our lives," I said, nudging her with a grin. "And who knows—maybe I wouldn't have met Dave."

We both laughed—the kind of laugh that comes from knowing how wild and beautiful the ride has been, and how little control we really had over any of it. Then, almost without saying a word, we grabbed our pens and started jotting down goals—plans for the contest and big-picture dreams.

"I guess we should stick to our plan—take the contest seriously," Tina said.

I began my list:

- **WIN EVERY EVENT.**
- **TEN PUBLISHED MAGAZINE PHOTOS.**
- **BE THE FIRST GIRL TO LAND A FRONTSIDE 720 IN THE PIPE.**
- **IMPROVE IN INTERVIEWS.** (Public speaking was my weak spot, but I wanted to get better at thanking my sponsors and encouraging girls to snowboard.)

I paused, pen hovering. Could I land that 720 in icy conditions?

I'd pulled it off in soft, slushy snow at Mount Hood over the summer—but doing it in a rock-solid winter halfpipe would be the real test.

Our *Prom* outerwear shipment arrived just in time—bright colors, feminine fit, and that effortlessly cool vibe. The waterproof overalls we designed stole the show. Finally, gear that reflected us—not just hand-me-downs from the guys.

With our goals set and gear ready, we packed up, feeling more prepared than ever. At the airport, Dave dropped us off with a grin and a wink. "Have fun in that icy pipe, girls! I'll be here riding fresh powder for ya."

We rolled our eyes, but deep down, we were stoked. We had a plan—and a head start on the competition.

But when we pulled into Ischgl, we were greeted by...no snow. Nichts. Nein. Zero. Zilch.

Tina stretched, yawning. "Maybe we should walk around to stay awake," she suggested. We bundled up and strolled through the quiet town, admiring the Edelweiss flowers displayed in shop windows. At a newsstand, we checked the forecast—five days of bone-chilling temperatures and clear skies. Not a flake in sight.

"What is it with Europe?" I muttered, feeling deflated. We'd come early to fine-tune our tricks, and now we were stuck with dry slopes and a bad case of jet lag.

Back at the hotel, we unpacked and tried on our new *Prom* outerwear.

"No one's going to recognize us!" I laughed, holding up my jacket with excitement. Tina and I had chosen each color to bring the designs to life, making each piece feel personal. Even if we were stuck practicing on a frozen halfpipe, at least we'd look stylish.

We hit the mountain—*brrr*, was it cold. With every foot of elevation, the temperature dropped. By the time we reached mid-mountain, the air stabbed my lungs with each breath. A cozy lodge beckoned—but we had to get to the halfpipe. Below us, the slopes shimmered like icy skate rinks—nothing like the soft Utah powder we'd just left behind.

"It's official—I'm complaining," I muttered, voice muffled behind my fleece neck gaiter.

Tina called out optimistically, "My feet already feel like ice blocks. Let's check out the pipe—maybe we can hike it, warm up a little."

But when we reached the top, it was obvious—the pipe was unrideable. Deep ruts had frozen solid, the walls shredded like spring slush, then flash-frozen. No way was I risking it.

"What a joke!" I said, frustration bubbling over.

Tina laughed. "Maybe we should just go back for hot cocoa."

"Or better yet, let's just book a one-way ticket to Hawaii," I joked, trying to laugh off the sting. The only silver lining? Our boards. My Burton *Dolphin,* with its pink base and smiling moon on the topsheet made me happy, even on ice. And Tina's Sims board—bright yellow, with a red-haired fairy she'd drawn herself—was a beauty. If only we had better conditions to enjoy them.

With little snow and even less to do, we did our best to stay upbeat. We turned our room into a creativity zone, brainstorming designs for *Prom* outerwear, sending silly postcards home, and having impromptu dance parties. The Beastie Boys blasted as we bounced around, our bed turning into an imaginary halfpipe where we'd "land" 720s and 540s like we'd stuck them in real life.

A few days before the competition started, things finally picked up. Competitors filed into our hotel, and the ISF meeting began. The International Snowboarding Federation oversees the World Cup events, and ahead of each contest, they hold rider meetings. In this one, we had plenty to say—the halfpipe wasn't just dangerous, it was unfit for use, especially considering the prestige of the event. The organizers promised to flatten and rebuild the pipe within 24 hours, though they couldn't guarantee perfection due to the icy conditions and limited snow. Still, it would be an improvement.

When the contest delay was announced, most competitors looked relieved—one more day to adjust and practice. But for Tina and me, it felt like adding salt to the wound. We exchanged a look that said it all: we just wanted this icy ordeal over with.

During the meeting, another bombshell dropped—the snowboarding world was buzzing with news that our sport was set to debut as an Olympic event by 1998. While most riders were excited, I couldn't shake my doubts, especially since the IOC (International Olympic Committee) had already vetoed snowboarding for the '94 Winter Olympics in Lillehammer. And now, the kicker: if snowboarding made it to Nagano, Japan, the Federation of International Skiing (FIS) would oversee snowboarding.

Let that sink in—skiing would control snowboarding. After years of being taunted by skiers, banned from slopes, and facing deep friction between the sports, now they'd be the ones calling the shots. It felt like a slap in the face. Snowboarding had gained enough traction to catch the IOC's attention, and suddenly skiing wanted in—not as allies, but as overseers. Why? Because they saw an opportunity to cash in on the wave of interest and money flooding into snowboarding.

This was about more than just an Olympic debut—it was about control, profit, and the very identity of snowboarding. And it had riders fired up.

The decision sparked outrage—how could a skiing organization control snowboarding? The animosity between the two sports was well-known. The sentiment among riders was clear: this was about money. European riders started handing out stickers reading "Snowboarders Against FIS Control," making their dissent loud and visible. Tina and I joked about making our own sticker: "Ride (Pow) or Die."

Snowboarders were rebels by nature. We entered the sport as outsiders, unafraid to break the rules or do things our own way. We weren't about neat rows or traditional paths, and that's what made snowboarding so electrifying. But that rebellious streak came with its own challenges. I always saw the value in uniting riders to stand up for our interests, to push contest organizers to prioritize competitors. A few of us—the trusty handful—showed up to meetings, hashing out ways to make the sport better for all of us. But we needed everyone on board to make real change.

The truth was, most contest organizers wouldn't put in extra time or money unless we demanded it. If things ran "well enough," there was no real incentive to improve. I stepped up often, trying to rally riders and get everyone on the same page, but most were too focused on their own runs to think about the bigger picture. Eventually, I started to pull back. As much as I cared, snowboarders as a whole weren't interested in coming together to push for structural change. It felt pointless to keep trying—so I focused on what I could control.

As the ISF meeting wrapped, we were still reeling from the politics of it all. But soon, we were out on the mountain, facing our own uphill battle in the icy halfpipe.

After days of practice on that treacherous pipe, contest day finally came. Both Tina and I fell during our first qualifying runs. On my last attempt to make finals, I caught my edge on the rutted wall during my first trick and slammed.

Tina dropped in after me, and I watched her disappointment as she fell mid-run. As she unstrapped her bindings, I gave her a side hug. "How did we both mess that up? I just want to go home."

No finals for us. That was it. I hadn't felt that kind of stuck, frustrated disappointment in a long time.

Tina sighed. "Let's figure out how to get outta here."

We rode straight to the mid-station lodge and made an emergency call to my dad—at 2 a.m. his time—begging him to book us the earliest Learjet home. Clearly, we weren't in our right minds.

"Shannon, a Learjet? Really?" he said, trying to suppress a laugh. "By the time you figure out how to get to France, you'll already be home on a regular flight."

"Dad," I said, lowering my voice dramatically, "I can't spend another day here. It's either a Learjet, hot air balloon—anything. Just get us outta here."

He yawned. "Fine. I'll check flights. Call me back in twenty. And Shannon, maybe relax and get something to eat."

When we called him back, every return flight was booked. We had no choice but to stick it out. As we trudged back to our room, Tina sighed. "One more contest with icy pipes, crappy hotels, and no practice—and I'm done."

I nodded. "What's the point if we're just gonna bruise our butts and crash out of the finals?"

"Right?" Tina threw up her hands. "I could be home in my PJs, eating popcorn. Or on a mountain with actual snow."

I agreed. "We definitely made the wrong choice to come early."

Our frustration turned into laughter—we cracked up, leaning on each other as we walked, two snowboarders stranded in Austria, laughing at how spectacularly everything had fallen apart. Still giggling, we stepped into the elevator—just the two of us at first. Then, out of nowhere, a pack of competitors piled in, loud and hyped. The elevator's max capacity was four, and now there were nine of us crammed inside. Daniel Franck, the Norwegian who'd just taken the win, stood holding his trophy, reeking of champagne and victory. We weren't in the mood, but we forced smiles and offered quick congrats. Against our better judgment, we stayed put as the doors slid shut.

One guy bounced on the floor, surprised when it rebounded like a trampoline. That was all it took. Suddenly, everyone—except Tina and me—started jumping in unison, shouting and laughing as the elevator bucked beneath us. With each jump, the floor flexed harder—like a rubber band winding tighter—every bounce launching them higher than the last. It was full-blown chaos: yelling, laughter, total madness.

"Not a good idea," I muttered, half-laughing despite myself.

"Hey! You're gonna break the elevator! Let's not all die today!" Tina shouted, trying to cut through the noise.

Daniel piped up in a mocking, high-pitched tone: "Ohhh, you're gonna breaaak the elevat—"

Midway through his impression, the elevator jolted, dropped five feet, and we all screamed. But instead of plummeting, it stopped.

Dead silence. Then the lights flickered out completely.

"Oh, great. Perfect," Tina groaned. "This is the icing on the cake."

People started pushing buttons and mumbling, trying not to panic—when suddenly, a massive fart echoed through the cramped space. Everyone froze, then tried to stifle their laughter. There was nothing left to do but laugh—and hit the emergency button.

Two sweaty, stinky hours later, repairmen finally pried open the doors, pulling us out one by one. We'd been stuck halfway between floors.

As I scrambled out, I turned to Tina, shaking my head. "This trip just keeps getting better and better."

Back in our room, we were wiped out—barely speaking—when Tina's brother Mikey burst in, grinning like he'd just won the lottery.

"Can you guys give me a lift to Innsbruck for the Red Bull Air & Style event? I got invited, but I'm short a ride."

"Definitely," I said, grateful for an excuse to ditch this place. Innsbruck and a Red Bull contest? Yes, please.

The next morning, as we dragged our bags through the lobby, the front desk lady greeted us with a stare that could melt ice.

"You're the girls who broke the elevator yesterday!" she declared in her thick Austrian accent.

Tina and I exchanged confused looks. "Wait, what?" I managed.

"You've got it all wrong," Tina said, raising her hands. "We didn't break anything! It was the others in the elevator. We just...survived it."

"Exactly! Not us!" I added, heart pounding. "We did not jump."

She crossed her arms. "I remember you two clearly—red hair, blonde hair. The Norwegian guy with the trophy said you two would handle the damages."

She grabbed a calculator and shoved the display at us. "$3,000. For repairs."

We both gawked in disbelief.

"No, no, no..." I said. "We're not paying for that."

She lifted her chin, her eyes gleaming. "I have your passports. I won't give them back until you pay."

Panic edged into my voice. "Dude..."

Mikey tried to reason with her, but it was no use. Our options were clear: pay the $3,000 or kiss our passports goodbye. So with dramatic sighs, we handed over our credit cards and split the bill.

As we walked away, I muttered, "We're now proud owners of an Austrian elevator. Do we get a deed with that?"

Tina snorted. "Right? Maybe we can rent it out as a vacation spot."

We finally burst out laughing—the kind of laugh that comes when you're so defeated it circles back to funny. With that, we walked out the door, lighter by $3,000 but more than ready to leave Ischgl behind.

Our next destination? Innsbruck. And this time, we'd have our eyes wide open—for sketchy elevators, icy pipes, and hidden fees.

CHAPTER 26

/ Flyin' Over Innsbruck /

STANDING AT THE TOP OF THE JUMP, I felt like I was staring off the edge of the world. Below us, a sea of more than ten thousand people packed the stadium, shoulder to shoulder, their cheers rising like a tidal wave. Blinding lights lit up the night sky, casting dramatic shadows across the massive setup. The sheer drop stretched out in front of us—so steep, it felt like the ground had vanished.

My heart pounded. This wasn't just a jump. It was a moment that could change everything.

I've always watched Olympic ski jumping in awe, wishing I could be that brave, but girls weren't allowed. I tried when I was twelve in Steamboat, but the coach told me no—until my mom spoke up, and her choice words changed his mind. But I wasn't bold enough to push it further. Now, standing at the top of this massive snowboard jump in Innsbruck, the memories came rushing back. A wave of recognition swelled in my chest—this was full circle. I was getting a second shot, and this time, it was on my terms. Not on skis, but on my board. This was my moment, and no one was going to tell me I didn't belong. Not today.

While the men competed for a $20,000 purse, Tina and I were riding for something bigger—something you couldn't put a price on. Especially since there *was* no prize money for us. We were here for passion. To make a point. Girls *should* be here.

The man on the loudspeaker called us out. Tina and I were the half-time show, launching off the jump between the guys' main event. His English accent boomed across the stadium—dramatic, full of flair: "The craaazy American girls! The only girls to everrr hit this jump!"

He introduced me first, then Tina. I lifted both hands and waved to the roaring crowd below, laughter bubbling up to release some of the nerves I'd been holding in. It felt wild—electric. We were about to do what no girl had ever done on that stage before.

From behind me, Tina shouted, "Strong legs, Shan!"

Other voices joined in: "Go big, Shan! You got this!"

I nodded, letting my focus lock in like it had so many times before. Everything else dropped away.

God, help me right now, I thought—not a desperate plea, more like a casual expectation. *Because let's be real: if you don't, my body parts might end up scattered across this Austrian arena, and my parents will be filing a lawsuit against Red Bull.*

The official signaled, and I took a steadying breath before pointing my board downhill. Speed hit me fast—*strong legs, strong legs,* I reminded myself, feeling the carve lock in perfectly. The jump rushed up, and I launched off the lip, soaring over the vast, open stretch below—sixty feet of sheer, empty space that seemed ready to swallow me whole. I held a steady method grab, eyes fixed on the landing, even as cold tears blurred the scene. Not tears of fear—just the cool wind generated from going Mach 3. If I'd allowed myself to think about that gaping chasm, my mind would've spiraled. That void below was a world of its own, a depth that pulled at you, daring you to look down, to slip up. But I didn't let my mind go there. Confidence was all I had to keep me from falling. My *Dolphin* board sliced through the Innsbruck air, trailing pink waves of destiny into the endless expanse.

Smooth as butter I touched down, and instant relief flooded over me as I coasted to a stop. The crowd went wild, but I kept my expression cool, trying to play it off as if it was just another run. Inside, my heart was racing with joy. I unstrapped my board and looked up, spotting Tina at the top, ready to drop in. I was nervous for her—and I shouted even though my voice wasn't going to reach her. "Go Tina—you got this!"

Moments later, she took off, nailing the jump with a clean, effortless landing. The announcer's voice boomed over the speakers: "Let's hear it for the American girls!"

The crowd roared, and as Tina rode over, I tackled her with a hug, both of us laughing and shaking from the adrenaline.

Right after, MTV Europe pulled us aside for interviews, the cameras rolling as we stood there, still buzzing with adrenaline, trying to make sense of what we'd just done. I didn't know exactly how or when it would matter—but deep down, I knew it would. There's always a first. A line that gets crossed so others don't have to wonder if it's even possible. We'd cracked something open. And even if the world hadn't caught on yet, I knew this was a door flung wide—for every girl who'd ever been told she couldn't.

We weren't supposed to be here.

A flashback tugged me to earlier that day—the first moment we laid eyes on the monster jump. It was around 10 a.m. and we'd just rolled in from Ischgl, stiff and bruised from the contest but stoked to step into a whole new snowboard scene. Since Tina's brother Mikey had been invited to ride in the Red Bull Air & Style big air event, we naturally tagged along to check it out. We had no expectations—and definitely no invitation. But that didn't matter. We were just hyped to see another side of the sport, to take in the energy of an iconic venue.

Still, here's the thing: it's not in my nature—or Tina's—to just show up and watch. If we were anywhere near a mountain or a jump, we were wired to get involved.

The moment we stepped into the Bergisel Olympic Ski Jump facility, my eyes widened. The scale of the place was staggering. On one side stood the legendary 90-meter jump, glinting in the late morning light and rising high into the clear mountain-city sky.

Opposite it, a massive scaffolding structure had been built to create the drop-in ramp—a snow-covered runway that started way up high. Riders would bomb down it to hit a giant jump that launched them across a humongous gap before landing on a steep hill below. That hill, called the outrun, is normally where Olympic ski jumpers glide to a stop after their flight. But for this event, the Red Bull crew had turned it into something entirely different.

They used the outrun as the landing zone—and stacked a colossal metal structure on top to form the jump. Concrete seating tiers fanned out around the landing, built to hold an army of spectators. The whole setup felt more like a gladiator arena than a snowboard contest venue.

It was beautiful and terrifying all at once—an arena built to crown legends...or swallow them whole.

We walked to the bottom of the jump with Mikey, taking it all in. From down there, the scale of the setup felt even more intense. Riders were launching off the lip and barely clearing the gap, their boards skimming the knuckle—the edge where the flat gap dropped into the landing—before touching down on the steep outrun.

As we stood there watching the guys send it, I already knew what was coming. It wasn't a matter of *if* we'd drop in—it was just a matter of *when*.

Mikey struck up a casual convo with one of the riders who'd just landed and was catching his breath near the fence.

"How's it?" Mikey asked.

"It's maybe sixty feet. Pretty big—you gotta point it," the guy said, wiping snow off his goggles. "It's tough to clear right now—kinda warm, slow conditions..." He nodded toward the top. "You going up?"

"Yeah, just got here," Mikey replied, cool as ever. But I could tell—he was fired up. The two of them started hiking up together.

Tina and I—still in jeans and sweatshirts—exchanged a glance.

We were already calculating. Neither of us said it, but we both felt the itch.

"Should we go off this thing?" Tina asked, her voice laced with excitement and nerves.

"Yeah, we should," I said—the words tumbling out before I could second-guess myself.

We watched the next guy take off, grabbing a method midair, and stomp the landing.

"Well, he landed it—it does kinda look gnarly, though, huh?" I commented, trying to play it cool. But inside, my adrenaline was already ramping up.

We hiked halfway up to get a closer look. Standing there, looking across that gap, I felt like an ant beside the jump's towering structure.

Tina looked up and said, "It's pretty huge, huh?"

"Yeah," I replied. "It's bigger than I thought...but we can totally do this."

She nodded toward an incoming rider. "Watch—just one little carve, then he points it straight."

We both leaned in, studying his approach like it held the key to unlocking the jump. But right in the middle of our quiet hype-up session, we got interrupted—an official in a Red Bull jacket appeared out of nowhere, frowning like we were vandals on sacred ground.

"Vat are you girls doing here?" he barked, his sharp Austrian accent slicing through the cold air.

"We're just checking out the jump. It's looking pretty good," Tina replied smoothly, but he cut her off.

"Well, there's no girls allowed off zis jump."

Tina gave me a sideways look that said, "Oh no he didn't."

My jaw dropped. Was he serious? We'd just watched a bunch of guys hit the jump—no problem—and I knew we could handle it just as well.

"Why not?" I snapped, my voice sharper than I meant it to be.

"Excuse me?" the official sputtered, like he couldn't believe I had the nerve to talk back.

"We're going off this jump," I said, standing my ground.

"We just came to check the speed," she jumped in. "We need to know what we're working with—"

"No, no, no! Zis jump is too dangerous for girls!" he barked, cutting her off mid-sentence, puffing up like his authority would scare us off.

"You can't tell us we can't go off this just because we're girls!" I fired back, stepping forward.

"Exactly!" Tina said, arms crossed, feet planted. "We're not here to watch. We came to ride."

His face turned red. He flailed his arms like we were unruly teenagers trying to sneak onto a closed rollercoaster.

"No! Zis is not possible. Zis jump is too dangerous for you. Too dangerous!"

"Says who?" Tina shouted.

"Says *me!*" he roared. "You are *not allowed!*"

Then he jabbed his finger downhill. "Come. You two are leaving. Now."

We exchanged a glance—both of us fuming—but turned and started walking, biting our tongues as frustration buzzed beneath our skin. He walked us partway down the slope, silent and smug. But just as we rounded a corner and slipped out of sight, Mikey popped out from behind a row of scaffolding like a snowboarding superhero.

"Pssst—hey," he grinned, eyes gleaming with mischief. "Don't worry. I know a back way up."

He threw an arm around both our shoulders and smirked, nodding toward a narrow stairway tucked behind the stands.

We exchanged a look—adrenaline flaring up all over again.

"Let's do it," I said, already feeling the shift.

Tina turned to Mikey. "Go take another lap. We'll suit up and meet you at the rendezvous."

We dressed in turbo time, tossing on our gear like we were clocking in for battle. Then, with boards in hand, we slipped through the maze of scaffolding and stairs, following Mikey up the hidden route, light on our feet to stay under the radar.

By the time we reached the top, my heart wasn't pounding from nerves—it was from the thrill of breaking the rules to do something no one thought we could.

As we emerged from the shadows, the guys already gathered at the top spotted us. They grinned wide and raised their hands, offering high-fives like we'd always belonged there.

"I can't believe that just happened," I said, shaking my head.

Tina just smiled, eyes lit up. "Let's do this."

"Hey! The girls made it!" Daniel Franck, our Norwegian elevator friend, shouted, laughing as he nudged my shoulder.

"Hey—by the way," I shot back, grinning, "thanks for stiffing us with the three-grand elevator bill. Dude, you've got to be kidding me."

Tina chimed in, "Yeah! You totally bailed. You owe us."

He cracked up, shaking his head—and honestly, we couldn't help but laugh too. At this point, it was just comedy. He said something back, but the noise up top was too loud to hear it. Whatever. We just chalked it up as a travel expense.

The energy at the top of the jump was too good to care. High-fives flew in every direction, and with each slap of a glove, the stress from earlier melted away.

Up here, on this towering structure, we weren't outsiders anymore—we were in the mix. These guys felt like our brothers. And for the first time that day, we felt like we truly belonged. The guys turned back to their prep. Tina and I exchanged a quick nod.

Mikey leaned over, face serious. "Just stick right behind me. Match my speed exactly," he said, eyes locked on mine. "You've got this."

I nodded and drew a deep breath, letting his confidence anchor me. I was locked in—steady, despite the storm of pressure buzzing all around. Tina slid into position behind me, our boards lined up like a freight train ready to roll. I could feel her presence—solid and strong—syncing with mine.

"Let's go, Shan," she said, her voice electric.

No backing out now. We were in this together—each pushing the other forward.

Just as I bent my knees and shifted my weight, ready to drop—

A hand shot out across my chest, stopping me cold. I froze, stunned. My eyes snapped up—and there he was.

The official. His face was carved in stone, arm blocking my path like a wall I hadn't seen coming.

"I told you," he growled. "You—are—*not*—allowed off zis jump."

Each word landed like a hammer—his last, desperate grasp for control. A surge of adrenaline spiked through me, but before I could speak, Tina leaned forward, fists clenched, fire already in her throat. The whole moment tightened—sharp, electric, like something was about to break wide open.

Behind us, the guys roared in anticipation—amped to drop in. This was practice, and there was a rhythm. A rhythm you didn't break. Testosterone was pumping, egos and a big-money prize was on the line. Stalling the flow? Not cool. Not now.

But before Tina could get a word out, a chorus of voices rose up from the guys around us.

"Come on, man!" one rider shouted.

"Let them go!" another chimed in. "They've got this!"

The voices rose around us—loud, united—cutting through the icy air and slamming straight into the official's resolve. You could see it waver.

The energy shifted. Suddenly, we weren't just two girls pushing back against the rules—we were riders. And everyone up there knew it. They'd seen us ride. They knew what we could do.

And in that moment, it felt like every single one of them had our backs.

"Fine. Okay zen—you can try out," the official relented, his voice clipped. "You get...three tries."

Tina and I nodded. *Fair enough.*

"If you land it, you can go off zee jump tonight. But you girls won't be part of zee main event—you ride at halftime. And if you don't pull it off now in practice?" He paused, eyes narrowing. "Zat's it."

Tina and I looked at each other, grinning like we'd just been handed the golden ticket. But the second he said *three tries*, my confidence cracked—just enough to let a little fear creep in.

It's one thing to defiantly say you're going to hit the biggest jump of your life. It's another to stand at the top, with every guy watching, the officials scrutinizing, and the pressure of proving you belong hanging heavy in the air. *Can I actually do this? Am I really that tough? Or am I just full of talk and adrenaline?*

But the second that doubt crept in, I shut it down. That flicker of fear was all I needed to light the fire. There was no way we weren't landing it. Not today.

Tina looked like she was having the same internal battle—but her eyes said it all: "Let's go."

Still, my nerves were spiking. Mikey pulled us aside and gave us the game plan one more time.

"Point it straight. Stay low. Carve heel to toe, but don't scrub your speed. Use your legs. Stay compact. Speed is your friend."

I nodded, locking it all in. Then it was go time.

Mikey dropped in, and I followed right behind. Every muscle buzzing, breath tight. As I hit the lip, I tucked into a method grab and launched into the air. The landing rushed up like a wave—boom. Landed it. I came into the bottom hot and turned my board sideways, spraying snow as I slid to a stop. My legs trembled, adrenaline crackling like electricity in my veins.

I looked back to see Tina dropping in. She cleared the gap but landed a bit backseat and slid out. Not a crash, but not clean either.

Try two—we both stuck it.

Try three—clean again.

We were officially in. The halftime show was ours. We gave each other a hug and some high-fives. We're really doing this.

Back at the hotel, we kicked off our boots and tried to rest—but the hype was too real. Soon enough, it was time to get ready. And we knew exactly what we wanted to do.

For the main event, we didn't want to blend in. We wanted to stand out—not as "just one of the guys," but as girls. Girly girls. Girls who could launch off a massive jump and still rock lip gloss doing it.

Our pink *Prom* outerwear sealed the deal. Tina rocked bright pink pants with a berry-colored jacket. I went bold with a pink coat over blue overalls. We braided our hair, curled our lashes, layered on mascara, dusted on blush, and topped it off with pink lip gloss.

By the time we stepped out that evening, we hadn't even touched the jump yet—and already, heads were turning.

We arrived at the dim, mostly deserted ski jump stadium parking lot, where Mikey, Tina, and I packed our backpacks with essentials: water, snacks, and an extra fleece for the cold. Tina had her CD player, ensuring we'd have tunes to get hyped.

"I forgot mine," I admitted.

"No worries—we can share my headphones," Tina offered with a grin.

The year before, Tina, Dave, the Livigno crew, and I had been part of the massive crowd—over ten thousand strong—screaming from the sidelines. None of us were competitors in this event, just spectators soaking up the energy of the place.

At the time, we'd only heard rumors about Red Bull—it was just hitting the scene—and we were hesitant to try it because of the wild myth going around that it contained "real bull ball juice." We had no idea what was actually in it.

One unforgettable highlight from that year's Air & Style was watching Bryan Iguchi—"The Guch"—launch off the massive jump and disappear into the dark abyss. We weren't even sure if he clipped the scaffolding, but he walked away just fine. He became our reminder to keep a straight trajectory.

As Tina and I started the climb up the jump, we took the secret stair route Mikey showed us. When we reached the top, we set our boards and packs down. Pausing to catch my breath, I took in the peaceful, almost surreal scene—the colored lights glimmered off the steel scaffolding, illuminating the space with a vibrant, unreal glow.

"Wow, we're the only ones up here," I said, taking in the quiet buzz of a light breeze. Tina pulled out her Walkman and handed me one side of her headphones. The moment I popped in the earpiece, the Beastie Boys' "So What'cha Want" kicked in—loud, gritty, perfect.

"Come on, Adam, we need your Beastie Boy vibes to amp up and hit this jump," Tina called out, egging on our invisible third member.

I laughed as we shared her headphones—each of us with one bud in our ear. With my hand on her shoulder, we bounced in perfect sync. She sang along, grinning, "I can't stand it, I know you planned it...I'm gonna set it straight..." Hands punched the air, arms stretched wide, karate kicks flying like the camera was rolling.

"Listen all y'all, it's a sabotage!" we shouted, jumping higher with each line. "Listen all y'all, it's a sabotage!"

The night was electric. We got two runs. I'd considered throwing a 360—just to show progression—but I hadn't practiced it, and there was too much at stake. It's hard to push progression when you're not even given the space to try. And right now, it felt more important to land clean. To prove we belonged. So I kept it simple—and solid.

After our final hit, the roar of the crowd hit like a wave. Cameras flashed. Reporters swarmed. MTV Europe pulled us aside for interviews, their crew scrambling to capture the moment as we stood there, still trying to process it all. Unforgettable.

We kicked back at the bottom, cheering as the guys threw down their biggest tricks. The after-party was already in full swing by the time we made our way over—still lit up from the adrenaline, still flying a little.

A few of the girls we'd competed against in Ischgl spotted us—faces full of curiosity, a mix of impressed...and maybe just a little envious.

"How did you girls get to go off the jump?" one of them asked.

"We wanted to, but they told us no girls were allowed."

Tina and I exchanged a grin.

"They told us the same thing," I said with a shrug. "We just...made it happen."

And this time—and every time after—no one was ever going to tell us we didn't belong.

CHAPTER 27

/ Japanese Blowout /

JAPAN HAD ALWAYS BEEN A PLACE OF ADVENTURE, but my first trip there with Morrow in 1992 was a whirlwind of laughter, surprises, and unforgettable moments.

One discovery that stands out? Learning how to say "I farted" in Japanese—"Watashi heshita." I'd mutter it just loud enough for people to hear in crowded hotel elevators, holding back laughter as people glanced around, confused, shifting uncomfortably.

Fast-forward four years. Snowboarding in Japan wasn't just a novelty sport anymore—it had exploded into a full-blown cultural obsession. In Tokyo, it was everywhere: people carried snowboards through the streets as fashion statements and strapped them to the roofs of their cars, even if they'd never been near a mountain. Just owning a board had become a status symbol. The media turned us into rock stars, portraying snowboarders as near-mythical, marveling at our abilities. Everywhere we went, crowds gathered, watching with a mix of awe and curiosity.

There we were—Tina, Tomo, and I—walking through the streets of Tokyo like rock stars, cameras flashing and people clapping, cheering, and shouting our names. Snowboards were strapped to the roofs of cars, cruising through neon-lit streets as if they were badges of honor. Snow gear was now Tokyo's hottest new trend. We had a front-row seat to this cultural shift.

Tomo, my Japanese friend, had crossed my path in my first trip to Japan, but we really bonded at Mount Hood's High Cascade Snowboard Camp. She had defied her parents to travel to America, immersing herself in the snowboarding scene. Working as a cook, she learned English and eventually became one of Japan's first pro women snowboarders. It felt like we were sisters, bound by humor, resilience, and a shared love for snowboarding.

When we arrived at a snowboard shop for a signing event, a long line of fans waited outside. As we passed, two girls burst into tears. Surprised, I turned to Tomo. "Did we do something wrong?"

"No, no!" Tomo smiled. "They're just happy. So excited to meet you guys!"

Inside, we sat at a table, posters in front of us. Fans handed us rice cookers, backpacks, and even pointed to their foreheads with markers in hand. We signed snowboards, arms, and yes—stomachs. Fans often mistook me for Tina and vice versa—we were in so many magazines together that we became interchangeable. It was a surreal moment, laughing, signing, and feeling grateful for all of it.

Then a woman approached me, cradling her newborn. "Please, picture...hold baby, Shannon," she said, her eyes sparkling with pride. I nodded with a small smile. "Yes—I'm Shannon." I hesitated for a moment, then carefully received the tiny baby she literally placed into my arms, doing my best not to look completely terrified. As the mother snapped photos, she smiled and spoke softly to Tomo in Japanese, gesturing from me to her baby.

Tomo turned to me, her eyes warm. "She named her baby...Shannon—in Japanese, it's Shiyano. After you."

"Wait...me?" I asked, stunned.

Tomo smiled softly. "She try many years to have baby. Then...she buy your Burton *Dolphin* pro model. Soon after...she got pregnant."

I was speechless. "You're telling me she believes the board helped her get pregnant?"

Tomo nodded, grinning. "Yes. She believes."

My heart swelled with awe—and at the same time, I couldn't help thinking, *Well, I'm not that amazing...* But I didn't want to dishonor her in any way.

"Wow," I said softly. "That's incredible."

Tomo chuckled, a twinkle in her eye. "She thinks you very special, Shannon. Very special."

I laughed, smiling warmly as I handed the baby back. "Please tell her I'm deeply honored."

After our Tokyo adventure, Tina and I parted ways. She joined her sponsor, Sims, for more events, and I flew to Sapporo with Tomo to meet the Burton team. Dave would join us soon.

Arriving at Rusutsu, the luxury resort in Japan, was a strange feeling. It was the same place I'd stayed on my first trip, yet it felt worlds away from those early years when the pros were getting kicked out for breaking the rules. Part of the hotel still had a carnival vibe—arcade games and even a rubber chicken launching station. Families lined up to shoot chickens at a target to win prizes—but, of course, some of the snowboard guys had turned it into their own game, hurling chickens at each other across the room, trying to see who they could take out.

Now, we were here for the Burton Japan Open—an extension of Burton's prestigious U.S. Open. The snowboarders were still edgy, but these days, most were at least sticking to the rules a little more.

As for me, I was struggling to find my focus. My energy was low—I was fighting the start of a cold and a cough—and though I'd hoped to win the contest, I didn't even make the top eight. I tried to brush it off, but the disappointment lingered.

Riding for Burton came with an unexpected weight—one I put on myself. Every event felt like a test, not just of my ability, but of my worth.

The harder I tried to prove myself, the heavier the pressure became. It wasn't just about results, it was about living up to the image—the media, the sponsorships, the interviews—and I felt overwhelmed, without the tools or capacity to handle it.

The other girls on the team were incredible, each with her own spark. I admired their energy, but I still felt like an outsider, struggling to find my place in a bond that had been built over time. Finding my place wasn't about reshaping myself—it was about honoring the foundation they'd built and figuring out where my journey fit into theirs.

Adding to the pressure, a close friend—a former Burton rider—had recently left the team. Burton hadn't given her what she felt she deserved, and while I admired her for standing up for herself, it created a quiet tension between us. Our friendship was never quite the same after that, and I understood why—it put me in an awkward position, riding for the company she'd just walked away from.

Meanwhile, Dave had arrived with the flu and was stuck in bed, his fever only deepening the sense of isolation I felt.

But as Adam Yauch once reminded me, I had to keep moving forward, trusting that things would work out. I tried to hold onto that belief, trusting God to guide me through this new chapter—but the truth is, it's hard to trust sometimes.

The night before we were supposed to leave the resort, fed up with a nagging cough that wouldn't quit, I picked up some Japanese cough medicine from the hotel pharmacy. The hotel was well-equipped, even with a clinic attached. I asked the pharmacist if it contained codeine—I'm allergic—and requested the kids' version since I'm super sensitive to medication. She assured me, "No codeine, no problem!" So, just to be safe, I took half the recommended dose before bed.

Within half an hour, I was hallucinating. The room spun violently, the walls warping as if they were melting into the floor. I gasped for air, desperate to anchor myself to something real. Dave, burning up with fever himself, reached out to steady me. When he handed me a glass of water, I tried to sit up—but the moment I lifted my head, it felt like I'd been flung to the ceiling. Disoriented and terrified, I flailed, knocking the glass from his hand as panic surged through me. My heart felt like it was slowing down, and I had to remind myself to breathe, taking deliberate, shaky gasps. I was terrified that if I fell asleep, my heart would stop. I literally counted down the minutes, eyes fixed on the clock, waiting for the madness to pass.

By morning, Dave was worse off than I was. Pale and barely able to breathe, I practically dragged him to the clinic, where they hooked him up to an IV. Once his fever broke, he finally started to feel better. We were both a complete mess.

Feeling exhausted, I headed to Tokyo later that day for a Burton promo event, while Dave stayed behind for a photo shoot. That night's big air jump event—though it had turned out to be more of a small, twenty-foot jump—was electric, with a couple thousand people packed in, cheering us on. Even though I was drained, I couldn't resist. The crowd was there to see their heroes fly, and the jump looked manageable. After a few practice runs, I thought, *Why not go for a 360?*

When the announcer called my name, the crowd erupted. I laughed, feeling a surge of confidence as I hit the lip. But I came in too fast, overshot the transition, and slammed into the flat bottom while still rotating. A sickening pop. My knee buckled. I knew instantly—it was my ACL. Just like the first time. But this time, it was the other knee. Again.

The realization hit hard. *How could I be so stupid?* Same mistake, different knee. I hated myself for not staying focused, for letting my guard down. My mind replayed it over and over, punishing me.

But I forced a smile and waved to the crowd, even as pain surged and tears burned my eyes. I came to Japan to rise—but this fall hit harder than I expected.

CHAPTER 28
/ Boobs, Boards, and the Beastie Boys /

THE IDEA THAT BECAME BOARDING FOR BREAST CANCER was finally happening on April 13, 1996, hosted by Sierra-at-Tahoe Resort, California. This snowboarding and music festival was more than just an event; it was a vibrant celebration of life and a cause born from Monica's vision. But as the festival took shape, there was a bittersweetness in the air. She wouldn't be there to witness it. Monica, our friend and inspiration, had lost her battle with breast cancer just three months earlier, at only twenty-eight years old. Her absence left a deep void in our lives and in the snowboarding community, yet her legacy had become a rallying force.

We wanted the day to be more than entertainment; it had to be something that might save lives. Our goal was a festival where people could celebrate, learn, and be empowered by the importance of early detection. The festival would feature a pro-invitational halfpipe contest, a big-air competition, and live music. Since my knee injury kept me from competing, I'd be handling interviews instead. If even one person left the event inspired to get a checkup, it would all be worth it.

Sierra-at-Tahoe's general manager, John Rice, had fully committed to supporting us, donating all ticket sales to cover event costs, while the resort staff volunteered their time. Local businesses chipped in, too. One of the behind-the-scenes heroes was Lisa Hudson. Despite a busy day job, she poured hours into organizing, pulling in sponsors, coordinating logistics, and setting up interviews. It was no small feat, yet Lisa made it look seamless. From wrangling donations from fifty brands for the auction to securing five incredible bands to play, she led the charge to make Monica's vision tangible.

The headliner? A little-known band called Quasar. Except...everyone knew exactly who they were. Due to legal issues with their label, the Beastie Boys had to perform under a pseudonym—but word had gotten out. Quasar was the Beastie Boys, and their low-key alias only added to the underground buzz.

The day before the event, Tina and I helped with setup, then headed back to the hotel. As soon as we walked in, she grabbed the phone to check her messages. Back then, it was all home phones and pay phones—no cell phones yet.

"You gotta listen to this message, Shan," she said, eyes wide as she dialed back.

Adam said something about the band needing a place to practice—somewhere mellow to dial in their set.

Tina called him back.

"Hey, Adam, what's happening? Okay…yeah, sure, I'll see what I can find. A pizza place? Got it. I'll call you back."

She hung up and grinned. "Yeah, the Beastie Boys blow up my phone all the time—to set up gigs," she said with a wink.

The next thing we knew, we were on a wild goose chase trying to find a spot for the Beastie Boys to warm up. After a few dead ends—places closed for the season and one worker shrugging, "The manager's not here"—I shook my head.

"Wow. I'm not sure she knows what she just passed up," I said.

Tina thought for a second, then snapped her fingers. "I'll call Shaun

Palmer! He lives in South Shore—somewhere around here. I just don't know his number."

We drove around looking for a pay phone until she finally reached her ex-boyfriend Andy, who was friends with Shaun. After a quick conversation, she had a number scribbled down. But when she called, a new renter answered and said Shaun didn't live there anymore.

Without missing a beat, Tina asked, "Well, would you want to host the Beastie Boys for a quick practice? They just need to fine-tune their set list."

When she hung up, her eyes were huge. "I think the guy just crapped his pants—he nearly hyperventilated," she laughed, jotting the address on her hand.

We weren't sure what to expect, but when we turned onto the street heading to the house around 10 p.m., we hit a bumper-to-bumper line of cars snaking all the way down the block.

"Whoa," Tina said, leaning forward. "I guess word travels fast—look at all these people."

There was no way we were going to sit there inching forward like everyone else. We needed to meet Adam and the rest of the guys.

Without hesitation, I cranked the wheel and veered onto the wrong side of the road.

Tina glanced at me and grinned. "We don't wait in traffic."

We zipped past a mile-long line of cars before squeezing into a narrow patch of dirt near the house, tucked between trees. As I threw it in park, I glanced at the crowd spilling off the front porch. A guy in a beanie waved us over.

"We're with the band," Tina said, hopping out with a smirk as we introduced ourselves, and he led us through the kitchen into a small, packed living room where he'd tipped over two couches to create a makeshift stage barricade. Moments later, MCA, Mike D, and Ad-Rock rolled in, dressed in black hoodies and ready to throw down the most intimate gig of their lives.

With the crowd growing, Adam asked Tina to introduce the band. Taking the mic, she welcomed everyone, thanked the owner, and hyped up the next day's event before shouting, "Kick it!"

Ad-Rock launched into "(You Gotta) Fight for Your Right (To Party!)" and the entire room exploded. The walls practically flew off as people screamed the lyrics, jumping in unison. Tina grabbed my hand, and we pushed our way toward the stairs.

"We've gotta get out of this crowd!" she shouted, laughing, though her eyes flickered with worry.

My knee was thrashed, and all I could picture was the headline: "Two Girls Trampled at Out-of-Control House Party."

From our spot on the stairs overlooking the packed living room, we had the perfect vantage point. We watched Adam—usually soft-spoken—transform into pure rock star energy. By the chorus, everyone was yelling, "You gotta fight...for your right...to party!"

As the night went on, the tiny room packed tighter and tighter, people hanging out of windows just to catch a glimpse. Some lesser-intelligent, or just really overconfident, guy launched himself from the stairs and grabbed onto the chandelier—it swung wildly, creaking under the weight, but miraculously, it held.

Four songs in, and the energy wasn't just electric—it was a ticking bomb, ready to go off at any second. The crowd was a frenzy, moving like one unstoppable force, thumping with the beat. The house itself seemed to pulse, every wall vibrating with raw power, like it could blow the roof off at any moment. People kept shoving forward, cramming into every corner, totally unfazed by the chaos. It felt like the whole place could detonate at any second. The band sensed it, too because they cut the music and made a quick exit out the back. Sweaty, exhausted, and buzzing with adrenaline, we said our goodbyes, already hyped to do it all again the next day.

A brutal 6 a.m. wake-up call jolted us from sleep, like getting hit by a train. Tina and I both had been traveling so much we were just running on fumes, but we shrugged it off. We'd pay for it later. Today was the day we'd been waiting for. The early morning sun hinted at a perfect spring day, and we made our way to the resort, barely able to believe what had just happened.

We cracked up the whole drive, replaying every wild moment from the night before. As we pulled into the resort and scored a front-row parking spot, I turned to Tina, grinning. "T, that kid is going to have the wildest story—he'll be telling people for the rest of his life that the Beastie Boys played in his house."

The festival got underway quickly, and people poured in. Sponsor tents dotted the venue, including a breast cancer awareness booth and the main stage, both ready to go. Lisa hustled us from one interview to the next. Between radio, TV, and magazine interviews, we barely had time to catch our breath or even go to the bathroom to pee. Finally, after hours of talking, we managed a quick water break.

We were heading toward the lift when we stopped at a booth with jellylike breast molds from the American Cancer Society, letting people

Quasar (aka the Beastie Boys) lit up the first-ever B4BC event. Best ever. Photo by Dawn Kish/Courtesy of B4BC

feel what a cancerous lump might feel like. "Let's remember to do these checks," I said, shoving a waterproof shower card with instructions into my pocket.

The vibe was electric—pros, fans, men, women—everyone from our industry was there, stoked to be part of something bigger. This wasn't just for women; it was for everyone, because, let's face it, almost everyone's been touched by breast cancer. Monica's spark brought us together, her memory lighting up every jump, every laugh. When Michelle Taggart, one of Monica's closest friends, nailed a backside 360 and followed it with a playful boob grab, the crowd exploded—laughter, applause, pure stoke. It felt like the mountains were cheering with us.

By mid-afternoon, John Rice shouted the news: 5,600 tickets sold. The grand finale was here; Quasar was about to take the stage.

"Now, for the grand finale...Quasar!" The announcer's voice boomed, and the crowd surged forward. Adam, Mike, and Ad-Rock—now in bright orange coveralls—stepped up, Adam still rocking his snowboard boots.

In seconds, the mosh pit exploded. Bodies crashed together, stage diving as security scrambled to keep control. The stage, softened by melting snow, started to sway under the weight of it all. At first, it was a subtle tilt, but then the platform groaned, a deep, ominous creak that made our stomachs drop. Security exchanged panicked glances as a radio crackled: "There's a mix-up in town—they think there's a riot up here."

Tina and I exchanged a sharp glance—it was time to bail before things went into full chaos. We jumped off the stage and sprinted toward the edge of the madness.

Suddenly, a low rumble filled the air, and a helicopter crested the peak, its spotlight sweeping across the crowd. All eyes shifted upward, momentarily awed, as the helicopter circled low. Overhead speakers boomed out, "Please clear the area..." But the energy was unstoppable; the moshers seemed to feed off the energy, testing the limits.

With each tilt and groan, the stage leaned more dangerously. It was clear that between the pounding crowd and melting snow, the stage was nearing its breaking point—and if it collapsed now, we'd be looking at a full-scale disaster.

The Beastie Boys cut the music, but the chaos just took a new form. Snowboarders pointed their boards downhill, bombing full speed toward a melted pond, skimming across the surface as their friends roared from the sidelines. Within minutes, a full-blown snowball fight broke out—chaotic, wild, hilarious—sending people sliding, dodging, and eventually splashing headfirst into the freezing water.

Gradually, the crowd's adrenaline began to ease, the wild energy fading as people finally started to disperse, a shared buzz of excitement and exhaustion settling over the slopes. In the aftermath, the grounds were littered with gloves, banners, and abandoned gear. We'd forgotten to hire a clean-up crew, but somehow, everyone pitched in, gathering trash and broken tents. Covered in grime and completely exhausted, we couldn't stop laughing as we recounted every wild moment.

Lisa tallied up the donations: $50,000. Every cent would go to the National Breast Cancer Foundation—at least until we figured out how to establish our own nonprofit. This was a cause worth building, and we knew this was only the beginning.

CHAPTER 29

/ Epipha-knee /

JUST A MONTH AFTER THE EXCITEMENT of Boarding for Breast Cancer, I lay in a hospital bed at the Vail Orthopedic Center, my knee bandaged and aching from ACL surgery. A Continuous Passive Motion (CPM) machine cradled my leg, moving it in a slow, steady rhythm—bending and straightening just enough to maintain circulation and prevent stiffness. It looked like a padded track, quietly whirring beneath my leg like a mechanical babysitter. I'd been through recovery before, but the long months ahead weighed on me.

Mom had just left the room with Dave to find some snacks for me at the hospital café. Dad flicked through TV channels, trying to lift my spirits. Then, a moment came that would shift everything. The TV in the corner flickered, and the announcer's voice broke the silence: "Snowboarding will make its official Olympic debut at the 1998 Nagano Games in Japan."

I looked at Dad, surprised. "Did you know this was happening?"

He nodded. "Saw it in the paper while you were in surgery. They're making it official tonight."

Of course I knew this was the plan, but nothing had ever felt certain. Until now.

The words struck me like ice water. The Olympics—every athlete's highest stage. Here it was: the big dream, my little-girl dream. But as I sat there in a hospital bed with a lengthy recovery, I couldn't even picture being back on a board, let alone at the Olympics. Part of me felt a thrill, but another part? I wasn't sure if this was what I wanted, or if I was ready for the intensity that the Olympics would bring.

As I tried to process my emotions, the TV showed a segment with teenagers talking about snowboarding's Olympic debut. Some called snowboarders "sellouts," others thought it was exciting, and a few mentioned how their idol, Terje Håkonsen, was boycotting the games.

"Terje," I murmured. He was our sport's Michael Jordan—untouchable, innovative, stylish to his core. His refusal to compete in the Olympics was already making waves. Norwegian snowboarder Terje Håkonsen had been outspoken about his distrust of the International Olympic Committee and, more specifically, their decision to hand control of Olympic snowboarding to the FIS.

The frustration ran deeper with context. Snowboarding had been denied even exhibition status at the 1994 Lillehammer Olympics—Terje's home turf. That could've been his moment. And now, just a few years later, the IOC hadn't just changed course—they'd handed the reins to FIS, a governing body created by and for skiers?

He was the best rider in the world—hands down—and without him at the Olympics, it almost made the whole thing feel less legit. Like, how could it be the highest stage in snowboarding if the best snowboarder in our sport wasn't even willing to show up?

"Snowboarding's about freedom," I said, shaking my head. "They're trying to control us, turn us into something we're not. I get why Terje's boycotting. But...would it even matter if I made a stand?"

Dad's face softened, and he leaned in. "I don't know about that. But what matters is what *you* think. You're the only one who decides what this sport means to you—not the Olympics, not the sponsors, just you."

I tried to take comfort in his words, but the reality was sinking in. Here I was, laid up in a hospital bed, feeling torn. On one side, the Olympics represented everything we athletes had trained for—years of sweat, dedication, sacrifice. But on the other hand, I felt that snowboarding's essence was slipping away. Skiing had never embraced us. They'd mocked us, excluded us, and now they wanted to mold us. The individuality that drew me to the sport in the first place was at risk of becoming lost.

Seeking comfort, I reached for my Bible on the bedside table, flipping it open at random, hoping to find guidance. The verse I landed on stopped me in my tracks: Psalm 16:11. "You will show me the way of life, granting me the joy of your presence and the pleasure of living with you forever."

I couldn't help but smile. It wasn't the first time I'd opened to exactly the verse I needed. This, right here, was what I needed. The Olympics, the injury, the politics—all of it felt huge, but I was reminded that I didn't have to get bogged down by every circumstance. God had a purpose for me that went beyond titles or medals. This was about pursuing what I loved with integrity, about doing something meaningful and true to who I was. Maybe the Olympics could fit into that, maybe they couldn't. But my purpose was so much bigger than a single event.

As I closed the Bible, a quiet peace settled over me. The road ahead would be tough, but I wasn't walking it alone. I didn't have to be Terje or anyone else—I just had to follow the path that felt right for me.

I reached for a pen and paper, jotting down the intentions that had been forming in my heart:

- **STAY TRUE TO MYSELF**—whatever the pressure.
- **EMBRACE CHALLENGES WITH COURAGE**—define my own success.
- **REMEMBER WHY I LOVE THIS SPORT**—be thankful. Don't seek others' approval.
- **TRUST**—God's guidance will help me create my own path.

Reading over my words, I realized I was ready to commit to my own journey, whether that meant competing in the Olympics or not. I placed my hand on my knee, closed my eyes, and said a silent prayer, *God, please heal my knee quickly and completely.*

I guess I had some more growing to do.

CHAPTER 30
/ The Inaugural X Games /

YOU KNOW THAT LIST I MADE THE YEAR BEFORE—the one before my trip to Ischgl, full of goals I wasn't sure I'd ever accomplish?

Turns out, they weren't gone. Just—delayed.

The season didn't start with a dramatic comeback or some big headline moment. It started quietly—my body steady, my riding smooth, my heart finally at ease. After everything—the ACL surgery, the doubt, the frustration—I felt like myself again. Maybe even better.

But yeah...I guess it ended up in the headlines after all.

I'd won every halfpipe contest so far, but this time, it wasn't about proving anything. The pressure I had been carrying had lifted, and in its place was something lighter. Gratitude. That injury had brought me to my knees—literally and figuratively—but it also gave me perspective. I saw how blessed I was just to be out there, doing what I loved.

And I wasn't about to miss a single chance to live it to the fullest.

When the invitation came to compete in a brand-new event called the X Games, I couldn't help but wonder if the hype was real. ESPN promised it would put snowboarding into every household around the world—calling it the "Olympics of action sports." Big words.

The first-ever event was set for Snow Summit, California, from January 30 to February 2, 1997. A whole new platform—and a massive new audience.

At competitor check-in, Tina and I scanned the itinerary of events: snowboarding, ice climbing, snow mountain bike racing, super-modified shovel racing... *Wait, what?*

"Super-modified shovel racing?" I asked, raising an eyebrow.

The woman behind the table lit up, clearly thrilled I'd noticed.

"Oh yes!" she said, eyes wide. "Think street luge meets mad scientist—sleds built from hardware store scraps, roll cages, nitrous tanks... the whole deal. And yep, they race them straight down the mountain."

Tina and I exchanged a look.

"What in the world...?" I muttered.

Welcome to the X Games.

Despite the quirks, a charged excitement hung in the air. ESPN had transformed Snow Summit's base area with towering banners, massive screens, and sponsor tents handing out free swag. Crowds gathered around a giant skateboarding halfpipe, while cameras captured every angle—both in the village and on the hill at each venue. Triple-story scaffolding rose at the base and alongside each course, giving judges and spectators a prime, bird's-eye view of the action.

This wasn't just another snowboard event—it was a full-blown media spectacle, the likes of which our sport had never seen.

Even with the hype and history being made, I couldn't ignore that some things still hadn't caught up. The X Games were a huge step forward for our sport—but not everything felt equal yet. That fight for equal prize money was still in the back of my mind, but it wasn't what was fueling me at that moment. I'd been outspoken about it for a long time, and I wasn't about to stop just because we were at a new event—even if I wasn't making a noticeable impact. I knew I'd have more of a voice if I was winning, so I kept pushing.

Truthfully, though, that wasn't why I wanted to win. I was competitive to my core. I loved the strategy, the adrenaline, the mental chess of it all.

Lisa—an all-around powerhouse—was at the X Games, working her magic and running the Boarding for Breast Cancer booth. She used the massive crowds as an opportunity to educate women about breast health right there in the village tent. But she wasn't just handling B4BC—she was also advocating for us.

Acting as our PR agent, she lined up interviews, organized an autograph session, and pushed hard for greater visibility for Tina and me. She believed in our presence—on the snow and in the spotlight—and she made sure others saw it too. She knew this was the event to capitalize on, to get us out there in the media. We needed that kind of behind-the-scenes support—and no one was pushing harder. Lisa was a major secret to our success.

The halfpipe event was held at the top of the resort, far from the noise and chaos of the base area. It was a relief to get some breathing room—but the stakes were still high. On competition day, the vibe was fun and laid-back. It actually reminded me a bit of the Burton U.S. Open, my favorite event—just with way more cameras and these random pauses for commercial breaks.

That part was new. Every so often, we had to stop the competition so the network could run ads on live TV. It felt strange—overly media-driven. Naturally, we all made fun of it. "Hold up! Gotta give the Pizza Pockets their moment." It added a layer of comedy that helped keep things light.

The best part of this contest was the format. Once you made the top eight for finals, everyone got two runs—but only your highest-scoring run counted. That took some of the pressure off, giving us the freedom to throw down riskier tricks and push progression.

In the final, I landed a solid run that included two of my biggest tricks: a backside 540 and a frontside 720. I was the first woman ever to land a 720 in the halfpipe, and sticking it sealed my win at the very first X Games.

Right after my run, an interviewer shoved a mic in my face. "Great run! What do you think about the X Games?"

I was still catching my breath, grinning wide. "The competition's a lot of fun. It's great to be out here with everyone. I just really love snowboarding, I guess."

I laughed, half-wondering how that answer would come across on air. People always wanted to hear the deeper meaning behind what we did—something that made snowboarding sound bigger than just riding down a mountain.

But honestly? It was that simple: I just really loved snowboarding.

That didn't mean it defined me. It just meant I was right where I was supposed to be. Life had its own twists and turns—just like the mountain—and I was learning that staying grounded and flexible was the key to not taking any of it for granted.

As I stepped off the snow, Don, one of the event's directors, waved me over. "Hey, Shannon, come with me for the awards ceremony. Ya know, there are over thirty thousand people here today, and we're broadcasting to millions across 168 countries. You're about to be a household name. The X Games are going to change snowboarding and probably your life forever!"

The enormity of it hit me. Snowboarding had gone from being perceived by the mainstream as a fringe sport—full of hoodlums and antiestablishment types—to prime-time TV in less than a decade. And now we were here, girls included, making history with the amount of TV coverage. I looked around at the crowd, the banners, the massive production, and realized: this was the moment. Snowboarding—our sport—was officially on the map.

No one gave us a blueprint for building a snowboarding career—we had to create it ourselves. We didn't wait on the sidelines for someone to tell us how it was done. We figured it out by connecting with the industry and proving our value—through every contest run, every photo, every story, every video part. And when you're building something from scratch, you can't ease up once the momentum kicks in. You have to keep evolving, pushing boundaries, and showing new ways you bring something to the table. It's not just about competing—it's about inspiring, connecting, and becoming someone the audience relates to.

As the X Games wrapped, it was clear we'd moved the needle for women in snowboarding. The riding spoke for itself—strong and technical. But the prize money gap still lingered like an unwanted echo. Visibility was only part of the equation—real change needed to happen behind the scenes.

It felt like the right moment to take the conversation higher. I decided to bring it to someone I respected deeply: Jake Burton Carpenter. Jake had always been approachable, with a calm, grounded way of making people feel heard. Even though I was nervous, I set up an appointment.

The opportunity came while I was at Burton headquarters, just before a big sales meeting. Jake liked to have the entire company involved in those gatherings, along with a few team riders. It was his way of keeping things connected—business and athletes in sync.

When I arrived at his office, it felt like an archive of snowboarding history. Vintage photos lined the walls—shots of Jake on an old Backhill snowboard, legendary moments with Craig Kelly and Jeff Brushie, and one of the original Burton boards from 1977. A leather couch sat across from the door, a coffee table in front welcoming you in. On it lay a neatly stacked pile of note cards. It was clear—Jake wasn't just building a brand; he was living it. He handed me a couple of 5x7 note cards—his signature move. He gave them to everyone he met with, a quiet reminder to take notes, to pay attention, to keep learning. Jake took his meetings seriously, and he was always a good listener.

I took a seat across from him, and he leaned in, fully present.

"So," he asked, "what's up? What would you like to talk about?"

At that moment, my nerves melted away. Jake had this energy like a dad—easy to talk to, genuinely eager to hear what you had to say. I took a deep breath.

"Well," I began, "I just wanted to say I think it's great you've always offered equal prize money at the U.S. Open—for the winners. But it's only for those top spots. I really think it's time we—women—have an equal total prize purse."

He immediately started jotting notes on his card. I was ready with my reasons—a whole list, in fact. But before I could even get rolling, Jake looked up, smiled, and said, "Yes—I totally agree with you."

Well, that was easy.

I didn't even get to explain what no one else seemed to grasp: people always said there weren't enough women to justify a full equal purse, or that only a handful of us could ride at the highest level. But I believed—and still believe—if you invest in women, they'll rise to it. More girls will go pro, and progression will accelerate. It might seem backward to invest before the results show up—but that's exactly what makes it work.

"Are you coming to the sales meeting this week?" he asked.

I nodded—that's why I was at the office, to join the Burton crew for the event.

Then Jake asked me something I didn't expect.

"Would you come onstage with me to introduce this idea?" he asked. "It'll be the perfect time to announce that we're implementing equal prize purses at the 1998 U.S. Open—this year." Jake didn't mess around.

At the sales meeting—in the conference room—there was a stage set up, with all the sales reps from around the world packed in. I was nervous to get on stage with Jake. Public speaking wasn't my thing, and my heart was racing. But Jake sensed it right away.

Before we went on stage, he handed me a few notes he'd scribbled on one of his 5x7 note cards.

"Don't worry—just follow my lead," he said, smiling. "Just tell the audience how you came into my office asking for equal prize money, no big deal, okay? You're going to do great. Then I'll do the rest of the talking."

And he was right. He led, did most of the talking, and when it was my turn, I kept it simple. But the energy in the room was electric. I could feel it—this was big for everyone. When the announcement was made, the entire room erupted in applause. You could feel the shift, like something important had just clicked into place.

I was grateful that Jake had made it feel so effortless. He was a fair, smart business guy—loved and respected by everyone, but also a little feared, because as he liked to remind us (with a smirk): "Don't eff it up." He had a profound connection with everyone. He wasn't just the founder—he was embedded in every part of the company. That's why, at events, we didn't say, "Thanks to our sponsor, Burton." We said, "Thanks, Jake."

It was instinctive, unspoken. Everyone just understood.

That moment with Jake wasn't just about prize money—it was about being seen. And from that point on, at the most important event in our industry, and in our history—the U.S. Open—we were equal, and it meant the world to me.

Thanks, Jake!

CHAPTER 31
/ Nagano or Bust /

NO WOMAN HAD EVER LANDED a McTwist in competition—but I was planning to try it, with my Olympic dreams hanging in the balance. For anyone not fluent in snowboard lingo, a McTwist is an upside-down 540-degree spin. The trick was originally done on a skateboard by Mike McGill (hence the name), and later adapted into snowboarding. You take off from the backside wall of the halfpipe—on your heels—and launch into a full flip and spin. You're upside down in the air, rotating, and then (hopefully) landing clean on the downhill transition.

That trick wasn't just another move. It was risky—and if I could pull it off, it might be the difference between watching the Olympics from my couch or standing at the top of the halfpipe, not only wearing the U.S. team jacket, but having a winning run once I got there.

We had three Olympic qualifiers—Sugarloaf, Mount Bachelor, and Mammoth. Only three men and three women would automatically make the team. One additional wildcard spot would go to either the men's or women's side, depending on who the coaches believed had the best chance of reaching the podium.

I didn't want to count on that.

Here's the thing to note—freestyle riders didn't have coaches. None of us did. Snowboarding just wasn't at that stage yet. We were still in the early days of competition, figuring things out as a crew. We traveled together, gave each other tips during sessions, and no one was analyzing video footage. You either landed the trick, or you worked it out with the help of your friends. Coaching wasn't even something we thought to ask for—we were the coaches.

So when it came time to assign a "halfpipe coach" for the first-ever Olympic team, there wasn't some deep pool of experienced snowboard trainers to pull from. There was exactly one: Pete "Delge" del'Giudice, from Mammoth.

Delge made sense—his son was a snowboarder, he was always around the Mammoth scene, and he genuinely cared. So they gave him the role.

Picture Delge—mustache, receding hairline, a voice like your local mechanic. A laid-back dad who sounded like he could rotate your tires while giving you pointers on your frontside air. He wasn't the clipboard type. He was the guy chatting with the riders at the bottom of the half-pipe and handing out encouragement.

Before the Olympics, Delge had run a steel fabrication business. He'd coached alpine skiing, and eventually became Mammoth's first freestyle snowboard coach. He was a surfer before he ever stepped on a snow-board. In a way, he was the perfect fit for that moment—because no one really knew what Olympic snowboarding was supposed to look like yet. And honestly? That felt about right.

As for the schedule and logistics beyond the qualifying contests—I wasn't about to jinx myself by planning that far ahead. If I made the Olympic team, my family would have to scramble to figure it out. Flights, hotels, all of it.

I'd finished fifth at the first qualifier at Sugarloaf, not ideal, but the conditions were icy and rough, and hardly anyone had a clean run. You could feel the high stakes in everyone's nerves. No one wanted to admit the pressure we were all under—so while the atmosphere still had the usual fun camaraderie, there was a personal tension we were all wrestling with.

Mount Bachelor went better: I took second place. That result put me back in the game—barely. Michelle Taggart and Cara-Beth Burnside had already locked in two of the three spots. Mammoth was my last shot.

Winning this final event would secure my place on the Olympic team.

So I poured everything into landing that McTwist before the final qualifier. Utah—one of the only places with a decent halfpipe at the time—would be my test run. If I couldn't stick it there, I knew I'd have to leave it out of my Mammoth run. And that might cost me the Olympics—because if I couldn't land it now, what were the chances I'd suddenly pull it off under Olympic pressure, with the world watching?

I pulled Dave in as my unofficial coach and hit the trampoline to break down the trick in a safer setup.

"All right, Dave, how exactly do I land this thing?" I huffed after what felt like my hundredth attempt—landing on my butt every single time instead of my feet.

Dave just smirked. "Easy. Just land it."

"Gee, thanks, Einstein," I shot back. "But, like...*how*?"

He shrugged. "Okay, okay. Just try a front flip and let me twist you midair."

I grabbed his hand, we gave it a try—and finally, I landed it. It felt like a breakthrough.

We drilled the motion over and over until it started to feel like second nature. But I knew doing it on the curved walls of a real halfpipe would be an entirely different challenge.

Still, I felt mentally ready.

I took it to the halfpipe on snow, but the conditions weren't ideal. I'd been hoping for warm and slushy spring-like weather, but instead it was windy, icy, and the walls were chewed up. Not exactly confidence-inspiring.

Each attempt got a little better—more rotation, more control, more spin. I inched closer with every try. And then...finally, two clean landings.

Not perfect, but solid enough for my body and mind to finally *get* the trick.

A storm started to roll in, and I took it as my cue. I'd done what I came to do.

Time for Mammoth.

The scene at Mammoth was festive—American flags and sponsor banners lined the pipe—but it was equally intense. This was our final shot to make the Olympic team, and the stakes were higher than ever.

The usual friendly vibes were thrown out in a last-minute frenzy of panic. We were all chasing a once-in-a-lifetime aspiration.

I hadn't landed the McTwist during qualifying practice. I made the finals with conservative runs, playing it safe just to get through.

The final format was simple: the top combined score from two runs would win it. We all wished it had been updated to the X Games format—best run out of two wins. That would've helped progression: land your safe run first, then push it on the second.

Visibility was poor. The halfpipe was icy, but at least we were given two practice runs before the finals. After those frustrating warm-up laps, I skidded to a stop at the edge of the pipe, where my parents, Sean, and Dave were waiting.

"I still haven't landed my McTwist," I said, the panic rising in my chest.

Sean gave my shoulder a squeeze. "You always mess up in practice, then kill it when it counts. Just go for it."

But this time felt different. My nerves weren't fueling me; they were shaking me.

Dave pointed to a steeper section of the wall. "Hit it higher. Ride off your tail—remember what we practiced—tuck your chin, look at your back armpit as you rotate."

They were right. Let the board ride longer so I didn't pre-spin—then commit. Just go for it.

I started the hike back to the top, clutching my board, heart pounding in my chest. At the top, I took a deep breath, exhaling the weight of every failed attempt. The cold air burned my lungs. The crowd buzzed behind the fences. Competitors were off doing their own thing—but I was oblivious to all of it. I blocked everything out.

I strapped in, waiting as the girls ahead of me took their turns. I went inward, visualizing my run over and over.

Then the starter's voice cut through my focus: "You're all set to drop, Shannon. The judges are ready." He smiled.

Somehow, I felt at peace. I smiled back at him and dropped into the pipe.

My body shifted to autopilot. The noise, the icy ruts—all of it disappeared. I moved through my run like I was watching it from the outside.

When it was time for the McTwist, I coached myself through it, Dave's voice in my head: "Wait for it...ride it longer...now."

My edge locked in. I waited. Committed.

And then—everything went blank for a split second. I honestly don't remember the motion.

But suddenly, my eyes were on the landing.

And I stuck it. Clean.

I pulled off the McTwist.

But I wasn't done yet—I couldn't let up. I kept my head down, my focus tight. I still had one more run to execute.

My turn came quickly. It was a repeat—solid execution—and I landed everything without a hitch.

I made my way over to where my family was waiting behind the competitor fence, their eyes locked on the scoreboard.

First place.

Dave and my family were in tears. We collapsed into hugs—crying, laughing, barely able to believe what had just happened.

All that pressure came crashing over me in one overwhelming wave. I'd done it.

I had become the first woman to land a McTwist in competition—and with it, I officially sealed my spot on the U.S. Olympic Snowboard Team.

On the men's side, Todd Richards, Ross Powers, and Ron Chiodi had secured their spots. Ron was being called "the dark horse" of the season—an East Coast rider who had only recently started landing podiums and wasn't widely known before the qualifiers.

The moment was still sinking in as I stepped off the podium. I was exhausted, overwhelmed, and buzzing with adrenaline—but there was no time to process it. There was still a lot more packed into the late afternoon: one wildcard spot left to fill, a press conference, and of course, all the questions about next-step logistics.

The final slot came down to Barrett Christy or Bjorn Leines. Word of the deliberation spread fast, and chatter filled the Mammoth lodge as everyone waited for the final announcement. It felt like it took forever.

In the end, the coaches—and whoever else was actually behind the decision—announced that they believed Barrett had the better shot at medaling. That was the deciding factor. Understandably, Bjorn—who had more overall points (earned at each Grand Prix qualifier)—was disappointed. Of course, I was excited to have Barrett on the team.

Next stop: the press conference.

The room was a mix of excitement, curiosity, and the usual clichés. One reporter tossed out the classic, "Shannon, can you tell me some snowboard lingo?"

I couldn't resist having a little fun with it. "Well, last I checked, we speak English. But if you're looking for trick names, there's a stalefish, roast beef..." I let the sarcasm hang in the air, hoping they'd catch on. I was rattling off the most ridiculous—though totally real—names for grabs. Anyone outside the snowboarding or skateboarding world would be completely lost hearing them.

Then came the inevitable team tension question.

"Barrett, there was some controversy about your selection over Bjorn Leines. How do you feel about that?"

Barrett handled it with grace, but you could tell the question made her—made all of us—feel awkward. I could feel the tension ripple across the table. We were making history as the first-ever Olympic snowboard team—and the media couldn't resist stirring the pot.

Another question went to Michelle about the uniform restrictions.

"How do you feel about not being able to choose your own outerwear?"

Michele sighed. "It's tough. We want to rep our sponsors—to look and feel like ourselves."

I nodded along. Our sponsors had been with us through everything—supporting us when the sport was still finding its footing, believing in us long before the Olympics came calling. Now, suddenly, we had no say. No input. No feedback. We were handed a standard-issue uniform from a ski outerwear company—approved by a committee that didn't even include snowboarders.

At the Olympics, individuality was replaced with regulation. And it cut deep.

Figure skaters were still allowed to design their own performance outfits—sequins, feathers, whatever helped them tell their story. But freestyle snowboarders weren't given that option. We couldn't express ourselves through what we wore, even though personal style was central to our sport.

Style mattered. It told the crowd who you were before you ever dropped in. And now, on the biggest stage in the world, we weren't allowed to be ourselves.

The irony wasn't lost on any of us. It felt like they wanted the snowboarding...without the snowboarders.

Then a reporter turned to Todd Richards. "How do you feel about Terje Håkonsen's boycott?"

Todd took a breath. "Honestly? A win without Terje feels hollow. But I'm here, and I'm ready."

It was the perfect response. Terje's absence cast a shadow, but we were all proud to represent snowboarding on this massive stage. We got through the rest of the questions with humor and the occasional eye roll, knowing the media still loved to paint us as the sport's rebellious outliers.

With the hoopla over, we had less than a week to prepare for Japan.

We were about to head to Nagano as the official U.S. Snowboard Team, and it felt like being launched into space—with no idea how we'd land. The U.S. Snowboard Team booked our flights and managed our logistics, so we assumed the same would go for our families.

But no—our families were left to figure it out on their own. They scrambled to find flights, book hotels, and navigate all the last-minute chaos no one had planned for. The stress was real, and the unknowns were piling up fast.

Ever tried to go to the Olympics last-minute? Turns out, nothing is available. Hotels were booked, flights were a mess, and we weren't sure if this was standard for every sport or just another "welcome to snow-boarding" kind of deal.

But one thing was clear: this was the chance of a lifetime.

I couldn't help but think back to the little-girl version of me—dreaming big, wishing I could become an Olympian someday. Years earlier, at my first World Cup contest, I'd watched my dad pick up an Olympic flag that had been blown down by the wind. Maybe that moment was a serendipitous glimpse of what was coming all along.

Now it was real. And I was going to soak in every single detail.

If I had anything to say about it—this trip was going to be fun. I was ready to embrace every twist and turn.

CHAPTER 32

/ Spirited Arrival /

WE WERE THE DIRTBAGS OF THE OLYMPICS.

Our plane descended through the clouds, snow-capped peaks of Nagano rising below us. We were snowboarders—unruly, unpolished, and still unsure if we even belonged here.

It was like someone had let the misfits crash the biggest, fanciest party on earth.

The mainstream didn't know what to do with us. We were more of a Jamaican bobsled team than a finely-tuned Olympic machine—rolling into Japan with baggy pants, mismatched gear, and a collective, "What now?" attitude. Not a single person on our team had grown up dreaming of this through snowboarding. The idea had never existed in our sport. No four-year plans. No podium manifestos.

And yet, here we were: the first-ever U.S. Snowboard Halfpipe Team.

We didn't even have a printed itinerary. Our newly assigned team manager, Deb, rattled off the plan: grab credentials, take Olympic headshots, pick up our gear, check into the Village, walk in the Opening Ceremony...then catch a bus to the halfpipe venue outside the city, where we'd be based for the rest of the Games.

None of us knew much about Deb—where she came from, what her background was, or how she ended up managing snowboarders. But she was clearly in charge of getting us where we needed to go. She was upbeat, approachable, and easy to work with. Deb became our go-to for everything unrelated to snowboarding: travel, paperwork, logistics, and uniforms.

We didn't bother her unless we had to, but it was comforting knowing she was there—someone to help us navigate the chaos of our first Olympics.

The flight had taken ten hours, and by the end of it, we were somewhere between delirious and amped. The stewardess had brought us champagne from first class after takeoff—a nod to the fact that we were, technically, Olympians. We clinked glasses and laughed at the absurdity of it all.

Cara-Beth Burnside—or CB for short—had been quietly nursing her own endless refills throughout the flight. Now she was blinking hard under the glare of the cabin lights, fumbling with her immigration form.

"Hey CB, you need some help with that?" I asked as she brushed her hair out of her eyes.

"Uh, yeah," she mumbled, squinting like the light itself was a betrayal.

I popped the cap off my pen. "Alright, what's your passport number?"

After some digging through her seatback pocket—and a few more groans—she found it. I started filling out the form like a school field trip chaperone, laughing to myself. Olympians. Right.

When we finally touched down, CB was up and wrestling with her backpack in the overhead bin, clearly off-balance from all the in-flight champagne. One moment, our whole team was grabbing their stuff to head out together; the next, I was alone with CB. *Thanks, guys! Way to keep an eye out for your teammates.*

I was a little annoyed that no one noticed her state or offered to help, but I couldn't just leave her to fend for herself.

"CB, you're gonna need this," I said, handing her the passport and immigration forms she'd left stuffed in her seatback pocket. "Let's put that inside your jacket pocket, okay?"

"Oh yeah, oops." She laughed as I tucked them into her coat. She started walking toward the back of the plane.

"This way...here, go ahead." I let her pass me so I could keep an eye on her, gently holding her jacket in case she swayed or wandered. Together, we made our way through customs and met up with the rest of the crew to board the bus to the next stop—getting our credentials and Olympic outfits.

CB was a legend, no doubt about it. Long before she became a pro snowboarder, she'd been one of the only women skating vert ramps—tearing it up in the male-dominated world of skateboarding. She had grit—that tough exterior and a keep-your-distance-from-me vibe. I respected it, even if I didn't always understand it.

And always tagging along was her friend and photographer—the queen of backhanded compliments.

"Did you see CB today? She's totally nailing her tricks." She would toss out lines like that right before my halfpipe run, always glancing at me to see if she'd thrown me off.

It didn't work. I knew exactly what she was doing. Her little digs only fed my competitive fire. Honestly? I should've thanked her. She was doing me a favor. Because when someone tried to throw me off, I doubled down. That kind of pressure made me laser-focused—like, bring it on. And when the contest was over? I let it go. I knew how weird people could get when emotions ran high. CB was always cool with me. She worked hard, rode strong, and kept to herself. We just weren't wired the same.

So yeah—we were probably the last two people on earth you'd expect to end up in this moment together.

But there we were.

We finally regrouped with the team at baggage claim and boarded the bus bound for the Olympic Village. Once again, no one seemed to notice CB was still out of it—so guess who got stuck as her unofficial chaperone? Yep. Me. Apparently, I'd been promoted to team babysitter.

Whatever.

When we arrived—somewhere—none of us really knew where we were going. We pulled up to this big, warehouse-looking building, and a guy in a Team USA jacket started herding us like cattle into a makeshift processing room.

Step one: grab your shiny new Team USA jacket.

Step two: *boom*—straight into the photo room.

"Hats off!" the photographer barked.

Cue the collective groan. Hat hair for our historic Olympic team photo? *Click*. Nailed it.

Would that happen to the figure skaters, the ones treated like royalty? Yeah, probably not.

Then they handed us our credentials, all official-looking, and proceeded to give the stern warning: "You need these everywhere—don't lose them. Wear them all the time, even when you're snowboarding."

Only the women had to go through the official gender test, which, thankfully, didn't involve getting naked—just a quick cheek swab. So, now I had an add-on badge that scientifically, officially declared me a girl. Guys posing as girls just to win an Olympic medal? I couldn't wrap my head around taking sports so seriously that you'd resort to cheating like that. Then again, I was a snowboarder—a world where we'd never even imagined Olympic medals in the picture.

After completing phase one, we moved on to the next stop: the gear stations—a massive warehouse alive with the energy of Olympians. Athletes of every build, yet all sculpted and powerful, America's finest, focused and single-minded in their purpose: bring home gold. I couldn't help but feel like an outsider in this realm. These were the elite, the finely-tuned products of years of structured training, while I was a snowboarder from a sport that was just starting to find its

way in the Olympics. Part of me wished I could've had the same regimen—a structured path, the discipline I knew and loved from my
gymnastics days. We were the mutts among purebreds, and though
I'd come to embrace that scrappy identity, the contrast hit harder
here than ever.

Our first stop handed us each a massive navy wheeled duffel bag
emblazoned with the Team USA logo, followed by a matching carry-on
and backpack. Our team was charging ahead, but instead of getting frustrated, I surrendered to hanging back and helping CB. Deb, clipboard in
hand, appeared beside us—ready to shepherd the stragglers through the
labyrinth of Olympic-issued gear with the efficiency and seriousness of a
general leading her troops.

"The small wheely bag is for your medal award outfit, okay?" she said.

CB and I nodded.

"I'll help you girls out. Those pieces are at the first stations here, so
don't worry. Everything else goes in the big duffel, okay?"

As I folded the medal outfit—navy outerwear pants and the jacket
we'd worn for our team photo—into that little wheelie bag, it hit me:
these weren't just clothes.

I'd read somewhere that only a fraction of Olympians ever made it to
the podium. But that tiny sliver of a chance—that was enough to light a
fire in me.

And I wondered—would I be wearing this?

Note to self: *Yes. It's going to happen. Might as well take the optimistic
approach.*

More than anything, I wanted to soak it all in—every weird, wild, unforgettable moment of the Olympics. We moved down the line piece by
piece, collecting all seventy-two items of Team USA gear from volunteers
stationed at each labeled table:

- **SHORT-SLEEVED TEE.**
- **LONG-SLEEVED TEE.**

- **COTTON SOCKS.**
- **THICK SNOWBOARD SOCKS.**
- **BASE LAYERS.**
- **NECK GAITER.**
- **AN EXTRA-LONG NAVY JACKET** for the opening ceremony.
- **HIKING BOOTS.**
- **A COWBOY HAT.**
- **A CRISP WHITE POLO.**
- **HIGH-WAISTED TAPERED JEANS**—not exactly on trend.

Then I held up the Norwegian-style wool sweater with a smirk.

"Fancy," I said, raising an eyebrow at its old-school skier vibe. But honestly? The quality was solid.

CB grimaced, still wrestling with her wheel bag's handle. I reached over and helped her out and kept moving—grabbing clothing and accessories for every possible Olympic occasion.

At one point, CB held up a pair of brown leather business pumps with a look of confusion. The volunteer explained they were for post-Olympics events and special occasions—like a visit to the White House.

"Oh no, I'm never—" she muttered, shoving them to the bottom of her bag.

"This outfit completes the look with those pumps," I laughed, holding up a pair of polyester pleated slacks, a white flowing blouse, and a silky scarf. "No way I'm wearing any of this. My mom wore stuff like this in the '80s."

We collected uniforms for every possible occasion—casual wear, outerwear, full business attire. There was a jean jacket, a leather jacket, a set of trading pins, and even a fitting for our Olympic ring—chunky, gold-plated, and straight out of a high school class ring catalog.

And one thing CB and I agreed on wholeheartedly: these outfits were hideous. Every single one of them. And yeah—it bothered us both.

Finally, I zipped up my overstuffed bag and helped CB with hers, making sure we were ready to roll. The team and the bus were already waiting. Deb must've figured that since I'd been helping CB, we were getting along great. So, as we shuttled over to our dorm-style apartments in the Olympic Village, she assigned us as roommates.

CB and me? Let's just say we didn't exactly mix. We were oil and vinegar. But hey—that's how you make a good salad dressing.

CHAPTER 33

/ Miss-Fits /

AFTER THE WHIRLWIND OF BUSES, credentials, and gear pickup, CB and I finally made it to our dorm room in the Olympic Village. We opened the door to find a spread of welcome gifts neatly laid out on each bed—like a personal celebration for just making it here. There was framed paper-cut artwork of a mountain scene, stuffed Snowlets (the four official Nagano owl mascots in bright aqua, purple, green, and pink), even more trading pins, keychains, chocolates, and cookies. All these tiny tokens felt like a reminder that—for once—we were the VIPs.

Seeing how thoughtful and beautifully curated it all was, I felt this unexpected rush of gratitude. *Wow. This is really happening.* Japan is known for thoughtful gifts, and I couldn't help but wonder if every host country treated their athletes this way.

Exhausted, I fell into bed, barely processing that tomorrow we'd be diving headfirst into Olympic life.

"Wake up, girls...breakfast in thirty minutes." Deb's voice floated through the door, jolting me out of a half-dream. Her voice had way too much cheer for this hour. I groaned a mumbled reply, pulling myself upright, feeling the kind of heaviness that only comes with serious jet lag—like gravity had tripled overnight.

"And don't forget," she added, "white collared shirt, jeans, belt, boots, and your credentials!"

I let out another groan, already dreading the uniform awaiting me. Across the room, CB grumbled even louder, her eye mask firmly in place as if she could will the morning away. Reluctantly, I dragged myself to the shower, and afterward, rummaged through my new Olympic bag for the clothes required. But as I pulled on the white polo and wrestled with the high-waisted jeans, I caught sight of myself in the mirror—and snorted.

"This is the ugliest ever," I muttered, half to myself. CB had shuffled into the bathroom to brush her teeth, and she stopped mid-scrub, squinting at me.

"Wait, we're really supposed to wear those mom jeans?" Her face was a blend of horror and disbelief.

I yanked the high-waisted pants up to my bra line with a deadpan expression. "Full commitment!"

CB shook her head in defiance, trying not to laugh. "No way, dude. Let's just wear our own clothes," she said, spitting into the sink.

I was in total agreement. We were the snowboarders—the rule-breakers. We didn't do "mandatory" unless it involved mandatory fun. I swapped the polo for my favorite black long-sleeve, threw on my usual jeans, and immediately felt like myself again.

"Much better," I said, grinning at CB, who had opted for her own jeans and a black sweatshirt. We strutted down to the dining area, a couple of renegades in a sea of conformity. But as we walked in, the stares hit us hard—every single person in the room was decked out in the official Team USA uniform, perfectly coordinated and crisp, looking like a catalog ad for national pride.

Leaning over to CB, I smirked. "Shredders represent."

We slid into seats next to Deb, trying not to crack up at our rebellion, but Deb's raised eyebrow told me she wasn't amused.

"Girls...you do know you need to wear your official Team USA outfits, right?" Her tone was gentle, but firm—there was no mistaking the directive.

Meanwhile, the rest of our team thought it was hilarious that we hadn't gotten the memo—or maybe that we ignored it on purpose. A few chuckles and smirks passed around the table as we stood there in our "non-regulation" jeans and black tops, clearly the odd ones out. CB rolled her eyes, and I quickly piped up, "But they're so...um, well, horrific!" I stammered, realizing a second too late that Deb was also wearing the uniform. "I mean, just not quite us," I added, trying to cover my misstep.

Deb just gave a knowing smile. "I get it. But here's the thing—you're no longer just pro snowboarders; you're Team USA Olympic athletes now. You're representing America, and that's kind of a big deal."

Her words hit harder than I'd expected. She was right. I sighed. "Fine. We'll change after breakfast."

Deb shook her head. "No, girls, run up and change now—your breakfast will still be here when you get back."

Defeated, CB and I exchanged a quiet look and trudged back to our room. But as I adjusted my collared shirt in the mirror, something shifted. This wasn't just about appearance—it was about accepting a responsibility I'd never imagined I'd carry.

Buttoning that shirt, I realized I really was part of Team USA. Pride and disbelief flooded my chest. I had made it—and even though I'd already been named to the team after the qualifying contests, it felt completely different now that I was actually living it.

The Olympics—growing up, watching them on TV, wishing I could be one of those athletes—had always felt like a distant, impossible dream. And now? This was wild. My wildest dream had come true—just not in the way I'd ever pictured it.

"Delight yourself in the Lord, and He will give you the desires of your heart." That verse had always resonated with me—but I never imagined it would unfold like this. Not through gymnastics or figure skating, but through snowboarding—the sport I loved, the one I never thought would lead me here.

It was clear now: God wasn't just fulfilling my dream. He'd been guiding every step, using each twist and turn to shape a path uniquely mine. I had stepped into the unknown, and he was revealing something far greater than anything I could have planned on my own.

Still, deep down, I sensed this wasn't the finish line. Maybe I was here for more than medals or moments. Maybe this was about purpose. His purpose. Looking back at that little girl with big dreams, it all felt light years away—but that's how he works. Quietly. Powerfully. And always on time.

I glanced over at CB, who was also reluctantly pulling at her uniform. We couldn't have been more different—me, the clean-cut, almost-cheerleader type (though I would *never* actually do that; cheerleading was beyond cringe in my high school), and she was the total opposite. Yet here we were, standing side by side, representing our country and embracing the quirks.

I guess this was part of the ride—uniforms, unexpected friendships, and the weird, wild honor of making Olympic history. What other surprises were in store?

CHAPTER 34
/ No One Gets Us /

I CALLED HOME TO SHARE A FEW STORIES—turns out, I was the headline. No hello, no how's it going. Mom skipped straight to it: "Did you know you and CB are all over the news as 'disrespectful snowboarders'?"

I nearly dropped the phone. "Wait, what?"

"Apparently, you and CB caused a stir by wearing untucked shirts and regular jeans to breakfast," she said, laughing. "Reporters are saying you snubbed the official team outfits."

I blinked. "Who even saw us? We were just in the dining hall for, what—five minutes? That's the scandal of the day?" I shook my head. "They must have spies or something."

"Guess so," she said. "They're calling you rebellious...ungrateful... even unpatriotic."

"Unbelievable," I muttered, more amused than annoyed. It was a perfect reminder to take media coverage with a massive grain of salt. We weren't trying to make a statement—we were just trying to feel like ourselves. Somehow, that got spun into a national headline.

When I told CB, she raised an eyebrow, laughed, and said, "Seriously? I'm calling my mom to see if she's seen it."

Mom also tossed in a quick update on Dad, Sean, and "Cousin Kevin"—who wasn't actually my cousin, just a close family friend. Sean couldn't get on the same flight as the others, but he'd make it just in time for the main event.

"Keep an eye out for your dad and Kevin during the Opening Ceremony," she said. "They've got nosebleed seats—oh, that's right—you haven't heard: Dad and Kev ended up sleeping in a restaurant."

Family didn't exactly get the VIP treatment. Classic Dad—winging it through Japan, probably loving every second of the chaos.

We updated the rest of our team with the "scandal," and it got a solid round of eye rolls. At least now we had something to joke about. It gave us a little momentum as we pulled on yet another outfit for the press conference.

They called us Olympians. But judging by the press room, no one quite knew what to do with us.

Our first Olympic halfpipe team press conference was finally winding down—but wow, it had been a full-on endurance event. The reporters were eager, sure—but also hilariously out of their depth.

We sat shoulder to shoulder behind a long table, each with our own mic, staring into a dense thicket of media chaos just feet away.

Cameras clicked like popcorn in a microwave. Notepads flailed. The air buzzed with questions—some sincere, some straight up off-the-wall.

When it was Todd's turn, he gave the press his usual unfiltered self—dropping words like "sick," "gnarly," and "air," leaving reporters cocking their heads and scribbling notes they probably wouldn't understand later.

One of them tried to keep up.

"Todd, how do you keep from getting bored with all the questions about your team's...irreverence?"

He was clearly referring to the headlines back home—about CB and me wearing our own jeans and shirts instead of the official Team USA getup.

Todd didn't miss a beat.

"I envision you all totally naked," he said with a mischievous grin.

CB and I locked eyes, trying not to crack up as the room shifted uncomfortably. It was classic Todd—deflect with humor, never explain, never apologize. He knew exactly what they were talking about, and so did we.

Then a reporter leaned in, looking serious. "Barrett, what do you think you'd be doing if it wasn't snowboarding?"

Barrett didn't even blink.

"I had three goals as a kid: to be a fireman, a Solid Gold dancer, or go to the Olympics," she said with a chuckle. "Though I couldn't have imagined what sport I'd go for."

A few reporters gave polite laughs. Most just stared, unsure if she was serious or kidding. Barrett was gold—unapologetic and fully herself, even in a room full of farty old men who didn't get her vibe.

Then another reporter turned to me. "Can you explain the sudden popularity of snowboarding, which essentially went from the X Games to the Olympics overnight?"

I took a second, then leaned into the mic.

"Honestly? I have no idea," I said with a laugh. "When I started, you pretty much knew everyone who snowboarded. There weren't that many of us—we were like this weird little family. Now it's like snowboarding's taken on a life of its own, like we created something totally new."

The reporter raised his eyebrows. Like it hadn't occurred to him that the sport started small, built from the ground up. I could tell some of them genuinely wanted to understand—even if they were completely fumbling it. The session wrapped up with the best mic drop moment we could've asked for. A writer from *Transworld Snowboarding* magazine came forward, flashed a grin, and said, "You guys rule, dude."

We all lit up. A little slice of home in a room that didn't quite get us. Finally—someone who spoke our language.

As we left, passing the figure skaters on their way to their press conference, the contrast was almost laughable. They looked flawless—zipped into sleek jackets and crisp turtlenecks, like they'd just stepped out of an Olympic magazine spread.

And us? We looked like we were late for school pickup—buttoned polos, awkwardly belted jeans, stiff and out of place.

Snowboarding was supposed to be cool—trendsetting. Now it felt like we'd been dressed by someone's patriotic grandma, and I felt a flush of embarrassment. This wasn't us.

Back in our dorm room, I glanced at the Opening Ceremony gear I'd laid out for the big afternoon ahead. It was really happening—we were about to walk in the Olympic Opening Ceremony as part of Team USA.

We had to wear a mash-up of American style: navy nylon insulated pants, a white turtleneck (*Who even wears those anymore?*), a thick wool sweater, a red-and-navy scarf, a long insulated jacket with shiny gold buttons, waterproof hiking boots, cowboy hats, and sunglasses. It was an odd blend, for sure—but seeing it all laid out made the moment feel real.

Before we headed out, we snapped a few shots of us girls together—grinning and a little giddy. We were just trying to soak it all in. This was one of those once-in-a-lifetime moments you can't believe is real.

The whole thing took me back to being a kid—sitting cross-legged in front of the TV, eyes glued as each country paraded out with their flags. I remembered the thrill of watching athletes wave to the camera, knowing their families were cheering from home. It felt like magic—like the whole world paused for something bigger than all of us.

I couldn't help but wonder, would the Olympics elevate snowboarding—or change it into something that didn't feel like ours anymore?

Either way, the moment had arrived. We were making history. There was no turning back—time would tell.

We hopped on the bus for a quick fifteen-minute ride to the Olympic ceremony stadium—freestylers and racers sitting side by side. Two disciplines, one team. For the first time, we were actually hanging out together as the complete U.S. Snowboarding Team.

But let's be real—we didn't exactly roll in the same circles. Snowboard racers were all gates, times, and rules. Freestylers? We were about style, expression, going big, and throwing tricks.

Sometimes I'd glance over and wonder, *If racing was the goal, why not just stick with skis?* Nothing against it—they were cool in their own way. But I never really connected with that side of snowboarding. It was a different vibe...and to me, a whole different sport.

Outside the stadium, reporters swarmed. We stood in line with athletes from around the world—trading small talk, cracking jokes, trying to play it cool, even though we all felt the weight of the moment. And as we waited—lined up under our American flag—I had to admit, it was kind of awesome.

It was one of those milky-sky days—clouds overhead, but warm enough that we were toasty in our heavy Olympic wear. I'll give those outdated uniforms one thing: they were functional. We passed the time sizing up everyone else's gear, trading quiet commentary about who looked sharp.Greece kept it simple—they wore all black. Clean, minimal, nothing flashy. Funny enough, it's the only outfit I actually remember.

With every passing minute, the anticipation swelled—every team, every athlete, lined up on the cusp of something historic.

When it was finally our turn to move through the tunnel and onto the main floor of the stadium, the moment washed over me all over again. The roar of the crowd rippled through the venue, pulsing in sync with the beat of traditional Japanese drums echoing into the open air. Dancers in flowing kimonos moved with quiet grace, while children with bright, joyful smiles added an unexpected warmth to the spectacle.

The nerves were real—but so was the pride. To the whole world, we were Team USA.

Leading each country was a revered sumo wrestler, hand-in-hand with an adorable child. It was the sweetest, most surprising mix of tradition and pageantry.

As we walked, I waved at the camera every chance I got, hoping my mom might catch a glimpse of me from her spot on the couch back home.

But most of the spotlight was on figure skater Tara Lipinski—the fifteen-year-old phenom and youngest U.S. Olympian. She was mic'd up and glowing, with cameras tracking her every move.

Somewhere in that massive crowd, my dad and Kevin were out there too. I knew my dad would find me—he always did. He always had a way.

In the meantime, we athletes took our seats to watch the post-walk show. It was distinctly Japanese—elegant, intentional, and poetic. Not flashy or over the top, but deeply meaningful. A quiet reflection of the culture that was hosting us.

The ceremony closed with a flyover, smoke trailing behind in the colors of the Olympic rings—a bold and beautiful finish.

As the final notes faded and the stadium buzz quieted, our snowboard team was led toward the exit. The stands were nearly empty now, just a scattering of spectators making their way out.

That's when I heard it—his unmistakable whistle. I looked up, and there they were—Dad and Kevin. I ran toward them, but the bleachers kept us just out of reach for a hug. Still, just seeing them made my heart lift. They were all smiles as Dad raised his camera and snapped a photo of me—grinning and waving, my all-American cowboy hat on my head with a tiny flag still tucked in the band.

They looked at me—faces lit with pride—and it said everything. Seeing them grounded me in the best way. My family was here. Cheering me on. And it felt really, really good.

Dad called out, "I've got a story for you later—about the crazy journey getting here!"

I just grinned, soaking it in—the pride, the disbelief, the overwhelming joy that they were actually here, witnessing this moment with me.

As we walked out of the stadium, one thought settled in: the celebration was over. *Let the games begin.*

Opening Ceremonies—captured by my dad. Just so happy to see him there.

CHAPTER 35
/ Monkey Business /

I EXPECTED OLYMPIC ENERGY.

Instead, we landed in what felt like a ghost town.

The halfpipe was at Kanbayashi Ski & Snowboard Park, and we'd heard it sat next to a hot spring famous for monkeys who lounged in steaming baths all winter. It had even flashed across Sky News on the flight over—quirky and kind of hilarious at the time, like a cultural bonus wrapped in a tourist magnet. I pictured our nearby hotel buzzing with visitors—packed with travelers snapping photos, sipping tea, and watching cheeky monkeys soak in the steam.

But the monkeys were the only ones living it up—because when we pulled up to the hotel, this was not what we got.

Everything felt frozen and deserted. Because of the Olympics, the hotel had been closed to everyone but athletes—no tourists, no locals, no energy. What I'd imagined as warm and bustling turned out to be cold and echoey, like we'd been dropped into a sterile athlete quarantine center instead of an Olympic Village.

The massive hotel at Kanbayashi, which we were told would be "home" for the next few days, had an eerie, almost desolate feel. Usually, when we arrived for an event, the vibe was alive—familiar faces everywhere—and it felt like stepping into a gathering of friends rather than competitors. Snowboarders, regardless of nationality, would typically mingle, sitting together and sharing stories as one big crew. But here, we were separated into countries, and the camaraderie was diluted. It felt strange and unsettling.

The entire hotel was overtaken by the 125 halfpipe riders plus our teams' coaches, yet it didn't hum with the usual excitement. The common areas felt empty, the gift shop was locked, and half the building was dark. Even the corridors we did have access to were lit only by the dull glow of emergency lights, casting odd shadows against stark white walls. The atmosphere wasn't warm or welcoming. It felt like the hotel itself was holding its breath, amplifying the pressure of what lay ahead.

To add to the weirdness, almost everyone seemed to be coming down with something. Coughs echoed through the halls, and flushed faces hinted at fevers. Most teams were battling some kind of bug, which only made us feel more isolated. I wasn't about to let a cold or flu ruin my shot, so I kept my distance from anyone who looked sick and doubled down on vitamins and obsessive handwashing.

Our room was tiny and bare-bones—two twin beds separated by a nightstand in a boxy space that felt more like a holding cell than a haven. CB and I unpacked in silence, the strangeness of it all settling in. I finally flopped onto my bed, mentally drained but determined to stay sharp.

As CB sorted through her things, I grabbed a notepad from the nightstand and made a quick list of what I needed to focus on in practice the next day. I scribbled a reminder to myself—"I can win"—and tucked it into my shoe. Overcoming doubts had always been key to my success, and I didn't want to forget that, especially here.

Dinner took place in a large, echoing dining hall. Snowboarders from every team gathered, but with the sickness spreading, we were all extra cautious. Our group stuck close, leaning on each other for normalcy.

So far, our team was healthy, but we kept our distance—not because we were the snobby Americans, but because we didn't want to get sick.

After our second night's dinner, I headed to the business center to call my mom, hoping for a quick chat and maybe some comforting words. She gave me more details about how Dad and Kevin stayed in the restaurant—after discovering all the nearby hotels were fully booked with Olympic visitors, they ended up at a local spot, unsure of what to do next. The owners kindly offered them futons and set them up on the floor—true Japanese hospitality.

I told her about my experience at the Opening Ceremony, and she mentioned how proud everyone back home was. But then she said something surprising—she hadn't seen any of the snowboarders on TV. In fact, the news barely acknowledged snowboarding as a new Olympic sport. The coverage focused almost entirely on figure skater Tara Lipinski. Then she shared news we hadn't heard yet: Canadian snowboard racer Ross Rebagliati had just won the first-ever Olympic gold medal in giant slalom. The racers had competed at a different mountain, so we hadn't seen any of it. I was grateful for a slice of the outside world. Inside our Olympic bubble, we had no idea what was going on beyond our little corner of Japan. No phones. No news we could understand. No real connection to life back home.

I checked my email and saw a note from Burton's PR team about how I'd been scheduled to be on the cover of *Newsweek*. It felt surreal—an unexpected kind of validation. But then came the twist: President Bill Clinton and Monica Lewinsky's affair had blown up, taking over every headline—and apparently, my cover story too.

I had to laugh at the irony. Here I was, a girl about to showcase one of the biggest moments for our sport—the first Olympic snowboarding competition—ready to show the world what snowboarding was all about. And yet, somewhere in a *Newsweek* layout file, I was already yesterday's news, bumped by a scandal.

It was a reminder to hold everything with an open hand. No matter how big the moment, life has its own way of unfolding, and sometimes the spotlight shifts before you even get your turn.

The days that followed settled into a strict rhythm of training, eating, and resting, each one stretching out the anticipation. Every evening, we looked forward to unwinding at the Japanese onsen. The mountains in Japan have natural hot springs, and each hotel has a special Japanese bath for men and women. First, you take a shower, then dip—naked. But most of us Americans weren't quite ready for that, so we wore bathing suits. It felt awkward at first, but modesty won out.

The ritual of rinsing, soaking in the hot mineral bath, dunking into the cold tub, and rinsing again became a cherished routine, leaving me feeling refreshed and centered. Even the faint scent of cherry blossom soap and a few moments in the massage chair area felt like rare luxuries in an otherwise stark, high-stakes environment.

As Wednesday rolled around, CB and I had found this easy, surprising rhythm together. For all our differences, we'd settled into a kind of friendship that felt natural. I mean, we weren't braiding each other's hair or anything, but we'd ended up in this unspoken buddy system. Every practice, we'd check in, cheer each other on, talk about what we'd dialed in or messed up, and set plans for the next run. And suddenly, it wasn't just me against the halfpipe—it was us. Maybe we both needed that. It felt grounding, a small comfort in a sea of big pressures. And tomorrow was the big day.

The forecast was calling for warm weather, probably even rain, which just upped the unpredictability. But at least we were healthy, a small miracle considering the flu that seemed to be taking down the other teams one by one. It seemed like half of every country's team was sick, but thankfully none of the Americans had come down with anything. We all felt tired, but with nothing to do between training sessions, it was hard to tell if it was jet lag, low-level flu symptoms, or just boredom. I still wasn't landing my McTwist consistently, but I had a feeling that once they cut the pipe for the main event, I'd find my line.

Then Deb, our team manager, popped her head into the open door of our room, casually asking if anyone wanted to check out the snow monkeys. Snow monkeys. Somehow, that felt perfect. I was ready for anything to distract us from the nerves that were piling up around us. No one else wanted to go, but CB and I both jumped on it without hesitation.

We headed down the snowy path, the heaviness of the day lifting as we went. "The Natural Wonder of the Snow Monkey—Japanese Natural Hot Springs," read a sign ahead of us. As we rounded a corner, there they were, lounging on the rocks in all their relaxed, carefree glory, steam rising from the hot spring.

CB pointed at a chunky monkey sprawled out like he owned the place. "That one's got the art of relaxation nailed," she said, laughing.

"Total spa day vibes," I agreed, snapping a photo as a baby monkey waddled to the edge, peering up at us like we were the real spectacle. They were so cute.

And for a moment, the Olympics and the press and the expectations faded away. The monkeys didn't care about any of it. They were just there, in their snow-draped hot spring, living in their moment. Watching them, I felt it too—a lightness, a reminder of what it was like to be in this for the love of it. We walked back in silence, but with lighter hearts. That field trip to monkey spa land? Exactly the mood reset we didn't know we needed.

CHAPTER 36

/ Snowboarding's Olympic Debut Came with a Bang /

THAT MORNING HELD A STRANGE STILLNESS—humid, heavy, like the mountain itself was holding its breath. The light filtered through a veil of clouds, which seemed ready to burst. Darker ones loomed in the distance, a warning of what was to come.

The warm air filled my lungs with a deceptive softness, tricking me into relaxing when every nerve should be on edge. Yet, there was a crackling energy, an electricity that woke every cell in my body. Just me and the mountain—snow rising beside the steel scaffolding, all standing still, ready for what was about to unfold.

Beyond that was the hum of the lift, the distant clinks of drills, and the synchronized movement of Japanese skiers sideslipping in perfect unison—dragging their edges down the walls to smooth out the snow, as if even they were reverent, preparing the ground for whatever was about to unfold.

I walked toward the lift entrance and noticed no other riders had arrived. Delge, our coach, would be at the top of the pipe today like he was at every practice, but this moment wasn't about coaching. He was there for support—because, really, there wasn't much left to say.

I was the first to grab my gear from the team van and head toward the empty lift. The stillness was almost thrilling. No other teams had shown up yet, and I relished the quiet. I glanced down at the bib in my hand—#1. I knew I'd been assigned it, but now it pulsed with new weight. A sign? A fluke? Either way, it grounded me.

Each rider had to wear a stretchy bib over our jackets so the judges could ID us. We received them days ago at the start of our practices. Mine felt heavier today.

I looked up at the halfpipe, its massive walls carved into the slope like a sculpture. With each step, my boots crunched against the snow—sharp, echoing—like a heartbeat. My actual heart beat in sync with my footsteps, louder with every breath.

This is it, I thought. *This is the moment. Snowboarding's first real step onto the world stage.*

As I settled onto the chairlift, the halfpipe stretched out ahead—fifteen-foot walls so smooth they looked sculpted from marble. Beautiful. Daunting. Ready to be carved by over a hundred competitors. I hoped the warmth wouldn't wreck it, but even if it did, nothing could take away the fact: this was the nicest pipe I'd ever seen.

I closed my eyes, took a deep breath, and let a quiet wave of gratitude wash over me. I hadn't made it here alone—not by a long shot. A prayer rose in me—a quiet conversation with God—asking for strength, for safety, and for the day to unfold however it was meant to.

It's strange—you can't see God, but you know he's there. I felt a warmth beside me, a steady presence. Today was going to be special, though I wasn't sure why. But deep down, I knew I was loved, held, like the embrace of someone who knows you so well.

I refocused on the tasks at hand—no time for getting emotional; that would just drain my energy. I whispered my goals to myself. "One: have fun. Two: make it to the finals. Three: when it's time, go all in."

But before I could stop it, a tear slipped down my cheek, surprising me. It was like everything I'd been through—every fall, every bruise, every sacrifice—rose up all at once, demanding to be felt. Part of me wanted to let go, to let it wash over me. But I knew I couldn't, not now.

So I gathered it all up and held it inside, like fuel. I'd burn it when I needed it most. I took one more deep breath, and a wave of peace settled over me, something deeper than anything this world could give. I knew—whatever happened next, I was exactly where I was supposed to be. It was a feeling of pure freedom.

Determined, I got off the lift, breathing it all in. I was getting in the zone.

Not gonna lie—this format was tough. For the 1998 Nagano half-pipe, each rider had just two qualifying runs. In the women's division, the top four riders from each run moved on to the finals, making eight finalists. For the men: eight riders qualified from each run, giving them a total of sixteen finalists.

Everyone preferred the updated formats of X Games and the U.S. Open—two final runs with the best score counting. This setup allowed riders to shake off mistakes and push their limits, whereas our Olympic format left no room for error.

And yeah, my first qualifying run was rough—low speed, low amplitude. I barely made my trick around, wobbled on the landing. When the score flashed—twentieth out of twenty-two—ugh.

I had one more shot. Riding the lift back up, I mentally replayed my first run. I'd drop in higher, clean up my spins, and hold the McTwist longer. Just like in Mammoth. Dave's voice echoed in my head: "Wait a little longer before starting the spin."

Subtle advice, but spot on. Most of all, I had to feel it. I took a deep breath and let out a quick laugh—because if I wasn't having fun, the run wouldn't come together.

Delge caught my eye at the top and said what I needed to hear: "You can do this."

Good enough.

And this time, it did come together. I knew I hadn't hit my ceiling—I had more in the tank—but I rode well enough to land in third overall, just behind CB. We exchanged a look—part excitement, part relief. We'd done it. We were through to the finals.

The thought of riding alongside CB in the final round gave me a jolt of energy. But the thrill was bittersweet.

Barrett and Michelle had both taken hard falls and didn't make the cut. Watching them miss out, knowing how much they'd poured into this, stung. In the men's division, Ron Chiodi didn't make it either.

Now it was down to me, CB, Ross Powers, and Todd Richards. If Team USA was going to reach the podium—this was it. We were the last ones standing.

The vibe at the top of the pipe had shifted from anticipation to something raw, crackling, ready to explode. The crowd was a roaring wave, noisemakers blaring, horns echoing off the towering walls of the pipe.

Up here, every last one of us—coaches, board techs, athletes—was in serious mode. Gone were the jokes, the banter, the casual warm-ups. We were locked in. The only voice cutting through the tension was the Japanese announcer, booming over the loudspeakers, warning everyone to tread carefully on the slick, rain-soaked sides of the pipe.

Then came the delay. A strange pause, a creeping sense that something was about to happen. And then—*Boom!*

Lightning ripped across the sky, close enough to send vibrations through the ground beneath us. The crowd hushed for a split second before the officials sprang into action, rushing people off the metal bleachers, urging everyone to clear the area immediately. Riders exchanged glances, wide-eyed, adrenaline now doubled as we tried to process the thunderous crack.

The talk at the top was tense. Should they postpone? Should they wait it out? The rain picked up, and just as people began moving off the bleachers, another *crack* split the sky. This one was louder, closer, like the whole mountain had shuddered. I looked up, heart pounding, feeling the thrill of something otherworldly in the storm. *What is happening?* It felt like the heavens had opened in some epic showdown, like the angels were throwing strikes in a bowling match above.

The mountain felt alive, buzzing with energy, the storm pouring down as if it had been summoned. I didn't know if we'd get another chance to ride today, but standing there, with the storm raging above, I knew one thing for sure—this was the kind of energy I'd remember forever.

The event was on—women first, then the men, which was the usual setup. But with lightning crackling close, it felt like they were rushing us out there, like they were saying, "Send the girls down first, and maybe the storm will pass before the guys hit the pipe." It wasn't actually that way, but in the moment, it sure felt like it. The rain was softening the walls of the pipe, and I had five riders before me. As I watched, I could see where the walls were starting to break down, snow softening with each pass. I decided to start a little lower to give myself a better chance—but that meant every trick would have to be on point if I wanted the space to pull off my McTwist at the end.

With each girl who dropped, I could feel my energy building up like a spring about to snap. My heart was racing, but in the best possible way, and every color felt brighter, every sound sharper, like I was super-charged. I couldn't wait to drop in and let it all out, but I kept breathing, trying to keep my body relaxed, even as I buzzed with excitement. Then, finally, my name was called.

I stepped into the start gate, and a rush of energy hit me like a wave. I let out a scream—couldn't help it—and threw my arms up, double-pumping, probably looking like a crazy person. But I didn't care. I loved Japan, loved these people who'd shown up in the rain, sticking it out just to feel the moment with us. I could feel it too—we were all in this together.

Sliding down to my starting point, I didn't even pause; I dropped in just as the beat of the Fugees' "Every Breath You Take" dropped on the loudspeakers. Each trick felt clean, solid—backside air, frontside 720, into a cab, then frontside air, Indy grab, lien air. And when I hit that final wall, I had the speed I needed. I launched into my McTwist, pulled it clean, and rode over the finish line. First girl to do that trick on the international level. No matter what happened from this point forward—I'd already made history.

Boom—first place. That was what I'd come here for. This was the moment, and it felt incredible, but I still had one more run left.

Being in first place meant I'd run last, so I had a front-row seat to watch all the girls throw down. We looked like drowned rats—cold, soaked, and probably smelling like wet dogs. It had been a long day. But as I watched each of them hit the pipe, that mix of admiration and anticipation in my chest grew. They were all holding their own, each fighting the same rain-soaked, slushy walls that awaited me. I cheered them on, then took a moment to breathe, to pull my focus back to my own last run. Just a few more riders, and then it'd be my turn to close out the women's competition.

The halfpipe was holding up, but just barely. The walls felt softer, looser, especially in that first hit, which had definitely changed since my last run. I'd have to drop in a little lower to avoid a kinked spot that was throwing some of the riders off. But the pipe was short, so if I wanted enough room to throw my McTwist at the end, I had to tighten up my line—carve a little harder on the backside wall to set it up just right. I had my strategies, and they worked for me. The crowd was relentless, cheering through the rain, the cold, and the general sloppiness of the day. More than anything, I felt grateful—to be here, to be in this moment with them. They deserved my best run.

When my name was called, I looked out at the crowd one last time and yelled out a scream of hooray for this amazing crowd, then paused for a split second of silence. I took a deep breath, and as I dropped in, the whole atmosphere seemed to hush, leaving only the steady beat of my heart. My first three airs came together seamlessly—clean landings, good height—a 720, a half-cab, and a frontside air. But on my next hit, I drifted a little too far down the pipe. Instantly, I knew I'd have to fight for space to set up my final trick. I dug in, leaning hard on my heel edge and carving to make up for lost ground. My board held steady beneath me—nothing out of the ordinary, just another quick adjustment I'd made a thousand times before.

But then—*whoosh*. My edge hit a slushy puddle, and in an instant, it felt like my board had a mind of its own. One second, I was in control; the next, I was sliding, my balance wavering as I fought to keep my momentum.

Do I stop? Do I raise my hand, ask for a rerun because of interference? I could picture it—a quick pause, maybe a reset, a chance to catch my breath and start over. Then a louder thought crashed in—urgent, defiant: *No. Keep going. Finish your run. Make it amazing.*

Gritting my teeth, I forced every bit of focus back into the run. The slip had stolen my momentum, but I still had two more tricks. Every muscle braced as I lined up for that final wall, locked onto one goal: finish this with everything you have.

And then—*I stuck it*. I landed my McTwist. It was like redemption. I rode through the finish line, chest heaving, heart racing. For a brief second, that slip earlier came back to haunt me, whispering about what might have been. But I refused to let it stick. I threw my arms up and screamed, letting out everything—frustration, joy, sheer exhilaration, everything I'd bottled up.

When the scoreboard flashed, I saw I'd dropped to third. It hit, but it didn't linger. Thankfully, I'd earned the highest score of the day on my first run, so even with my mistake, I was still going to stand on the podium. And just like that, relief and pride washed over me. I'd done it. It was done.

My coach was waiting at the top. I looked around at my fellow riders and saw Nicola in first, tears streaming down her face as her coach wrapped her in a hug. Stine stood in second, cheering with every ounce of energy she had left. They'd given everything—just like I had.

And then I caught CB's eye.

She'd landed in fourth, just a fraction behind me. I saw the flicker of disappointment on her face—but only for a moment. She walked over, smiling, and pulled me into a hug, congratulating me with this whole-hearted, genuine joy that said more than words ever could.

"I'm sorry you didn't make the podium... You rode really, really well, and I thought you deserved to be up there."

"Thanks, Shan." CB's voice was full of admiration. "You did great...I'm so happy for you. I thought you were gonna win... You ruled it."

"Thanks, CB." My voice was tinged with relief that the competition was over.

"Ya know, I'm so glad we got stuck together as roommates," she said, her words oozing with gratitude.

"Stuck," I chuckled, beaming at her. "Yeah, me too, buddy."

The whole moment swelled, bigger than any medal, bigger than rankings or scores. I looked around at Nicola, Stine, CB, and all the others. We were in this moment, *making history*. Right here, right now.

And then, through the crowd, I spotted my dad, pushing his way forward, his face beaming. He wrapped me up in a hug, kissed my head, his voice thick with pride as he said, "Shannon, I'm so proud of you."

His words hit me, and suddenly, tears mixed with the rain on my face.

Just then, I noticed my agent, standing a little off to the side, looking somewhat out of place amid the swirling emotions. Right before I left for the Olympics, a friend had pulled me aside.

"Listen," she'd said, "if you win a medal—especially gold—it's going to be chaos. Everyone will want a piece of you, and you'll need someone to shield you from that madness. You need an agent."

So, at the last-minute, I met with a guy and signed him on. I hadn't given it much thought since, and I definitely didn't know he'd come all the way out here to watch. I was surprised to see him, but I thanked him for coming. He just sighed and said, "Well, you almost did it. Unfortunately, everyone loves a winner. I'm not sure what I can do for you with third place."

Before I could say anything, my dad turned to him, fire in his eyes, and said, "She's the first-ever American snowboard medalist."

In that moment, I felt something bigger than any medal, any podium, any place in the rankings. I felt a pride that went beyond the competition itself, something that filled me up, knowing I'd won something more profound than any contest could ever give me. It wasn't about meeting expectations—it was about owning my story. And for the first time, I truly felt like I had.

CHAPTER 37

/ Postpartum Podium /

NO ONE TELLS YOU WHAT ACTUALLY HAPPENS AFTER THE CONTEST ENDS.

One minute you're flying high. The next—it's a blur of soggy gear, security fences, and microphones in your face. As soon as the results dropped, everything went into overdrive.

I suddenly remembered my backpack—still at the top of the half-pipe. No way I was hiking back up. Hopefully, Delge would grab it. If not? Well, goodbye forever, backpack.

Meanwhile, I was at the bottom of the pipe, hooting and hollering like a total maniac—obnoxiously loud, full of nerves and leftover adrenaline. I felt like I needed to sprint laps just to burn it off, but instead, I stood next to Stine—second-place finisher—and a few other competitors, screaming into the void. They didn't join in, but to their credit, they were kind enough to pretend I wasn't making a complete spectacle of myself.

Honestly, if it had been someone else, I probably would've rolled my eyes hard enough to shut them up—or, depending on my mood, maybe I'd have screamed right along with them.

But no one knew—I wasn't celebrating a medal. Definitely not third place.

I was releasing everything I'd carried to get here.

I'd landed the hardest run of my life. Scored the highest of the day on my first of two final runs. Then slipped on my second—random, irreversible. It cost me, but I'd already let the outcome go. I was thankful to get on the podium. I gave everything I had—and that had to be enough.

As the men finished their final runs, I bounced between press interviews, hugging my dad, and soaking up his hilarious play-by-play.

I knew my dad had muscled his way through security without a media pass—but then he gave me the quick version. Kevin—built like an NFL lineman—"convinced" the guard by accidentally knocking him over. My dad made a break for it. There was no love for family unless you had credentials, and no one had helped him get one. But there he was—breathless, misty-eyed, and full of pride for me. Sean got stuck behind the fence, running interference to make sure no one chased Dad down.

Dad told me Sean had been waving the giant American flag through the whole event. I hadn't known it was him at the time, but I'd seen that flag from the top of the pipe—you couldn't miss it. Knowing it was my brother? That hit me hard. It made me proud. It meant something.

From the top of that Olympic pipe, I felt national pride. It's a real thing—something I didn't quite get at that first breakfast with CB. But by the end? I got it. And honestly, it felt pretty rad.

Then, like a little miracle, Delge showed up—my backpack in hand. He gave me a side hug and said, "Good job, girl."

And then, it was time for the flower ceremony at the bottom of the halfpipe. Quick. Surreal. We stepped onto the podium in a full downpour, took our bouquets, and smiled through a storm of camera flashes. We were soaked to the bone, but I was still buzzing—lit up from the inside, running on pure fumes. It felt like a dream sequence, everything moving in slow motion except the electricity still firing through my body.

As I stepped down from the podium, I spotted Bruno—now serving as Burton's team manager after Eric had moved on earlier in the season. I hadn't seen him all day. He opened his arms, and I collapsed into them.

That's when the tears hit. Hard. My peak energy cracked wide open. The floodgates let loose. I just needed a hug—needed to let it all out. It was so much. My body was begging to chill, to come down—but at that moment, it just couldn't.

Deb leaned in and gave me the next plan.

"You've been flagged," she said. "Time for drug testing."

No more hugs. No contact. Once you're tagged, you're in Olympic lockdown. Apparently, people have faked it before.

She guided me away from the bottom of the halfpipe—my dad still standing just beyond the fence. He was already asking how to get tickets for the medal ceremony that evening in Nagano, but Deb didn't know. She mentioned we'd be on a tight schedule and might not have time to stop at the hotel.

Good thing we'd packed our little wheely bags that morning with our official medal outfits and tossed them in the team van—just in case. I was so stoked I'd actually get to use mine.

As we walked, a soft-spoken woman from the Olympic Museum in Lausanne stepped into our path. "Would you like to donate something?" she asked gently. "Your bib, maybe?"

I peeled it off and handed it over like it was sacred. "Sure. Take it."

She wrote up a small receipt and smiled. "Please come visit—your bib will be forever on display at the museum!"

All I could think about was peeling off my soggy gear and taking a long, hot shower—but that would have to wait. The rain was coming down harder now. As we made our way toward the testing hut beside the venue, my dad—soaked through in his wool jacket—called out that he'd figure out the tickets and meet me in Nagano. Sean and Kevin had been ushered out with the rest of the crowd, so now Dad had to track them down, too.

Then everything turned cold.

The testing hut was small and sterile, lit by a buzzing fluorescent bulb that flickered like something out of a bad motel. I was soaked to the skin. Just me, Deb, one stone-faced official tracking my every move, and another seated at a table, silently logging it all.

The official followed me into a stall with no door and watched—watched me pee in a cup like I was a criminal. No privacy. No comfort. Just protocol. Just humiliation.

I handed her the cup.

And then—my body cracked.

A cramp hit out of nowhere, so sharp it knocked the wind out of me. One wave, then another. I braced against the wall, knees buckling. I hadn't eaten all day. I'd chugged water like it was my job. My nerves had finally short-circuited. The pain was primal—rolling, deep, and violent. Like contractions in my gut. It felt like labor—but crueler, because there was no new life on the other end. Just pain—just collapse.

What was left was me, folded over in a freezing Olympic hut, shaking, breaking, in the shadows of history.

I hit the floor, clutching my stomach, gasping for air. My body was staging a full-on revolt. I had no idea what was happening—only that it hurt more than anything I'd ever felt. I curled up on the freezing concrete floor, tears streaming, groaning through the pain.

"God, help me—I'm dying," I whispered, half to Deb, half to the fluorescent buzz above me. The words just fell out, shaky and small.

Was I really going to die here? Alone in this Olympic hut, miles from my loved ones, and without any way to reach them? Abandoned in the shadow of the biggest moment of my life?

And then, the official returned, utterly oblivious to the state I was in.

"Your sample is too diluted," she said flatly, as if this were just another day. "There's too much water in your urine. You were over-hydrated. You'll have to give another sample."

Another sample? I could barely breathe, let alone function. My body was trembling, cramping, unraveling—and now they wanted me to *what*? Pull it together and pee again?

Anything that hadn't made it into the cup had already gone swirling down the toilet. I was completely empty.

"Can't you just take a blood sample and be done with it?" I asked, my voice cracking, barely above a whisper.

The official shook her head, unmoved. "No. We don't do that."

That was it. No empathy. No plan B.

"Okay, well... I need some water and food," I said, trying to hold it together. "I drank all my water. Do you have any snacks?"

She handed me a bottle of water. "Here. But don't drink too much—you already overdid it once."

I stared at her. "Then how long does it take to pee again without drinking?"

She shrugged. "Could take an hour or more. It just depends."

Another cramp caused me to curl instinctively inward.

"I need food," I said, shaking. I get hypoglycemic sometimes—low blood sugar—and I could feel my body crashing hard.

Deb turned to the woman. "Do you have any snacks?"

"No."

"Can I go get her something?"

"No. She can't leave."

Another cramp hit. I doubled over, tears blurring my vision, and I broke. Deb crouched beside me, rubbing my back. I wanted to be anywhere but here. But I was trapped. I tried to focus on relaxing. Slowly, the cramps eased into a dull ache.

Then, maybe out of guilt—or just plain fatigue—the official relented.

"You can get something," she said. "There's a 7-Eleven nearby. Be quick."

We bolted.

At the store, I grabbed whatever I could carry—rice snacks, pretzels, chocolates. I didn't even make it back to the hut before tearing into them. I stood just outside the sliding doors, shivering, stuffing bites into my mouth like they were oxygen.

"Don't drink too much," the official's warning echoed.

I downed half a Japanese version of Gatorade anyway, hoping it wouldn't be too much—but needing something, anything, to steady me.

Slowly, I felt myself coming back. Breath by breath. Bite by bite. The panic began to fade.

"I'm so sorry I'm so dramatic," I kept apologizing to Deb on our walk back to the hut.

She smiled gently. "You aren't dramatic. You're just human."

And in that moment, I needed that grace more than anything. I looked up at her, unsure if I was about to laugh or cry. This was supposed to be one of the most exciting nights of my life—Olympic medal in hand, adrenaline still pumping—but instead, I was exhausted, starving, soaked to the bone, and praying for one more ounce of strength to get through it all.

At the hut, I took a seat, and Deb patted my back gently. "Think you can try to pee again? You just need a little." She glanced at her watch. "They've postponed the medal ceremony for you. We've got a forty-five-minute drive back, but if we leave soon, we'll make it—otherwise, they'll have to push it to tomorrow."

I took a deep breath, steadied myself, and tried. Miraculously, I managed to fill the cup just enough to reach the designated fill line. Moments later, the official looked at me, nodded, and said, "All good to go. You cleared the drug test."

It felt like the best moment of my life—total freedom. After two hours of chaos, of cramps and tests, we were finally on our way to the medal ceremony.

I changed in the car. Everything I'd worn that day was soaked through—even my underwear—so I climbed into the back of the van and discreetly swapped it all out. I kept my bra, peeled off the rest, and wriggled into my dry, designated podium outerwear pants and Olympic T-shirt, jacket over the top.

Thankfully, past me had stashed some essentials in the front pocket: mascara, a couple of barrettes, a mini brush, and lip gloss. My hair was dripping wet, so I asked Deb if I could crank the heat and use the vents as a makeshift blow dryer while I brushed it out. I used the visor mirror to clean up my face.

A few minutes later—bam. Freshened up. Back to (some version of) normal.

I was led into the athlete waiting room, where all the podium finishers were gathered—men's and women's halfpipe, along with the singles and doubles luge teams. My dad and Sean were already inside, arms open wide, and I walked straight into their hug. Only direct family members were allowed in the lounge, so "Cousin" Kevin didn't make the cut.

When I joined the other riders, it felt like a reunion. We'd just come through a war together—storm, slush, media chaos—and somehow made it out standing. I apologized for holding up the ceremony and explained the situation. Everyone got it.

Once the event kicked off, Dad and Sean would be ushered into the crowd. This wasn't just a medal presentation—it was a full-blown show. A ticketed spectacle. While we waited backstage, Dad passed around a giant Olympic poster for us to sign.

Sean and I couldn't resist cracking jokes about the doubles luge teams.

"Seriously," he whispered, smirking. "Who wakes up one day and says, 'You know what I want to do? Slide down a frozen track lying on top of another dude at eighty miles per hour.'"

My dad, meanwhile, was bursting at the seams. He fired off a hundred comments and questions like he'd been saving them up since breakfast.

"Oh—and I talked to Mom!" he said, lowering his voice like it was top-secret intel. "She said the only way she could watch the contest was on Canadian TV. Thank God we have satellite. None of the U.S. channels aired it—so Grandma didn't get to watch."

So yeah...snowboarding's Olympic debut, and all of my relatives missed it entirely. On American TV, it was like it never even happened. Classic.

Then his tone shifted again—conspiratorial, serious. "You're in the news again," he said. "Mom saw something. Rumor is...you failed your drug test. Just like Ross Rebagliati."

"What?" I blinked. "What happened with him?"

"They took his gold medal," Dad said, eyes wide. "Said he tested positive for marijuana. A trace amount. Total controversy. The Canadian team's fighting it. But now the news is saying the same thing happened with 'the American girl.' That's you, Shannon!"

I just rolled my eyes. Of course. I couldn't be more of a straight arrow if I tried—I'd never even touched a drug in my life. I gave him the quick version of what really happened, leaving out the messy parts. I figured the full meltdown could wait.

Right now, I was soaking in the relief, the reunion, the surreal electricity of what was about to happen. I was finally ready to step onto that podium. I peeked out at the crowd below. The place was packed, roaring with energy. The media might not have cared much about snowboarding, but the crowd? They were all in—Japanese fans, international travelers, flags waving in every direction. Snowboarding had officially won the hearts of the people.

And now, it was our time to take the stage.

I was called out first.

My name echoed through the stadium as I stepped onto a high-rise platform that stretched thirty feet above the crowd like a runway. Music was blasting. The lights—blinding.

Through the glare, I spotted them—Sean, Kevin, and Dad—my whole heart, right there in a sea of faces. Sean was going absolutely wild, waving that massive American flag like his life depended on it.

I grinned so hard it hurt.

The walkway to the podium was about fifty feet long, so I threw in a little moonwalk—just to make them laugh. I could hear them cheering over the music, louder than anyone else. *I actually can't believe this is happening!*

And then, I stepped up.

I took my position on the podium. Heart pounding. Lungs tight. The moment was overwhelming—not just joy, but something heavier, layered with longing. I wasn't in the center. I wouldn't be hearing my anthem. That stung. I was used to making history—not watching someone else's moment unfold from the side. That familiar hunger to be the best flickered inside me—just enough to burn. But then I looked out at the crowd, at my family, at the flag waving wildly in Sean's hands—and the sting softened.

This was still a victory. A big one. And I was standing on an Olympic podium.

An official stepped forward, shook my hand, and slipped the Olympic medal over my neck. It was heavy—weighted with meaning. He handed me flowers, and in the medal's shine, I caught a flash of my younger self—like a movie reel playing in my head. I looked out and saw Sean still waving that giant flag, saw my dad's face lit up with pride, and smiled so big my cheeks hurt.

They announced the rest of the girls, and as the German national anthem played, I just kept smiling. What a moment—for all of us.

We took photos on the podium, arms around each other, soaked in gratitude and disbelief. It was surreal and sweet—and I didn't want it to end.

Only a select few ever reach this level. It was rare air. And I was in it—representing my country. Pride swelled in my chest. Not the kind that needs applause, but the kind that hums quiet and steady. The kind that knows—third place or not—this moment mattered.

I glanced to my right, smiled at Stine and Nicola, and surrendered to the belief that everything had worked out exactly the way it was meant to.

Me on the Olympic medal podium—a surreal moment I'll never forget.

CHAPTER 38

/ Keep on Truckin' /

WHEN I GOT HOME FROM THE OLYMPICS, I half expected something—anything.

Maybe a glass of champagne on the flight, a few letters in the mail, or even a shoutout on the local radio station. But the reality? Silence.

A few national outlets ran short pieces on snowboarding's Olympic debut, and my hometown paper in Steamboat Springs wrote a small article—but that was it. Then again, I had moved away. And like my agent warned me, "Nobody celebrates third place. They want the gold."

I didn't expect a parade or a key to the city. But still—not even for myself, but for the *sport*—snowboarding had just debuted in the Olympics. You'd think that would be a big deal. A milestone for action sports in America. I had just medaled in the first-ever Olympic snowboard halfpipe event. That should've counted for something.

But snowboarding hadn't hit the mainstream yet. Our event aired at odd hours on a network barely anyone watched unless they were specifically hunting for it. And even if someone did tune in, the only snowboarding headline that broke through was Ross Rebagliati—the

Canadian alpine racer who had his gold medal stripped after testing positive for marijuana, only to have it reinstated a few days later.

The rest of us? Ghosts.

A few days after I got back, I went with Dave to a combined surf/snowboard event he was competing in at Huntington Beach and Bear Mountain Resort, just a few hours outside of LA. Two reminders of my early snowboard experiences—the crazy guys demolishing the house and then the Damian party at Huntington. What a long way we'd come. Me in my career and snowboarding as a sport—from outlaws to Olympians.

Dave had stayed home during the Olympics. Crowds and contests weren't his thing, and at first, I was bummed he wasn't there. I figured he didn't really understand the intensity, the pressure, or the emotional crash that comes with high-level competition. But after everything that went down in Japan—and the ordeals Dad, Sean, and cousin Kevin dealt with—I was actually glad he hadn't come. In a way, he was ahead of the curve. His calm, grounding presence reminded me of what truly mattered in life.

I believed in competition. Like Dad taught me, it teaches you compassion. It pushes you into uncomfortable places—those high-stakes moments where you either rise or flop. And even if you botch it, you grow. You walk away with more empathy for anyone who's ever stood in that fire.

That's why, even if contests made Dave cringe—including the one he was in—I still genuinely enjoyed being there for him. I understood what it took to show up. He'd always been the buffer who softened everything when I felt stretched thin or overwhelmed, and this time, I got to be that for him.

Turns out, he didn't really care how his contest went—and he definitely wasn't overwhelmed the way I get. He doesn't have that competitive drive, and honestly, I don't relate to that. But it didn't matter—we were just happy to be together again.

That was also my first time back on a board post-Olympics. And at that event, one person—just one—asked how it went.

It was Wing, the owner of Wahoo's Fish Tacos—a true board-sports enthusiast who'd been sponsoring surf-snow crossover events for years. He cared. He followed the sport. He *got* it.

But beyond that one moment?

Nothing.

So when five months later an envelope arrived in the mail with a gold seal from the White House, I didn't know what to think.

Every Olympic and Paralympic athlete gets invited to the White House for a handshake and a "well done" from the President. But it felt so far removed from everything I'd experienced. No one around me seemed to care that I'd been to the Olympics—so why should I care about shaking hands with the President?

At the time, I barely followed politics. Bill Clinton's policies meant nothing to me. But the headlines about his affair with a White House intern—Monica Lewinsky—were everywhere. It was all anyone could talk about. He just seemed...gross.

Still, how often do you get the chance?

So I flew out with some of the U.S. Snowboard Team. We were handed a full itinerary—everything professional, polished, and meticulously planned. There was a formal Olympic luncheon, followed by bus rides to the White House for a private tour led by decorated military members who had earned medals of their own. They walked us through the rooms, sharing history, pointing out details—the paintings, the decor, even where certain presidents had once lived and worked.

That part felt special. Quiet and sacred, in its own way.

Then came the main event: the President's speech, a quick meet-and-greet, and the photo op.

I'd even come up with a zinger: "Hey, thanks for stealing my *Newsweek* cover, Bill!" Because yeah—his scandal had bumped my Olympic snowboarding feature right off the newsstands.

But when I actually stood face to face with President Clinton, there wasn't even time to deliver the sass. I didn't mention the magazine.

Instead, I just held out a golf ball I'd picked up at the White House gift shop.

"Can you sign my ball?" I asked, probably sounding a little too sarcastic to pass for polite.

He squinted at it, confused—like I'd just handed him a foreign object.

"Where'd you find this?" he asked, studying it like it was some kind of national security threat.

"The gift shop. Right next door."

He took his time looking it over—maybe trying to decide if it was legit. Or maybe just zoning out. He seemed very relaxed. Not rushed. His head looked even larger in person—honestly, kind of bobblehead-ish. That was one of the first things I noticed. He had this smooth, easy demeanor, like nothing fazed him.

He signed the ball with a Sharpie. Nodded. Shook my hand while we smiled for the camera. Click—got the shot.

And just like that—next athlete.

The next morning, at the official Olympic breakfast in our hotel, someone I didn't know—some official-looking guy from the Olympic Committee—tapped me on the shoulder.

"Hey, can you do a school visit this afternoon?" he asked casually, like he was inviting me to grab a sandwich. No details. No prep. Just, "The bus leaves in thirty. Bring your Olympic medal jacket."

Of course, I said yes. I figured I'd smile, wave, maybe answer a couple questions about snowboarding. Easy.

I was on a bus with absolutely no one I knew, winding through a DC neighborhood I wasn't familiar with. Bars on windows. Graffiti on buildings. It wasn't what I'd pictured. The school was gated. Security stood at the entrance. We were escorted inside.

And then...there I was. Standing in a packed gym, expected to inspire a crowd of at least two thousand high schoolers.

The Olympic rep had never mentioned a speech. But based on the way the principal introduced me—like I was the evening's headliner—

I realized they were all expecting a ten-minute motivational saga about grit and glory. I had...nothing.

A gold-medal women's hockey player went up first—confident, composed—and launched into this incredible story about growing up playing hockey with boys, how her family even moved to support her dream. She was every bit the hero in her own epic: a story of battles fought and won. The gym was pin-drop silent. Every kid was locked in. And if you've ever tried to hold the attention of a gym full of high schoolers, you know that's basically impossible.

I was trying not to cry from her tear-jerking story. And then it hit me: I had to follow her.

Panic set in. What was I going to say? Since the Olympics, I'd done zero public speaking. And to be honest, the Olympics still felt like a fleeting novelty in my world—like a blip on anyone's radar. Now I was supposed to somehow make my journey sound like a clear path from medal to enlightenment?

My face started to burn. Sweat beaded on my forehead. My heart pounded so hard I was half afraid it might knock me over. I had never felt so overwhelmed and underprepared in my entire life. And here I was—on a stage, in front of thousands of expectant teenagers. No one could save me.

God, help me.

As much as I wanted to be clear-headed and come up with some quick talking points, my brain was frozen. Like everything had been blacked out. I had absolutely no plan—no thoughts. And talking wasn't my strong suit. My default button was silence.

The principal said my name, and somehow I made it to the stage, gripping the microphone like it was the only solid thing in the room.

"Hi...thank you for having me," I started. The students stirred—probably expecting some epic Olympic tale.

Good, I thought. *At least I know how to start.*

"I started snowboarding in Steamboat Springs, Colorado, when I was sixteen..."

My voice was shaking, but I told them about learning to ride, about entering competitions. And then—nothing. My story ran out. I glanced at the students. A few started giggling.

I couldn't help it—I started laughing too, my nerves spilling everywhere.

"So...after I learned," I stammered, "I was kind of like Forrest Gump. I just happened to be in the right place at the right time, doing well in contests. And then—boom—suddenly, snowboarding was an Olympic sport."

The laughter got louder. They thought I was joking, which, honestly, helped. I didn't know what else to say.

Grasping for something—*anything*—inspirational, I blurted out, "So, um...I decided to go for it. If you can dream it, you can do it! And... work hard! Believe in yourself! Perseverance will get you through!"

I sounded like a walking Hallmark card. And they knew it. Giggles bubbled up across the gym. I was laughing too now, fully leaning in. I threw up my hand and said, "When you don't know what to do next, you gotta just...keep on truckin'!"

My arm shot into the air like I was pointing to the ceiling tiles, and the entire gym *lost it.*

Keep on truckin'? Where had that even come from?

As I walked off the stage, cheeks flaming, the principal met me with a half-smile, half-smirk. I extended my hand.

"Thank you for having me," I said, trying to sound like I hadn't just totally bombed.

He nodded, amused. "That was...an interesting speech."

I let out a shaky laugh. "Yeah, I didn't really know I needed a speech—I was thinking it was going to be more of a Q&A thing."

He finally cracked a smile. "Well, you definitely kept them entertained."

Back on the bus, the gold medal hockey player sat with her entourage—Olympic officials, reps, what looked like a whole team of handlers. Meanwhile, it was just me, myself, and I. I sank into my seat and stared out the window, doing everything I could to avoid eye contact.

I had to block it out just to keep from emotionally unraveling. I cringed, covering my face with my hands. *I'm never doing public speaking again. Ever.*

But as the bus pulled away from the school, something softened. I replayed "keep on truckin'" over and over. *Why the heck did I say that? How dumb!* I watched the streets blur past and thought...

That ridiculous line—*keep on truckin'*—actually meant something. It was awkward, for sure. But kind of...true. And weirdly honest.

Keep going for it. Even when it's messy. Even when it's not what you expected. Even when you're unprepared. Just keep going.

Next time I spoke somewhere, I'd ask more questions. Get the details. Don't assume someone else is thinking the same thing I am. I'd show up prepared.

But I wouldn't stop showing up.

CHAPTER 39

/ Marry Me /

IF DAVE WASN'T GOING TO MARRY ME, I WAS DONE.

I wasn't trying to be dramatic; I'd just reached that quiet, clear kind of knowing. After nearly five years together, I needed to know if we had a future. I loved him, but I wasn't going to keep floating in limbo.

I was relieved the Olympic whirlwind was behind me. I was still recovering from the cringe of my "keep on truckin'" speech—I'd sounded like a terrible, walking motivational calendar.

Thankfully, the snowboard world snapped right back into our scrappy, normal routines. For me, that meant Utah for the winter and Southern California in the off-season. I had a low-maintenance condo near the mountains and a beachside duplex—living in one unit and renting out the other.

Tina had just bought a house tucked against the jagged peaks of Big Cottonwood Canyon. It had belonged to a former Utah Jazz player, so everything—from the sinks to the ceilings—felt like it was built for giants. I'm 5'2", so walking through that house was like wandering through an NBA-sized funhouse. Dave was renting a room in the loft.

Thanksgiving rolled around, which also happened to fall on my birthday.

Tina hosted a big dinner, and after the feast, she and I found ourselves at the sink doing dishes while everyone else lounged on the couches, watching the NFL game. I couldn't hold it in any longer.

"Hey, Tina," I asked, trying to sound casual. "Has Dave said anything to you about...proposing?"

She paused. "Honestly, Shan, he hasn't. But maybe he's just waiting for the right moment?"

I nodded, but the truth sat heavy. "I thought he was the one from the start. I could've married him the week after we met. But if he doesn't know by now..."

That night, I cried myself to sleep. I loved him—but I couldn't wait forever for someone who wasn't sure I belonged in his future. After tossing and turning, I made up my mind: I was going to end it.

The next morning, Dave called. "Wanna go ride Brighton?" he asked.

A storm was rolling in, and there might be powder. "It's not supposed to hit until late morning," he said. "Let's just take a few laps—I'll pick you up around noon."

I said yes, figuring I'd bring up the dreaded conversation over dinner later. One last day on the mountain.

As we rode the lift, snowflakes started to fall. By the time we reached the top, it was a full-on storm. We took a few runs, but I was cold, tired, and ready to call it a day.

"Wanna just take one more run?" he asked, hopeful.

I shook my head. "Nah, I'm good."

He sighed, unbuckling his bindings like he was ready to head back with me. But I saw the look on his face—he really wanted that one last run. So I caved.

"Okay, why not," I said. "Let's make it a good one."

We rode the lift again, talking about Thanksgiving, our past five years, and the first time we'd met. Dave put his arm around me, and I felt that old warmth creep in—the kind that made me question everything I'd decided the night before.

At the top, he turned to me with a smile. "Follow me."

We snowboarded halfway down the run, then dipped into a quiet patch of trees. The mountain was hushed. The storm muffled everything. Thick snowflakes fell like we were inside a snow globe.

I leaned on him to balance.

And then—he unstrapped his board and dropped to one knee.

My heart skipped.

"What are you doing?" I asked, half in shock, half in hope.

He didn't answer—just pulled a Tiffany-blue box from his jacket pocket. He opened it. Inside was a delicate diamond band that sparkled in the low light.

Tears welled in my eyes, blurring my vision.

"Shannon," he said, steady and full of love, "I love you so much. I want to be with you forever. Will you marry me?"

I was stunned. Breathless. Finally, I managed to squeak out, "Yes."

He pulled off my glove and slid the ring onto my finger. We hugged. We kissed. The snow swirled around us like a movie scene, and for a moment, the whole mountain faded away.

As we pulled apart, I laughed through tears. "What if I'd said no to that last run?"

He grinned. "Then I guess I would've had to come up with plan B."

He kissed me again—and just like that, the storm didn't feel so cold anymore.

/ Full Circle /

THEY FOUND IT BURIED AT THE BOTTOM of a plastic bin in my closet. My Olympic medal. The one they'd seen in pictures, heard stories about—but never actually held.

That moment—watching my elementary-school-aged sons turn it over in their hands, wide-eyed—brought everything full circle. It reminded me how much life had happened since those days on the podium.

Their curiosity cracked open a flood of memories. As the years rolled on during my pro career, so did life—and I changed right along with it.

Not long after the Nagano Olympic Games, I got married. We held a small, intimate ceremony on Catalina Island—just family, close friends, ocean breeze, and a deep sense of peace. Betsy stood beside me as my bridesmaid, a grounding reminder of where I came from.

Snowboarding had taken me to places I'd never imagined—from the vast, wild mountains of Alaska to podiums around the world. I earned Grand Prix titles, X Games medals, and, in 2001, the thrill of being named X Games Overall Athlete of the Year for top results in halfpipe, slopestyle, and big air. Winning a few cars and trucks along the way didn't hurt—it was icing on an already wild ride.

Somewhere in those seasons, I became the first woman to land a frontside inverted 720, pushing the boundaries of what was possible for women in the sport. Every victory—every new milestone—felt like progress. Not just for me, but for snowboarding as a whole.

Creating the Feelgood board line for Burton felt like another way to shape the future of women's products. I approached Burton's marketing team with the idea of building a women's-specific line alongside Victoria Jealouse, and together, we helped launch the original Feelgood series. A few years later, I took over the line's design, working closely with Burton engineers to refine it using everything I'd learned from years on snow. That board outlasted my competitive career and continues to sell to this day—a lasting testament to its impact.

By the time the 2002 Olympics came around, I was still at the top of my game, qualifying first and setting my sights on the podium again. But as the season wore on, I could feel my fire dimming. The U.S. Snowboarding Team had taken on a serious tone and structure that, for me, felt restrictive—less about the joy of riding and more about meeting expectations. I'd thrived on freedom, but this felt confining. There was a small voice inside me whispering that I'd done it all, that maybe it was time to start a family. But I also knew it's never ideal to approach life with the mentality of "I just can't wait to get to what's next."

When I finished in fifth place at the Olympics, I was disappointed, but I also knew I was witnessing something much bigger than my own journey. Kelly Clark, a powerhouse of raw talent and drive, was right there, ready to push women's halfpipe snowboarding further than we'd ever imagined.

Salt Lake City was the perfect stage for a new era. The U.S. men swept the podium in the snowboarding halfpipe—a historic first. The pipe itself had evolved into a towering superpipe with eighteen-foot walls, allowing riders to soar higher and push the limits in ways that would've seemed impossible just a few years earlier.

And this time, the format supported that progression: riders qualified, then took two final runs—best run counted. Finally, a system that encouraged risk, innovation, and next-level riding.

My first son, Logan, was born in 2003, followed by Dillon in 2004. My life shifted from podiums to playgrounds, medals to motherhood, and I threw myself into raising my boys. The next twenty years were a beautiful, chaotic blur, and I embraced every part of it.

While I stepped away from competition, snowboarding continued to evolve. Years later, another shift took place—one I could see coming, but it was still exciting to watch unfold. Slopestyle, a discipline blending rails and massive jumps, brought a whole new dimension to Olympic competition. By the time it made its Olympic debut in 2014, it opened doors for a new generation of riders to showcase their creativity and technical skill on a global stage. The halfpipe continued to grow, eventually reaching a monstrous twenty-two feet high, enabling pros to boost to the moon—spinning upside-down tricks that were once unthinkable.

That growth was everywhere. Now, girls are leveling the playing field with the men. With access to year-round training facilities, airbags, and advanced progression tools, female riders are pushing boundaries like never before—proving that, with the right opportunities, they can throw down just as hard. Watching this evolution has been incredible—seeing how far the sport has come while knowing that the groundwork we laid helped make it possible.

BOARDING FOR BREAST CANCER (B4BC.ORG)

Snowboarding wasn't the only thing that mattered. Over the years, my work with Boarding for Breast Cancer has grown into something more impactful than I ever imagined. When we first started, the mission was simple: use the power of snowboarding to educate young women about early detection.

Now, decades later, I've heard countless stories from women who attended our events, felt the breast lump in the jelly mold demonstration, and later found their own—catching their cancer early. Those moments hit me in a way competition never could. This nonprofit isn't just about awareness; it's about saving lives.

What makes it even more special is that we bring the same passion and energy to it that fueled my riding career. Whether it's on the mountains, at a skatepark, or in the surf community, we've expanded beyond snowboarding, making sure this message reaches as many people as possible. It's also been an incredible way to stay connected to the snowboard industry, working alongside Tina Basich and Lisa Hudson—two longtime friends who helped shape B4BC from the beginning. Because life is better when we lift each other up and ride this journey together.

2023—A LEGACY RESURFACES

Burton rereleased my *Dolphin* board.

And wow—what a comeback.

People were freaking out over it. Some were drawn to the nostalgia, remembering the impact it had on their younger selves, while others just loved the bold, bright graphics that stood out.

And as if that wasn't enough, that same year the Smithsonian's National Museum of American History included my original *Dolphin* pro model in its *Change Your Game* exhibit, on display from 2023 to 2028 for its contribution to sports innovation.

I mean—no pressure or anything—but that board is now an actual artifact of history.

And then there's my *Sunflower* board, already in the Smithsonian's collection, waiting for its own exhibition honoring its contribution to women's sports.

Let's just say—my younger self would've cracked up at the idea of my snowboards sitting in a museum next to, I don't know, actual historical treasures.

And speaking of surreal honors—Tina Basich and I were inducted into the U.S. Ski and Snowboard Hall of Fame alongside Terry Kidwell, the godfather of freestyle snowboarding, as part of the Class of 2022. We were the first women snowboard athletes ever inducted, which made it even more meaningful. Years earlier, in 2016, I'd also been honored by the Colorado Snowsports Hall of Fame. These recognitions felt like a nod to the long road we paved—not just for ourselves, but for every female rider coming up behind us. Thank you to everyone who believed in our vision from the beginning.

AN INVITATION THAT CHANGED EVERYTHING— MAY 2024

Pat Bridges, the founder of *Slush* snowboard magazine, invited me to the World Quarterpipe Championships.

At first, I thought the email was a joke and laughed it off, almost deleting it, thinking it was junk mail.

This was a legit, serious pro event—have you seen the top snowboarders these days? The tricks they're pulling off are borderline supernatural, death-defying stunts. Snowboarding has evolved into an entirely different sport.

But here was Pat, inviting me—a fifty-one-year-old mom who hadn't hit a freestyle jump, much less a quarterpipe, in over twenty years.

Yet, I've never been one to turn down a challenge when someone believes in me. So I contacted Pat and told him, "Yes, put me in, coach."

I played it cool, like it was no big deal.

Inside, I knew it was a very big deal.

Most everyone I told tried to talk me out of it or just gave me a look. "You don't have to do this," they said.

"You have nothing to prove."

"Be careful. Seriously, don't."

I smiled and shrugged it off, but in the back of my mind, I wondered if they were right.

FAST FORWARD TO THE EVENT

I did a secret drive-by mission to check out the venue the night before the event, slipping in under the cover of darkness like some kind of undercover agent. No crowds, no distractions—just me and the towering behemoth I had agreed to ride.

The second I laid eyes on it, my stomach dropped.

The quarterpipe was even bigger in person—thirty feet tall, sitting there in the vast darkness like a beast waiting to be tamed. It was a quarterpipe on steroids. Imagine looking up three stories of snow and ice, a towering wall built to send riders sky-high. No joke situation.

Unlike a halfpipe, where you flow side to side as you ride downhill, a quarterpipe is a single wall that you charge at head-on, like hitting a skateboard vert ramp. The goal? Launch as high as possible, throw a trick if you've got it, and then land back on the transition you came from. This size wall could send riders into orbit in a way that makes my early competition days look like child's play.

There wouldn't be any practice except the next day at the event. No time to test it out. No warm-ups. No easing into it. I had to show up and commit.

That night, I couldn't shake the weight of what I was about to do. For the past twenty years, ever since I retired, I'd had the same recurring nightmare where I was suddenly back in a pro contest, modern-day, completely unprepared. Standing at the top of a massive drop-in, heart racing, knowing I had to throw down like my career depended on it. The panic would hit—I was out of my league, totally lost. Right before I had to drop in, I'd wake up in a sweat, heart pounding, relieved beyond belief that it was just a dream.

But this? This was real.

I tossed and turned all night—wide awake at 2 a.m., mentally berating myself.

What were you thinking? Agreeing to enter this competition? Can't you just let it go?

I could practically hear the industry laughing, mocking this poor old lady trying to keep up with the pros. I could see the headlines already: "51-Year-Old Mom Attempts Quarterpipe, Ends in Total Disaster." *What the H-E-double L was I thinking?*

No one would care if I backed out. I could walk away right now. In the morning, I could just let Pat know that I had been a little overambitious with his invite and save myself the embarrassment. No one would even notice.

But in the morning…something shifted. There was this quiet, stubborn part of me that wouldn't let it go. That reminded me why I was here.

This wasn't just about the quarter pipe. It was about showing up. About redefining what "older" can look like in snowboarding.

I wanted to ride with style, to prove that experience isn't just a relic of the past but something that matters, something worth honoring, and that I actually still had skill.

I let myself off the hook from feeling like I had to throw a McTwist or prove I could hang with the new generation. Instead, I focused on what I could do—get a great shot. A stylish, timeless photo that showed I was still here, still riding, still loving every second of it. I didn't get to plan anything with the photographers, so that part was left to chance.

So, despite the nerves, the doubts, and the fear of looking ridiculous, I decided it was time to show up—really show up—and carve out another unforgettable line in my story.

With each step up the never-ending runway, there was plenty of time to think, plenty of time to observe. I could feel the eyes of the other riders, probably wondering what I was doing there. The energy was intense—this wasn't just some casual session.

To gain speed, you had to hike that runway, strap in, point it straight down, and charge full speed at the massive thirty-foot wall—no hesitation, no second-guessing. Plenty of time to think on the way up. Zero time to think on the way down.

And that's when reality hit me. Every single rider was either in their twenties or younger. Two of them were actual kids. I was the oldest rider there—by decades.

I felt like a total outsider, like I had stepped into a scene where I no longer belonged. I truly felt like a nobody at this event—I'd been out of the snowboard industry for so long that I was just some random fifty-year-old poaching the contest. I was convinced no one knew who I was. And honestly? That was kind of humiliating.

To top it off, at one point, I said hi to a pro rider judge who had started her career just as I was retiring mine. I was just trying to be friendly, but she completely blew me off. She had no clue who I was and probably wondered why this random older woman was even talking to her. I found out later that she hadn't realized who I was at the time—but in the moment? Talk about an uncomfortable situation.

And then, there was the crowd.

Snowboarding, or any athletic sport, doesn't give you a waiver if you don't perform. It doesn't care how long you've been away or how old you are. You either show up and do it, or you don't belong there. And I had to perform.

Yet, in the midst of that awkwardness, something unexpected happened.

A couple of the female competitors came up to me, telling me how much they appreciated what I had done for women's snowboarding. Their words caught me off guard.

One of them was Ellie Weiler—a name I had never heard before. She was my son's age. And yet, here she was, taking the time to introduce herself, looking me in the eye, genuinely thanking me for paving the way. I didn't expect it. I hadn't even considered that this new generation of riders might know who I was.

I thanked her, smiled, tried to keep it cool—but I had to rein in my tears to keep riding.

I was getting used to the speed, throwing in a few grabs where I could style it out—hoping at least one of the many photographers would catch the shot I'd been chasing. I was feeling good, getting comfortable with this thing—like a relationship. And with that comfort came the itch to go bigger. I was hanging with the other girls in height, feeling strong, but I wasn't about to pull a catastrophic event by throwing a trick without having practiced anything in two decades. Still, I knew I could send it huge, although my legs were tiring from so much hiking and riding.

I straight-lined it for speed. The announcer's voice crackled over the speakers: "Shannon is coming in with tons of speed."

As I went up the face of the wall, I felt it—the g-force on the transition hit hard, my legs buckled, and time slowed down.

At the top, the photographers standing on the snow platform scattered—they could see what was coming before I even had time to react.

I froze, knowing in that split second that whatever happened next was out of my hands. I was either going to fly high above the lip and crash flat on the deck or somewhere below.

God's will. That's my outcome.

And somehow, in the chaos, I felt relaxed.

Next thing I knew, I landed perfectly on the transition, gently sliding on my back down to the bottom. Best case scenario—no impact, no injury, no problem.

That was enough. I wanted to go bigger. I wanted to send it. But it wasn't the time or place for that kind of progress.

Stick to the plan, Shan. Just get a good photo, I told myself.

And I did—thanks to photographer Mary Walsh, who captured a shot I was proud of.

At the end of the day, *Slush* Magazine handed out just two honors: Best Overall Rider—awarded to the competitor throwing down the hardest tricks with the strongest riding—and the Best Time Award, given to the rider who, in the judges' eyes, was simply having the most fun out there.

Ellie took home Best Overall Rider for the women. Nixon, sponsor of the Best Time Award, gifted a gold watch to the top male and female riders who embodied the purest spirit of snowboarding—style, joy, and just going for it.

To my surprise, they handed me the women's Best Time Award, while Raibu Katayama, a Japanese rider I deeply respect, took it home for the men.

I came to the event feeling like the underdog, unsure if I even belonged among this new generation of snowboarding. But in the end, I realized—it wasn't about proving I could ride like I used to.

It was about showing up, pushing myself, and reconnecting with the part of me that still comes alive on a snowboard.

That mattered more than any result. That reminded me who I am.

BRINGING IT HOME: FULL CIRCLE

When I got home, I set the watch on the table in front of my boys. "Check it out," I said. "My latest prize."

They leaned in, inspecting it like treasure.

"Wait—this was for having the most fun?" Logan asked, eyes lighting up.

"Yep," I said. "Pretty cool, right? Stepping outside our comfort zones—pushing ourselves to see what we've really got in us—that's what it's all about."

Dillon nodded, slipping the watch onto his wrist. "That's pretty sick."

And just like that, the story came full circle.

The medal I'd won decades ago? The one they'd once helped me dig up from the depths of my closet like buried treasure? *That* was their mom, the Olympian.

But this watch? This moment?

This was their mom, the snowboarder—*still* showing up, *still* pushing herself, *still* living the lessons that got her there in the first place.

Slush World Championships Quarterpipe contest—photo by Mary Walsh. Thankful she captured this moment for the memories.

THE TAKEAWAY: KEEP ON TRUCKIN'

Looking back, I realize I've built my life around love, resilience, and lifting others up. Snowboarding taught me that—and so did motherhood.

In the end, that's what matters: choosing the meaningful path, leaning into the hard things, loving others well, and living beyond yourself. You never know where God will lead when you finally loosen your grip and let go of control.

And when you have no idea what you're doing or where you're going...maybe that phrase I randomly threw out during my cringe-worthy post-Olympic speech had a deeper meaning than I realized.

Just throw your hands in the air like you just don't care—and keep on truckin'.

Because sometimes, all you can do is have faith, keep going, give it your all—whatever that looks like—and trust that somehow, it will all work out.

I tucked the Nixon gold watch next to my Olympic medal.

Two trophies. Decades apart.

Bound by the same heartbeat:

A love for the ride.

/ Acknowledgments/

FAITH

First, I want to thank God, Jesus, and Holy Spirit. To be fully known and deeply loved is a mystery, yet such a simple gift offered to everyone. Not religion, but a personal, relational walk in spirit and truth with God. I'm eternally grateful to live by faith in the promises of the Bible—through a life of both peaks and valleys.

FAMILY

To my husband, Dave, and our sons, Logan and Dillon—your love, encouragement, humor, and endless sense of adventure have been my greatest gifts. You've kept things real, sharpened my edges, and challenged me in the best ways. You've lifted me higher than any contest podium ever could.

To my mom and dad and my brother, Sean—thank you for the foundation of love and support that gave me the strength to chase big dreams, and for showing me that life's messes are overcome by love.

FRIENDS, MENTORS & LIFELONG SISTERHOOD

To my friends and mentors in snowboarding—those who cheered me on, pushed me harder, and believed in me when I wasn't sure I believed in myself—I'm forever grateful.

Especially to Leslee (Olson) Schader: I got to travel the world while connecting on faith and laughing harder than I ever could have imagined. I couldn't include every character in my book—I had to stick to a structure and storyline—but that doesn't lessen the impact you've had on my life. You are my sister, and I'm so happy I get to be "Auntie" to your daughter. Walking alongside Andee Grace and supporting her snowboarding goals has been such a gift.

Arigato to Tomo—my Japanese sister and forever my tour guide!

To my Bible study crew, my beloved "Shan Fans"—thank you for praying me through this book, encouraging me when I wanted to quit, and reminding me that God's timing is always perfect. Your support carried me through the painstaking process of writing page by page, draft by draft. I am forever grateful for your sisterhood.

To Tina Basich—my partner in crime in this book and in life. Can you believe the fun we've had? I love your friendship, and your beautiful daughter, Addie.

To Betsy—my forever bestie! My life is forever shaped by our friendship. Love you forever.

PIONEERS & PROS

Thank you to the pioneers who came before me, paving the way and setting the tone that girls belonged in this sport. To the women who rode alongside me—thank you for pushing me. We all helped open the door for more women in snowboarding while living through the sport's coolest era. Good job, ladies!

SPONSORS & INDUSTRY FRIENDS

To my sponsors who supported me and were instrumental in my career: Morrow, Sims, and especially Burton. Donna and Jake Carpenter—you've done more for this sport than anyone. Thank you, and thanks also to all of my team managers along the way for your guidance and support.

To Eric Kotch—for getting me on Burton and always being a plumbline for what's up in the industry.

To Lisa Hudson and Gaylene Nagel—two women with the grit and positivity to put on a smile no matter the situation and keep charging forward. "I can't do this" has never been in your vocabulary.

To Brad Steward—pioneering force in snowboarding—thank you for seeing me, approaching me, and taking a chance on me.

To Chad DiNenna and Andy Laats—founders of Nixon watches. You guys have done so much to support my career. Thank you.

To Chris "Gunny" Gunnarson—for building the kind of terrain parks and playgrounds that fueled progression and continue to give riders a place to dream big.

To all the characters in this book—I'm so thankful our paths crossed. You impacted my world.

MEDIA: PHOTOGRAPHERS, FILMERS, & MAGAZINES

To the photographers who captured it all—especially those I worked with the most:

Jeff Curtes—always pushing for perfection: "Hike it one more time, let's make sure we got the shot!"

Trevor Graves—always getting creative.

Jon Foster—"You quit, I quit." We never really stopped—maybe just slowed down a little, right?

To the filmers who brought snowboarding to life on screen:

Mike "Mack Dawg" McEntire, Mike and Dave Hatchett, and Whitey McConnaughy—thank you for including me in your videos and giving our sport inspiring action to replay countless times. You helped define snowboard culture.

TO THE MAGAZINES THAT SHAPED THE SPORT AND GAVE SNOWBOARDING ITS VOICE:

Transworld Snowboarding Magazine: founding editor Kevin Kinnear and the entire TWS crew—thank you for the coverage and for believing in women's riding from the start.

Snowboarder Magazine: Doug Palladini—thank you for your vision and for filling the pages with snowboarding's rawness and energy. And to Kayte Peck-Guerrero—publisher, friend, and a strong woman influencer behind the scenes—thank you for your impact.

Slush Magazine: founder Pat Bridges and crew—thank you for keeping the stories authentic, full of humor, and unafraid to be unhinged.

FANS

To all the fans who stood on the sidelines cheering me on—thank you. As athletes, part of our role is to inspire and entertain, and your energy fueled me every step of the way.

BOARDING FOR BREAST CANCER

To everyone at B4BC—co-founder and president Lisa Hudson, event coordinator Maggie Gonzalez, co-founder Tina Basich, and all who have been involved, along with the countless volunteers since 1996—let's keep charging forward, taking this mission further than ever before.

To Monica Steward's family—her legacy continues to shine on.

BOOK TEAM

Thank you to my editors, and to Brad Pauquette—founder and director of The Company. I signed up for a writing class, never imagining it would lead to a whole book…oops. Best mistake I ever made. Your approach—using your gifts to serve others—spoke to me deeply.

COMMUNITY

And finally—thank you to the entire snowboard community, past and present. This book is as much yours as it is mine.

/ Author Bio/

SHANNON DUNN-DOWNING is a trailblazer in snowboarding and a two-time Olympian who made history as the first American woman to win an Olympic medal in the sport, earning bronze in the halfpipe at the 1998 Nagano Games. Over her groundbreaking career, she helped shape women's snowboarding from the ground up—pushing progression in competition, designing some of the first women-specific snowboard products, and mentoring the next generation of riders. Her influence has been recognized with induction into the U.S. Ski and Snowboard Hall of Fame, and her signature board is on display at the Smithsonian.

Beyond competition, Shannon co-founded Boarding for Breast Cancer (B4BC), a nonprofit dedicated to health education and support, and continues to be a voice for empowerment in both sports and life. Today, she shares her journey through speaking, writing, and mentorship, blending stories of courage, faith, and creativity to inspire others to pursue their calling with boldness.

She lives in Southern California with her husband and two sons, where her love for snowboarding, surfing, fishing, and the outdoors still fuels her everyday life. *Snowboard Girl* is her debut memoir.

Scan to listen: "Snowboard Girl Soundtrack" on Spotify.

Thanks for riding along. For behind-the-scenes photos, blog posts, and updates related to Snowboard Girl, visit **SHANNONDUNNDOWNING.COM**

Made in the USA
Columbia, SC
11 December 2025